A MATTER OF TRUTH

The Struggle For African Heritage & Indigenous People Equal Rights in Providence, Rhode Island (1620-2020)

The examination and documentation of the role of the City of Providence and State of Rhode Island in supporting a "Separate and Unequal" existence for African heritage, Indigenous, and people of color.

By the Rhode Island Black Heritage Society and 1696 Heritage Group
Research and writing - Keith W. Stokes and Theresa Guzmán Stokes
Editor - W. Paul Davis

Our Report Production Team gratefully acknowledges the time and involvement of the many individuals who made their vital contribution to this work. These include Dr. C. Morgan Grefe (Executive Director, Rhode Island Historical Society), Richard J. Ring (Deputy Executive Director for Collections and Interpretation, Rhode Island Historical Society), Brent Runyon (Executive Director, Providence Preservation Society), Caleb Horton (Providence City Archives), Lane Sparkman (Rhode Island State Archives), Joanna Dougherty (The Rhode Island Historical Preservation & Heritage Commission), Clifford Monteiro, (Providence NAACP), and Raymond Watson (Providence Cultural Equity Initiative). While their comments and suggestions were gratefully taken into account, the sole responsibility for the content of this publication is ours.

978-1-917054-87-4 (**Paperback**)
978-1-917054-88-1 (**Hardcover**)

Table of Contents

I. **Introduction:** Organizing Research Content & Narrative ... 1

II. **The Process:** Truth Process Research Objectives ... 3

III. **The Truth:** Mayor's Truth, Reconciliation & Reparations Initiative ... 4

IV. **The Narrative:** Seven-Part Narrative Documenting 400 Years of History ... 6

    Part 1. Founding Enterprises Indigenous People Land And African Labor (pre 1600 - 1800) ... 7

    Part 2: Separate & Unequal in 19th Century Providence (1800-1899) ... 35

    Part 3: The Great War & The New Civil Rights Era (1900-1940) ... 66

    Part 4: Fair Employment During WWII Era (1940-1955) ... 80

    Part 5: Fair Housing & Urban Redevelopment (1950-1970) ... 87

    Part 6: School & Community Integration & Tribal Sovereignty (1970-2020) ... 111

    Part 7: Continuing Legacy (2020 & Beyond) ... 122

V. **The Resources:** Contributing Historical Institutions & Libraries ... 134

    Appendix A: Endnotes ... 135

    Appendix B: Bibliography & Resources ... 161

I. INTRODUCTION:
Organizing Research Content & Narrative

Why History Matters

2020 was a year of racial awareness, providing America with a long-overdue awakening to the systematic racism that has created measurable socioeconomic disparities between Black and White communities across the country and here in Providence, Rhode Island. Systematic racism, a form of race-based discrimination embedded as a normal practice within a society and its governmental system, has a long history in America, and cities like Providence approved discriminatory and dehumanizing laws and policies that created and exacerbated inequality in almost every sphere of life. This report documents 400 years of discrimination in The Ocean State, including the detribalization of Indigenous people and the enslavement of those of African heritage. From the moment when the English colonists settled Providence and Rhode Island, African heritage and Indigenous people were denied equal standing and a chance at self-determination. Although some within the colony sympathized with the oppressed, any laws that would have empowered them were largely ignored. Instead, laws were employed to further subjugate and control early people of color.

The history of Providence, Rhode Island, is the collective memory of its entire people. Throughout the year—not just on Native American Day or during Black History Month— citizens must recognize the important roles that people of all walks of life played in building our city, state, and nation. The interdependence between these people is what makes our history unique. To tell the story completely, it must be inclusive. African heritage and Indigenous people have made and continue to make major contributions to our capital city's history, commerce, and culture. This legacy has its roots in ancient Africa and America, particularly in Providence. The city's very names of places and rivers — Woonasquatucket, Weybosset, Tockwotten, Moshassuck, and Wanskuck — are part of its Native American past. And what would be the history of important contributing neighborhoods and historic buildings such as College Hill and the Providence Art Club without its ample African heritage contributions? This rich Providence history has remained hidden in plain sight from most of its residents.

Historically, Indigenous people and, beginning in the 17th century, African heritage people have been a part of our city. Today, the city's residents include African, bi-racial, Latino, Cape Verdean, Caribbean, and Native people. Yet, the accomplishments and contributions of African Americans, Indigenous people, and people of color have generally been invisible, lacking in public acknowledgment.

On July 15, 2020, Honorable Mayor Jorge O. Elorza signed an Executive Order that identified and created a process of Truth, Reconciliation, and Municipal Reparations to address institutional and systemic bias and racism affecting Black, Indigenous people, and people of color within the City of Providence. Working together, a team of city and state historical institutions has crafted a comprehensive narrative for public education, public interpretation, and future policy-making efforts.

They have collected over 600 primary and secondary documents and historical artifacts highlighting 400 years of Providence and Rhode Island history. The account is divided into seven sections. Each includes detailed examinations of the people, events, and places that have shaped the history of the city and state.

Research, recovery, and interpretation help us understand how the City of Providence's treatment of nonwhite people evolved, which people and institutions benefited, who got left behind, and how these past legacies still influence us today. The findings, which document and validate the struggle by African heritage and Indigenous people to thrive in the City of Providence, will help to create an environment and future policy platforms for positive change that fosters fairness, equity, and justice.

Images courtesy of the Rhode Island Black Heritage Society Archives

II. THE PROCESS:
Truth Process Research Objectives

African Heritage & Indigenous People History Truth Process Research Objectives

- Apply objective analysis of the recovered documents to ensure an accurate and comprehensive interpretation.

- Recognize that historical remembrance is best understood through public education and engagement.

- Define African heritage and Indigenous people as a vital part of the earliest settlement of the City of Providence and the State of Rhode Island, greatly influencing the region's economic, religious, and social origins.

- Document and affirm the development of the city and state through the enslavement and genocide of African heritage and Indigenous people.

- Examine the state and municipal laws that discriminated against formerly enslaved African heritage and Indigenous people and their descendants.

- Examine the lingering adverse effects of the institution of slavery, Indigenous genocide, and the seizure of Indigenous lands.

- Present evidentiary documents for public education, public interpretation, and future policy-making recommendations at the municipal, state, and federal levels.

III. THE TRUTH:
Mayor's Truth, Reconciliation & Reparations Initiative

On July 15, 2020, Honorable Mayor Jorge O. Elorza signed an Executive Order that identified and created a process of Truth, Reconciliation, and Municipal Reparations to address institutional and systemic bias and racism affecting Black and Indigenous people (Indians) and people of color within the City of Providence. The Truth process requires identifying, compiling, and presenting the evidentiary documentation of the institutions of slavery, the genocide of Indigenous people, and the ongoing discrimination that resonates to the present day. The Executive Order provides detailed instructions on how evidentiary documents shall be compiled and made available for public interpretation and future policy-making efforts:

> **The Truth** process shall begin by identifying, compiling, and synthesizing the relevant documents on the institution of slavery, the genocide of Indigenous people, and the forced assimilation that existed within the State of Rhode Island and the City of Providence; and

> **The Truth** will include the documentation and examination of the facts related to the capture and procurement of Africans; the transport of Africans to Rhode Island for enslavement, including their treatment during transport; the sale and acquisition of Africans as chattel property in interstate and intrastate commerce; the treatment of African slaves in Rhode Island, including the deprivation of their freedom, exploitation of their labor, and destruction of their culture, language, religion, and families; and the extensive denial of humanity, sexual abuse, and chatellization of persons; and

> **The Truth** will include the documentation and examination of the facts related to the capture and procurement of Indigenous people; the sanctioned genocide of Indigenous people, the treatment of Indigenous people in Rhode Island, including the deprivation of their freedom, exploitation of their labor, seizing of their land, and destruction of their culture, language, religion, and families; and the extensive denial of humanity, sexual abuse, and chatellization of persons and property; and

> **The Truth** will examine the role of the State of Rhode Island and the City of Providence in supporting the institution of slavery, the genocide of Indigenous people, and the forced assimilation and seizure of land in constitutional and statutory provisions, and

> **The Truth** will examine the state and municipal laws that discriminated against formerly enslaved

Africans and people of color and their descendants and Indigenous people from when they were deemed United States citizens to the present, and

The Truth will examine and document those laws, policies, and customs that created a "Separate and Unequal" existence for African heritage people in Providence and Rhode Island after the abolishment of slavery and continued throughout the 19th and 20th centuries, and

The Truth will examine the other forms of discrimination in the public and private sectors against freed African slaves and their descendants, Indigenous people, and people of color from when they were deemed United States citizens to the present, including but not limited to redlining, educational funding discrepancies, and predatory financial practices, and

The Truth will examine the lingering negative effects of the institution of slavery, Indigenous genocide, and seizure of Indigenous lands, and

The Truth will examine and document that although slavery was abolished at the end of the Civil War, the brutalities of racial discrimination persisted under the guise of Jim Crow laws in the South and Jim Crow traditions in the North.

MAYOR JORGE O. ELORZA
CITY OF PROVIDENCE

"As a country and a community, we owe a debt to our Black, Indigenous People, and People of Color, and on the local level, we are using this opportunity to correct a wrong. Though this does not undo history it is the first step in accepting the role Providence and Rhode Island has held in generations of pain and violence against these residents, healing some of the deepest wounds our country faces today. May this process of truth bring us education and awareness of these wrong-doings and may our reconciliation change the systems that continue to oppress our communities, while reaffirming our commitment to building a brighter, more inclusive future,"
            -Honorable Mayor Jorge O. Elorza.

IV. THE NARRATIVE:
Seven-Part Narrative Documenting 400 Years of History

Part 1: Founding Enterprises: Indigenous People Land and African Labor (Pre-1600-1800)   7

Part 2: Separate & Unequal In 19th Century Providence (1800-1899)   35

Part 3: The Great War & The New Civil Rights Era (1900-1940)   66

Part 4: Fair Employment During WWII Era (1941-1950)   80

Part 5: Fair Housing & Urban Redevelopment (1950-1970)   87

Part 6: Community & School Integration & Tribal Sovereignty, (1970-2020)   111

Part 7: Continuing Legacy (2020 & Beyond)   122

PART 1. FOUNDING ENTERPRISES: INDIGENOUS PEOPLE LAND AND AFRICAN LABOR (PRE 1600-1800)

First People: Rhode Island Before European Colonization

Before the arrival of the first European colonists, the Algonquian-speaking tribes inhabited New England. From coastal Maine to the Mid-Atlantic region, they represented highly structured societies with defined cultural, religious, and social identities. The populous and vibrant tribes included the Wampanoag, Massachusetts, Nipmuc, Pokanoket, Mohegan, Pequot, and Narragansett peoples within present-day Rhode Island boundaries. As detailed by historian Howard S. Russell, *"The native inhabitants whom they (Europeans) met, strange in customs, food, implements, and costumes, they termed savages: yet well settled."*[1] Experts estimate between 70,000 and 100,000 Indigenous people lived in New England alone at the beginning of the 17th century.[2]

The various Indigenous tribes congregated around the coastal areas adjacent to dense forests where they would hunt *"deer, beaver, fowl, and sea birds, as well as fished and harvested clams and oysters from the bay."*[3] They traveled on foot and in canoes made of birch bark from the forest's readily available trees. Their clothes, as well as their homes, were fashioned with animal skins. Their enduring self-sufficiency and success were tied to their unbridled access to the seashore, woodlands, and natural environment. The arrival of the English and their colonization of New England would fundamentally change Indigenous peoples' lives, land, and culture.

The Great Dying 1616-1619 & "God's Will"

Before the Mayflower landed in 1620, possibly the first epidemic in America came from a deadly disease that swept coastal New England from Maine to Cape Cod. Known as the "Great Dying," it was part of a wave of diseases—including smallpox, influenza, and the bubonic plague—brought to the New World by early European explorers. The deadly diseases reduced the Indigenous populations by up to 90 percent.[4] For thousands of years, Europeans lived near a variety of domesticated animals. Over time, animal-borne infections crossed species and became deadly to man. Diseases like smallpox, influenza, and others would become a fatal inheritance of the European farming life.

Indians Lament Death by Disease, New England Historical Society

As European colonizers arrived and settled in America, they brought their farm animals and their illnesses with them. The Indigenous people had no natural resistance to the new diseases. The devastation was so complete that entire village populations perished. Tisquantum, a Wampanoag man kidnapped from the village of Patuxet in 1614, returned five years later to find it empty.[5] French sailors shipwrecked in Massachusetts Bay recorded the first cases of the plague. Soon after, another colonizer captured by the Indians said the natives boasted, *"their number was too great to ever be conquered.*

Then in a short stroke, that they died in heaps."[6] The plague decimated nearly all Indigenous tribes in its path. As an early colonial Governor noted, the affliction created an unintended opportunity for the English colonists:

> *"For the natives, they are near all dead of the smallpox, so the Lord hath cleared our title to what we possess."*
>
> –John Winthrop, Massachusetts Bay Colony founder & governor.[7]

Initially, the plague did not cross Narragansett Bay, and the Narragansett people were spared. But when Roger Williams settled and colonized the area that would become the Town of Providence and the Colony of Rhode Island in 1636, the disease followed. Williams cataloged the descriptions of the devastating sickness suffered by the Narragansetts in his 1643 *Key Into the Language of America*:

> *I have a swelling He*
> *is swelled*
> *All his body is*
> *swelled He hath*
> *the Pox The Pox*
> *The last Pox*
> *He hath the plague*
> *The plague*
> *The great plague*[8]

Conveniently, for the English colonizers, the Great Dying of Indigenous people was seen not only as an unintended consequence of two cultures interacting for the first time but as part of "God's Will" and a divine plan. Providence had taken the form of a "miraculous pestilence" that had swept the land clean so that they could establish a new Christian society. As clearly stated by one New England settler:

> *"[How] strangely they have decreased by the Hand of God… and it hath generally been observed that where the English come to settle, a Divine Hand makes way for them."*
>
> – Daniel Denton, early American Colonist[9]

A few generations after the colonists arrived, New England was virtually emptied of its Indigenous inhabitants. This combination of colonization, disease, and the belief in divine intervention would dramatically shape and justify the sweeping European settlement of New England generally and the formation of Providence and the Colony of Rhode Island as the new "English Israel."

New England as "English Israel"

The English colonists, with their deep Puritan beliefs, hoped to establish a land of religious freedom without persecution. "New" England offered them the opportunity to live as they believed the Bible demanded. As they set out to create a reformed Protestantism model, a new English Israel belief system took hold as part of their divine right to settle and colonize under "God's Will." The New England Puritans' fascination with the Old Testament of the Bible and the Jewish religion's legacy is well documented.[10] They saw themselves as the Old Testament's Hebrews, directed by God to seize land, prosper, and expand "God's word" in the new world. John Winthrop, a Puritan lawyer and one of the founders of the Massachusetts Bay Colony, explained it this way:

"That which is common to all is proper to none. This savage people ruleth over many lands without title or property; for they enclose no grounds, neither have they cattle to maintain it, but remove their dwellings as they have occasion, or as they can prevail against their neighbors; Nay why may not Christians have liberty to go and dwell amongst them in their waste lands and woods, (leaving such places as they have manured for their corn) as lawfully as Abraham did among the Sodomites?"

-John Winthrop, General Observations, 1629[11]

This belief that God would enable the Puritan colonists to gain control of New England was deeply embedded in a singular belief that as God delivered the Jews to the Promised Land, so God would deliver the Puritans to an English version of Israel in New England. Indigenous people who were fortunate enough to survive the plague (and the wrath of God) would be required to submit themselves to the "gifts of Christianity and English civilization."[12] Rhode Island Baptist minister John Callender embraced this belief in an English Promised Land, declaring, *"The wonderful and unsearchable Providence of GOD in the whole Affair of driving out the Natives and planting Colonies of Europeans, and Churches of Christians, in the Place of Heathenism and Barbarity."*[13]

This imported religious system of single-race destiny and power clashed with the beliefs of most Indigenous people. Though the Indigenous people also worshiped an all-powerful, all-knowing creator, sometimes referred to as a "Master Spirit," the important difference was that they believed human beings, nature, and animals had a shared spirit, with none having dominion over the other.[14]

This dramatic difference in religion and man's relationship with his natural environment would form the basis of heightened tensions between the Puritans and the surviving Indigenous people. As an example, Indigenous people viewed elk, deer, and other woodland animals as openly available for shared hunting and consumption. Conversely, Puritan colonists considered livestock such as pigs, sheep, and cows as their possessions. They fenced off the land for homes and animals, restricted traditional hunting, and blocked native access to seashore forests—a recipe for future conflict.

Roger William's Providence

While New England settlement may have begun as a Christian religious impulse, it soon shifted into a demand for control of native land. English pastor Roger Williams arrived in Boston, in 1631 and immediately refused to align himself with the Puritans' religious views, particularly those of the Anglican church. While he is remembered for his heroic stance on the separation of church and state, Williams also believed Indigenous people were the lawful proprietors of all the lands they occupied. A King's patent from faraway did not automatically endow colonists with land rights in New England, he argued.[15] His position on native land rights sealed his fate. The Massachusetts Bay Colony expelled him in late 1635.[16]

Roger Williams left the Massachusetts Bay Colony and proceeded south towards Narragansett Bay. Because of his previous interactions with Indigenous people, he may have first visited Ousamequin, the Sachem

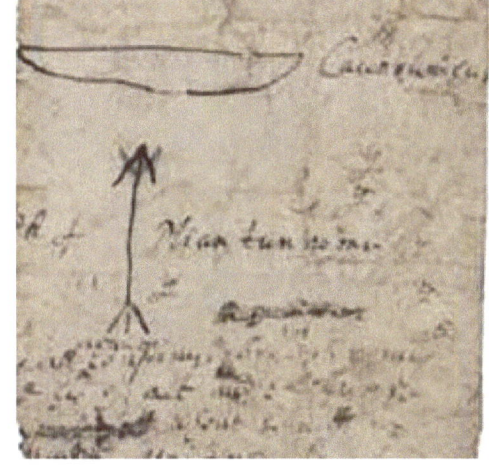

Deed to the Settlement at Moshassuck March 24, 1636, Providence City Archives

of the Pokanoket tribe who resided in today's Bristol. From Ousamequin, he obtained a grant of land near Seekonk. Once the Massachusetts Bay Colony learned he was still within the colony's borders, he was urged to leave. Williams crossed the river into the Narragansett tribal area and secured a deed from the two chief sachems of the powerful Narragansetts, Miantonomo, and Canonicus.[17] An original March 24, 1636 deed in the City of Providence archives represents a formal agreement between Williams and both sachems for what would become the Town of Providence settlement. Both sachems signed the document with the symbols of a bow and arrow.

By 1637, Williams arranged a deed between the Narragansetts and William Coddington for Aquidneck Island.[18] The town of Portsmouth was established in 1638, and Newport would follow in 1639. The Colony of Rhode Island was becoming a new English colony. The Narragansett Indigenous people would now encounter the diseases, land encroachment, and culture clashes that their Wampanoag rivals had faced within the Massachusetts Bay Colony.

1641 Rhode Island Hunting, Property & Harvesting Act

In 1641, the fledgling Colony of Rhode Island passed a law relating to property, hunting, and harvesting on Aquidneck Island. The law, which prevented anyone, including Indigenous people, from encroaching on private land, said:

> *It is ordered, established, and decreed, unanimously, that all men's properties and their lands of the Island, and the jurisdiction thereof shall be such, and so free, that neither the state nor any person or persons shall intrude into it, or molest him in it, to deprive him of anything whatsoever, or shall be within that or any of the bounds thereof, and that this tenure and propriety of his shall be continued to him or his, or to whomever he shall assign it forever. It is also ordered that no Indian shall fell or peel any trees upon the Islands, and that if any be found so doing, or carrying of bark (so peeled upon the Islands) away, it shall be lawful for all that so finds them to bring or cause to be brought the parties so offending, before the magistrates, who shall order and punish them according to the law.*

> -The Orders & Laws made at the General Court held at Newport, 17th of September, Anno 1641[19]

The rush to colonize and obtain land in 17th century Rhode Island was dramatic. Thirty years after Roger Williams established the Town of Providence, new colonists aggressively sought land for their economic prosperity and security. They struck land deals with Indigenous people that, in many cases, were grossly unfair to the native. In 1663, four months before Rhode Island received its formal charter from England, the colony enacted a law to restrict private land acquisitions that exploited the Indigenous people, declaring:

> *FOR AS MUCH as divers Persons have made Purchases of Lands in this Colony of the Indians, without the consent or approbation of the General Assembly, which manifestly tends to the Defrauding, and Manifest Injury of such Native Indians, as well as defeating the just Rights of this Colony.*

> *BE it therefore Enacted by the General Assembly, and the Authority of the same, That no Person or Persons for the future, shall purchase any Lands or Islands within this Colony, of or from the Native*

Indians within the same, but such only as are so allowed to do by the General Assembly, upon Penalty of forfeiting all such Lands or Islands so purchased, to this Colony; And to pay for every such Purchase by them so made, the Sum of Twenty Pounds as a Fine, to and for the Use of the Colony; And all such Purchases shall be Esteemed and Adjudged Null, Void, and of none Effect.[20]

While the law was designed to reduce native abuse, there is little evidence of how effective it was in stemming the tide of colonist expansion that would soon become—through the King Charles II Charter of July 2, 1663— the Colony of Rhode Island and Providence Plantations. Ironically, the English colonists' laws, regardless of the intent, were enacted with no recognition of sovereignty, historic land ownership, or use rights of the region's original inhabitants. The beginning of Rhode Island was directly related to the dramatic land loss and demise of the descendants of the aboriginal people who had thrived within the region, dating back more than 15,000 years ago.[21]

Rhode Island Charters: Conflicts in Content

Roger Williams, John Clarke, and Anne Hutchinson deserve full historical credit for their vision in founding an English Colony in Rhode Island that advanced the notion of a separation of church from civil functions. At the time, Rhode Island stood alone as the single settlement in New England to embrace a "liberty of conscience" for its English colonists. As aptly acknowledged by historian J. Stanley Lemons, *"The rest of New England looked with undisguised horror at what was happening around Narragansett Bay and moved to overpower and stifle the bay towns. They called Rhode Island the 'sewer of New England,' not because its people were thieves and murderers, but because Rhode Island was a 'hive of heretics.'"*[22]

The charter conceived by Williams and others embodied a dynamic set of governing laws for a people who would settle, colonize, and prosper within a new world. But what effect did these laws have upon the Indigenous people who had occupied the land for thousands of years before English arrival? Ten years before the Charter of 1663, Williams secured a patent from England to unite Providence, Portsmouth, and Newport. This early patent recognized the existence of the Narragansett people, indigenous to Rhode Island. It included a peaceful acquisition of the land between colonizers and natives. It also clearly expressed an intent by the English to use the land for multiple economic endeavors:

The Royal Charter of 1663, Rhode Island State Archives

And whereas there is a Tract of Land in the Continent of America aforesaid, called by the Name of the Narragansett Bay; bordering Northward and Northeast on the Patent of the Massachusetts, East, and Southeast on Plymouth Patent, South on the Ocean, and on the West and Northwest by the Indians called Nahigganneucks, alias Narragansetts; the whole Tract extending about Twenty-five English Miles unto the Pequot River and Country.

And whereas divers well affected and industrious English Inhabitants, of the Towns of Providence, Portsmouth, and Newport in the tract aforesaid, have adventured to make a nearer neighborhood and Society with the great Body of the Narragansetts, which may in time by the blessing of God upon their Endeavors, lay a sure foundation of Happiness to all America. And have also purchased, and are purchasing of and amongst the said Natives, some other Places, which may be convenient both for Plantations, and also for building of Ships Supply of Pipe Staves and other Merchandize.[23]

It is crucial to note the English colonists in 17th-century New England and Rhode Island ignored the many tribal sovereignties and boundaries. For the Narragansett natives, there was no question that Rhode Island was theirs. They were willing to deed land to Roger Williams and those who followed him under the belief that everyone would share in the numerous resources offered by the fertile land. But under English laws embedded within their charters, the colonizers had a "right" to settle, expand, and privately possess the land—a right granted directly by a European king who had little thought or care for the Indigenous people.

The Colony of Rhode Island Charter of 1663 further advanced these beliefs into a set of settlement laws. Land ownership and economic investment would occur not only through the consent of the native people but also through their "orderly conversion" into Christianity:

"The purchasers and free inhabitants of our island, called Rhode Island, and the rest of the colony of Providence Plantations, in the Narragansett Bay, in New England, in America, that they, pursuing, with peaceable and loyal minds, their sober, serious, and religious intentions, of godly edifying themselves, and one another, in the holy Christian faith and worship, as they were persuaded; together with the gaining over and conversion of the poor ignorant Indian natives, in those parts of America, to the sincere profession and obedience of the same faith and worship.

By the good Providence of God, from whom the Plantations have taken their name, upon their labor and industry, they have not only been preserved to admiration, but have increased and prospered, and are seized and possessed, by purchase and consent of the said natives, to their full content, of such lands, islands, rivers, harbors and roads, as are very convenient, both for plantations, and also for building of ships, supply of pipe-staves, and other merchandize and which lies very commodious.

To direct, rule, order and dispose of, all other matters and things, and particularly that which relates to the making of purchases of the native Indians, as to them shall seem meet; whereby our said people and inhabitants in the said Plantations, may be so religiously, peaceably and civilly governed, as that by their good life and orderly conversation, they may win and invite the native Indians of the country to the knowledge and obedience of the only true God and Savior of mankind.

And upon just causes, to invade and destroy the native Indians, or other enemies of the said Colony. Nevertheless, our will and pleasure is, and we do hereby declare to the rest of our Colonies in New England, that it shall not be lawful for this our said Colony of Rhode Island and Providence Plantations, in America, in New England, to invade the natives inhabiting within the bounds and limits of their said Colonies, without the knowledge and consent of the said other Colonies. And it is hereby declared that it shall not be lawful to or for the rest of the Colonies to invade or molest the native Indians or any other inhabitants inhabiting within the bounds and limits hereafter mentioned, they having subjected themselves unto us, and being by us taken into our special protection, without the knowledge and **consent of the Governor and Company of our Colony of Rhode Island and Providence Plantations."**[24]

The conflict over private land use, possession, and Christian obedience and conversion quickly led to a devastating war by the end of the 17th century. A century later, Crowfoot, Chief of the Blackfeet tribe of Canada, would make an age-old observation regarding the universal ownership of land:

> *Our land is more valuable than your money. It will last forever. It will not even perish by the flames of fire. As long as the sun shines and the waters flow, this land will be here to give life to men and animals. We cannot sell the lives of men and animals; therefore, we cannot sell this land. It was put here for us by the Great Spirit, and we cannot sell it because it does not belong to us.*[25]

West Africa Before European Colonization

It is commonly forgotten that West African history did not start with the transatlantic slave trade. Well before European arrival on the African continent, African societies were civilized, organized, and contained technologically advanced peoples. Major empires would emerge in West Africa, most notably the Ghana Empire, Mali, Kingdom of Nri, Yoruba, and Akan Empire of Ashanti. Gold, rice, and salt were all major trade products. The people along the African West Coast have traditionally been among the most skilled and productive African artisans. Craftsmanship has a long history in West Africa, with iron-working dating to the 4th century. Blacksmiths, weavers, leather workers, and silver and goldsmiths were all active long before European arrival. Many early Africans held complex spiritual and religious belief systems that included a supreme power or God controlling everyone and everything.[26]

These skills, along with sophisticated religious and cultural beliefs, were transported with the enslaved to the Americas. Skilled Africans helped build the massive wealth found in the cash crop commodities of sugar, coffee, tobacco, and rice, along with the maritime trade economies of Colonial Rhode Island. In the South, slaves worked on big plantations. In Rhode Island—a tiny colony with less land—enslaved Africans worked at the trades. As interpreted by historian William D. Pierson, *"Nature as much as Christianity carved a puritanical character on the New England way of life. The region's rigid climate and parsimonious soil, far more than its morals, banned the prodigal excesses of plantation slavery from the Yankee colonies."*[27]

While Africa was comprised of tribes that embraced sophisticated civilizations, human bondage was also a part of African culture before European arrival. Nonetheless, the European-dominated slave system within the Americas was unique in two important respects: the manipulation of race as a means of controlling the enslaved and the extent of the system's economic rationalization.[28] Unquestionably, the most devastating condition of African enslavement in the Americas was the law of "inheritable slavery." Children born to enslaved mothers were slaves for life.[29] This law provided generations of free labor for the wealthy owners of plantations, seaports, or homes.

This slave-trading system would bring, as estimated by the Trans-Atlantic Slave Trade Database,[30] 12.5 million men, women, and children from the African continent to the Americas and West Indies over a three-and-a-half-century period.

1663 - Rhode Island Royal Charter & Royal African Company Charter

In Rhode Island history, King Charles II of England is recognized for granting the Royal Charter for the Colony of Rhode Island in 1663. He also granted a second charter for the Royal African Company, officially sanctioning England's entry into the West African slave trade. The Royal African Company transported an average of 5,000 slaves a year and constructed slave forts along the West African coast, or the "Gold Coast." The charter gave the company a slave-trade monopoly stretching trade from Morocco to the Cape of Good Hope.[31] Of the several forts operated by the company, Cape Coast Castle and Fort William at Anomabo would become active centers for Rhode Island slave trading throughout the 18th century. The establishment of the Royal African Company also fortuitously coincided with Charles II's marriage in 1662 to Catherine de Braganza, princess of Portugal. Her dowry included the legal right to Portugal's castles on the African coast.[32]

Ironically, before either charter was finalized, Indigenous and African people were already facing bondage in 17th-century Rhode Island. The earliest enslaved Africans arrived in Rhode Island with English families from the Massachusetts Bay Colony. The early natives, meanwhile, were forced into servitude through English laws and trickery. According to historian Margaret Newell, *"the practice of judicial enslavement—the sentencing of Native Americans to long periods of involuntary service to settle debts, as well as civil and criminal penalties,"* was widely practiced in early Rhode Island.[33]

The Emblem of the Royal African Company, Department of Economic History, London School of Economics

The enslavement of both Indigenous people and Africans soon clashed with the principles of a colony founded on religious freedom. As early as 1637, Roger Williams wrote a letter to John Winthrop of Massachusetts shortly after the Pequot War rejecting the "perpetual servitude" of native captives.[34] With Williams' support, Rhode Island enacted a 1676 law—in direct response to King Philip's War—that sought not to enslave Indigenous people but place them in indentured service:

> *Every Indian servant in the Colony, from twelve years old and upward, should be provided with an attendant in the daytime and be locked up at night, but that no Indian in this Colony shall be a slave, save only for debts, covenants, etc., as if they had been countrymen not in war.*[35]

Even earlier, on May 18, 1652, Williams, along with Thomas Olney, would lead an effort in Rhode Island to enact one of the earliest laws in New England to prohibit African enslavement. It remained silent on Indigenous people, declaring:

> *Whereas, it is a common course practiced amongst English men to buy negroes, to that end they have them for service or slave forever: let it be ordered, no black mankind or white being forced by covenant bond, or otherwise, to serve any man or his assigns longer than ten years or until they come to be twenty-four years of age, if they be taken in under fourteen, from the time of their coming with the liberties of this Colony.*[36]

Despite the actions by Rhode Island founder Roger Williams, the 1652 law went primarily ignored, and by the end of the 17th century, the fledgling Colony of Rhode Island and Providence Plantations would actively enter the African slave trade. In 1696, 47 Africans from Barbados arrived at Newport on the brig *Seaflower*.[37]

These intersecting histories of Rhode Island's founding and the introduction of African and native enslavement become a uniquely Rhode Island irony when the persecuted becomes the persecutor. Those escaping the tyranny of religious oppression would become founders of a colony that would build its early personal wealth and economic prosperity through the seizure of native lands and the use of African bondage. This peculiar institution would only accelerate after King Philip's War.

King Philip's War: "I am Determined Not to Live Till I Have No Country"

Early tensions between the English and the native people in southern New England reached a boiling point by 1675. As the English aggressively expanded into the native territory, European land cultivation increasingly disrupted native life. Growing towns, animal pens, and grazing pigs and cattle interfered with native hunting and access to forests. These strains sparked King Philip's War, an armed conflict that led to the near-extermination of the Indigenous people in Rhode Island. Increase Mather, a Puritan clergyman and early president of Harvard University, justified the war this way:

> "That the Heathen People amongst whom we live, and whole Land the Lord God of our Fathers hath given to us for a rightful Possession, have at sundry times been plotting mischievous devices against that part of the English Israel."
>
> -The History of the King Philip's War, Increase Mather, 1676[38]

Although the Narragansetts had aligned with the English in their war with the Pequots between 1636 and 1638, there was still, nearly forty years later, concern with English advancement within Rhode Island. Miantonomo, the Narragansett sachem who had deeded the land to his friend Roger Williams, was distrusted by some Englishmen in Massachusetts and Rhode Island because he commanded a large number of warriors and controlled a vast land area.[39]

The Sachem Metacomet, known as King Philip, was particularly vocal about English encroachment. The English, he said, let their animals roam on native lands.[40] This threat to Metacomet and all Indigenous people of 17th century New England cannot be understated. As Scholar David Silverman notes:[41]

> "Livestock would have compromised the mobility Indians needed for winter hunting, destroyed Indian crops, competed with wild game for resources, transcended Indian conceptions of property and human-animal interconnectedness, threaten the Indian's gender division of labor, and clashed with rooted Indian hostility toward the trespassing of beasts."

The fuse that likely lit the explosion of war came with the death of a converted Christian native named John Sassamon. In January 1675, Sassamon reportedly warned Josiah Winslow, the governor of the Plymouth Colony, about an impending attack planned by Metacomet. Metacomet had Sassamon murdered for his betrayal. A jury of colonists and Indian elders convicted and executed three members of the Wampanoag tribe for the murder, setting in motion tensions that would lead to war. These historical details come not from an Indigenous source but Rhode Island Deputy Governor John Easton.[42]

Philip, King of Mount Hope, "The Entertaining History of King Philip's War," Line Engraving, Colored by Hand, by Engraver and Silversmith Paul Revere. Yale University Art Gallery

The two cultures clashed for land, sovereignty, and survival. What may have been Metacomet's declaration of war came in a statement attributed to him through English sources:

> *"The English who came first to this country were but a handful of people, forlorn, poor and distressed. My father (Massasoit) was then Sachem. He relived their distress in the most kind and hospitable manner. He gave them land to build and plant upon. He did all in his power to serve them. Others of their countrymen came and joined them. Their numbers rapidly increased. My father's counselors became uneasy and alarmed lest, as they were possessed of firearms, which was not the case of the Indians, they should finally undertake to give law to the Indians and take from their country. They therefore advise him to destroy them before they should become too strong, and it be too late. My father was also the father of the English. He represented to his counsellors and warriors that the English knew many sciences which the Indians did not, that they improved the cultivated earth and raised cattle and fruits, and that there was sufficient room in the country for both the English and the Indians. His advice prevailed. They flourished and increased. Experience taught that the advice of my father's counsellors was right. By various means they got possessed of a great part of his territory. But he still remains their friend until he died. Soon after I became Sachem, they disarmed all my people. They tried my people by their own laws and assessed damages against them which they could not pay. Their land was taken. At length a line of division was agreed upon between English and my people, and I myself was to be responsible. Sometimes the cattle of the English would come into the cornfields of my people, for they did not make fences like the English. I must be seized and confined till I sold another tract of my country for satisfaction of all damages and costs. But a small part of the dominion of my ancestors remains. I am determined not to live till I have no country."*[43]

Narragansett War & Enslavement

The Pequot War and King Philip's War decimated the Indigenous people. Many of the Pequot and Narragansett survivors were enslaved.[44]

The first, the Pequot War between 1636 and 1638, virtually eliminated the Pequot tribe and people from southern New England through either death, capture, or enslavement. As historian Katherine Grandjean notes:

> *"Largely because of English eagerness to chase them down, kill them, capture them, enumerate them, or pin them down on paper, we do know a fair amount about where the survivors went. Captivity is perhaps the best-known destiny faced by surviving Pequot's. Many endured swift capture and servitude, having been caught up in the great dragnet dispatched by the English in the aftermath of Mystic. Most of the captives, other than the ones that were killed, were women and children. These Pequot captives landed everywhere from Mohegan and Narragansett to Boston and Providence, where they were disposed of to particular persons in the country. Others found themselves shipped to more distant and exotic locations."* [45]

The Wampanoag and Narragansett people feared capture and enslavement in the aftermath of the Pequot War. As allies to the English, they likely witnessed the victorious actions of the colonists as they consigned captive Pequot men, women, and children to a life of permanent slavery. As Brown University historian Linford D. Fisher notes: *"Fear of enslavement and, more specifically, the fear of being sold as a slave out of the country played a major role in the waging of King Philip's War, perhaps even more than scholars have typically acknowledged. The terrifying prospect of being sent overseas as a slave was constantly present for natives, even in times of peace."*[46]

This threat of enslavement and banishment for Indigenous Rhode Islanders is graphically illustrated in the colony's records before and after King Philip's War. One example from 1727 centers on a native youth named Peter:

> *"Whereas, it has been made to appear to this Assembly, that a certain Indian lad, named Peter, belonging to Jacob Mott, Jr. of Portsmouth, did sometime past, maliciously endeavor to murder his said master by discharging at him a gun. For the preventing of future danger, and for the terror of evil doers hereafter, do order, enact and it is hereby ordered and enacted by this General Assembly that the said Indian lad, named Peter shall on the 17th day of this instant June, be branded on the forehead with the letter R with a hot iron, and be publicly whipped at a cart's tail, throughout all the most public corners and places of the town of Newport, not exceeding ten lashed in one place; and that the said Jacob Mott shall hereby have the power to sell and dispose of said Indian, named Peter, so that he be banished into some foreign part, never to have liberty of returning into this government again."*[47]

The Pequot War ended the threat of native aggression in western New England, and King Philip's War marked the beginning of the end of Wampanoag and Narragansett agitation in the east. In 1675, the United Colonies of Massachusetts Bay, Plymouth, and Hartford amassed a large army to attack those Indians perceived to be Narragansett allies in Rhode Island. The colony's leaders relied on both legal and religious justifications for the adoption of a proclamation on June 22, 1675:

Proclamation of the Plymouth Colony Council, To The Elders Of The [Churches Of] Plymouth

> *The Council of this Colony taking into the serious Consideration the awful hand of God upon us in permitting the heathen to carry it with great insolence & rage against us, appearing in their great hostile preparations & also some outrageous carriages as at all other times so in special the last Lords day to some of our neighbors at Swansea to the apparent hazard if not the real loss of the lives of some already, do therefore Judge it a solemn duty incumbent upon us all to lay to heart this dispensation of God, & do therefore commend it to all the Churches, ministers & people of this colony to set apart the 24th day of this instant June, which is the 5th day of this week wherein to humble our souls before the Lord for all those sins whereby we have provoked our good God so sadly to interrupt our peace & Comforts, & also humbly to seek his face & favor in the gracious continuance of our peace & privileges, & that the Lord would be intreated to go forth with our forces & bless, succeed & prosper them, delivering them from the hands of his & our enemies, subduing the heathen before them & returning them all in safety to their families & relations again, & that God would prepare all hearts humbly to submit to his good pleasure concerning us & yours.*[48]

> *By order of the Council of War*
> *Nathaniel Morton, secretary*

On December 19, 1675, armed men from the United Colonies marched into Rhode Island and attacked the winter village of the Narragansett tribe. Ironically, as early as October of that year, Canonchet, the Chief

Sachem of the Narragansetts, had traveled to Boston to pledge neutrality in the conflict. Unfortunately, the English would reject Narragansett neutrality because they believed they had aided King Philip and might join him.[49] The colonists burned the wigwams in the winter fort and killed an estimated 600 or more men, women and children in the Great Swamp Massacre.[50]

After King Philip's death and the capture and execution of the Narragansett Sachem Canonchet in the spring of 1676, the war came to a bloody end. The task for victorious English was what to do with the native survivors. As an outcome of the Pequot war, slavery, and banishment were the most practical options. At a town meeting held in Providence on August 14, 1676, a committee led by Roger Williams, Thomas Harris, Thomas Angell, Thomas Field, and John Whipple, Jr. determined the fate of the captured natives. They would become slaves or servants. The committee reported:

> "We, whose names are underwritten, being chosen by the town, to set the disposal of the Indians now in town, we agree, that Roger Williams, Nathan Waterman, Thomas Fenner, Henry Ashton, John Mowry, Daniel Abbott, James Olney, Valentine Whitman, John Whipple, Ephraim Pray, John Pray, John Angell, James Angell, Thomas Arnold, Abraham Mann, Thomas Field, Edward Bennett, Thomas Clements, William Lancaster, William Hopkins, William Hawkins, William Harris, Zachariah Field, Samuel Windsor, and Captain Fenner, shall each a whole share in the product. Joseph Woodward, and Richard Pray, each three fourths of a share. John Smith, Edward Smith, Samuel Whipple, Nelle Whipple, and Thomas Walim, each a half share. Inhabitants wanting to have Indians at the price they sell at Rhode Island or elsewhere:
>
> All under five years, to serve till thirty; above five and under ten, till twenty-eight; above ten till fifteen, till twenty-seven; above fifteen to twenty, till twenty-six years; from twenty to thirty, shall serve eight years; all above thirty, seven years."[51]/[52]

Within a little over 50 years, from 1620 to 1675, New England's Indigenous people were nearly exterminated by disease, war, enslavement, and banishment. Rhode Island colonists used bondage and permanent removal against the Narragansett survivors as part of the victor's spoils, thereby reinforcing English manifest destiny and their "God-giving" right to settle and expand across New England. It would be Indigenous people, not Africans, who would become the victims of the early slavery laws and actions in New England and Rhode Island.[53] And Roger Williams, the father of "liberty of conscience," founder of Providence and a friend of the native people, would take a captive Indigenous boy for himself, separating him from his mother and renaming him Will.[54]

War Aftermath: Narragansett Land Claims – 1709

Immediately after King Philip's War, the Colony of Rhode Island looked to expand its borders and control land previously held by the Narragansett tribe. Rhode Island needed to expand and secure its western boundaries against the Connecticut Colony, increase land acquisition and white settlement, and reduce future native uprisings.[55] In 1707, the General Assembly authorized a survey of the Narragansett tribal lands within the colony's southwestern area. The General Assembly then settled conflicting native claims to titles and negotiated with the Narragansett Sachem Ninigret. Lawmakers wanted to know how they might compensate

Ninigret and his people for access to native lands. As a result of these concessions, Ninigret, on March 28, 1709, deeded his interest to 130,000 acres of Narragansett land to the Colony of Rhode Island, nearly all of today's South County.[56] The compensation received by the Sachem Ninigret for such a vast amount of land included the declaration:

1. For expense the Colony had been to in defending their title and property against Englishmen residing outside of the Colony limits.

2. For gratitude, good will, love and confidence the Indians had in them, and respect they had for their honesty and integrity, that is the Rhode Island Colony.

3. For considerations of the future, that after surrendering up a vast tract of land, they were to be forever protected in their title to the pittance which was reserved. That this was not to be taken from them without consent being had of both the Tribe and the Colonial Government.[57]

Undoubtedly, the most important of these considerations was the assurance that the Narragansetts and their remaining land would be "forever protected" by the Colonial Government. The agreement also required the Narragansetts to receive General Assembly approval for any future disposition of their land. Under the pact, the Colony of Rhode Island assumed the guardianship of the Indians and appointed an overseer or agent to represent the Narragansett Tribe at all times.[58] This trade-off for government protection would set the stage for further native land sales and transfers over the next 50 years.

Enslaved Africans in Rhode Island: Strangers in a Strange Land

> *To All the Africans in Providence*
> *Newport, July 27, 1789*
> *"We the members of the Union Society in Newport, taking into consideration the calamitous state into which we are brought by the righteous hand of GOD, being strangers and outcasts in a strange land, attended with many disadvantages and evils, with respect to living, which are like to continue us and on our children while we and they live in this Country."*[59]

Those honored men, women, and families that first settled in Providence and Rhode Island nearly four centuries ago brought to these shores an unconquerable sense of religious toleration. As persecuted religious minorities, they built not only a new home but created a place where anyone, regardless of religious beliefs, could settle and prosper. But Rhode Islanders lived a double life. Its early settlers, ardent believers in religious freedom and civil liberties, were slave traders too. Their business ventures turned Rhode Island into the leading slave-trading port in British North America. As pointed out by historian Christy Clark-Pujara, *"In Rhode Island, slave trading and political power went hand in hand. During the colonial period, most Rhode Island governors were of the merchant class. Many were slave traders."*[60]

The African Slave Trade and Rhode Island share common origins. Rhode Island's seaports—Newport, Providence, and Bristol—experienced unprecedented growth during the 18th century, mostly through the production and export of rum, spermaceti candles, horses, codfish—and slaves. More than 60 percent of the

North American ships involved in the African slave trade in the 1700s were based in Rhode Island.[61] Many of the enslaved Africans that arrived in Rhode Island originated from Guinea, Gold, and Cape Coasts of West Africa. Others came from Barbados, Antigua, and Jamaica. The enslavement of African people in the Americas differed markedly from slavery throughout world history. Slavery in the Americas confined bondage to a single race and ensured that the children of enslaved mothers remained unfree for the rest of their lives.[62] This brutal system of inheritable servitude impacted the lives of tens of millions of displaced Africans and dramatically shaped the settlement and formation of the Americas and, particularly, early Rhode Island.

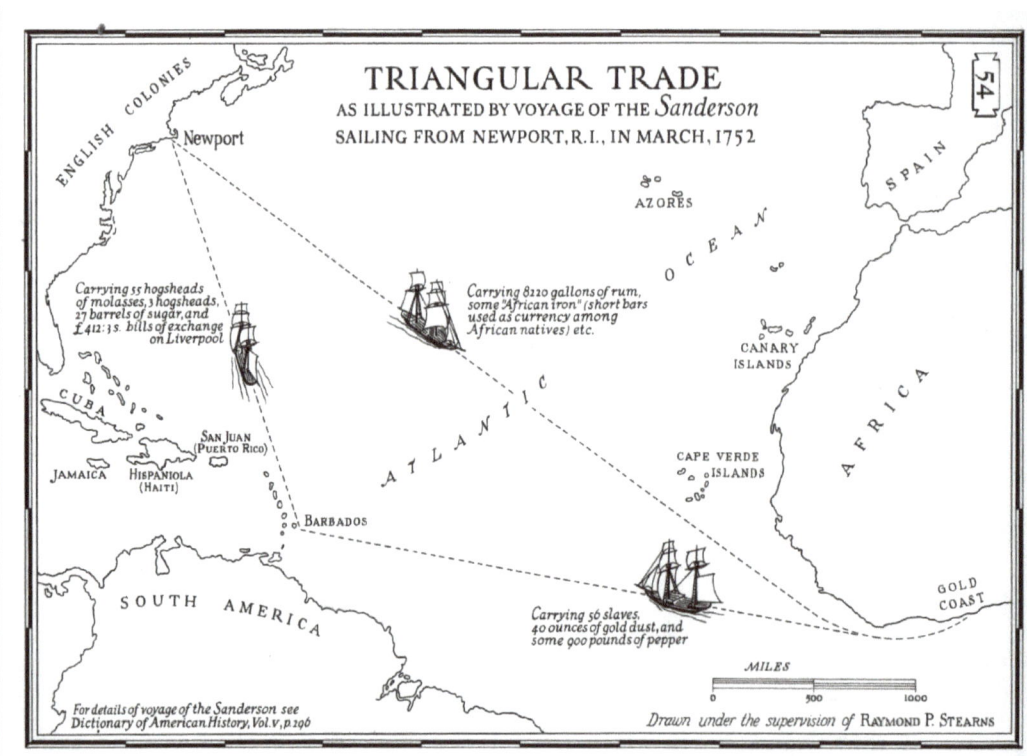

Voyage of the Sanderson Sailing From Newport, R.I., in March, 1752

From the beginning, African heritage people who were enslaved and transported to early Rhode Island were legally rendered chattel property, movable personal property like hogs, horses, and cattle. A 1695 Rhode Island law declared:

> *We enact and order, that the Magistrates of every respective town shall by warrant forthwith warn in the inhabitants of each town, to choose two or three honest and able men to take a true list of every "man's rateable estate; and of all lands and meadows, housing, merchants, and tradesmen, shall be by these said men rated at their wisdom and discretion, according to the yearly profit.*
>
> *And for Negro servants and cattle, we set these certain prices, for these men to make this rate by:*
>
> | | |
> |---|---|
> | *As oxen, four years old and upwards, at three pence per head,* | 00 00 5 |
> | *Steers, three years old, and all cows at two pence per head,* | 00 00 2 |
> | *All two year old, a penny per head,* | 00 00 1 |
> | *All year old, at half penny per head,* | 00 00 1 |

All sheep at one "' "year's old and upward, at five pence per score,	00 00 5
All swine above a year old, at a half penny per head,	00 00 1
All horses and mares above three years old, at three pence per head,	00 00 3
All two years old horses and mares, at one penny per head,	00 00 1
All year old horses, at a half penny per head,	00 00 1
All Negro men servants, per head,	00 01 8
All Negro women servants, per head,	00 00 10[63]

The first of these "forced immigrants" entered the Colony of Rhode Island with their Massachusetts owners sometime around 1650, and the first documented slave ship, the *Sea Flower*, arrived in Newport in 1696.[64] By the early 18th century, enslaved Africans outnumbered white indentured servants in the Colony almost 8 to 1. As early as 1711, the Rhode Island General Assembly enacted a tax on African (Negro) slave importations into the Colony, stating:

> *"That every Master of any ship or vessel, Merchants or others, that shall import or bring into the Colony, an Negro slave or slaves, of what age forever shall enter their Number, Names, and Sex in the Naval Office; and the Master shall insert the same into the Manifest of his landing and shall pay to the Naval Officer in Newport, Three Pounds per Head."* [65]

Throughout the 18th century, Rhode Island enacted numerous laws with defined restrictions to enforce social control over enslaved Africans and surviving Indigenous people. A 1703 enactment restricted the very movements of both enslaved Africans and natives by stating, *"If any negroes or Indians either freemen, servants, or slaves, do walk in the street of the town of Newport, or any other town in this Colony, after nine of the clock of night, without certificate from their masters, or some English person of said family with, or some lawful excuse for the same, that it shall be lawful for any person to take them up and deliver them to a Constable."* [66]

An Act to Prevent All Persons Keeping House & Entertaining Indian, Negro or Mulatto Servants or Slaves, 1755, Stokes Family Collection

Laws regulating movement and public conduct, later known as "Negro Codes," were enacted throughout the 18th century, including a 1757 law *"To prevent all persons keeping house within the colony, from entertaining Indian, Negro or Mulatto servants or slaves."* The penalties included fines for white offenders, imprisonment for slaves, and indentured servitude for free Africans and Indigenous offenders.[67]

Even in the rare cases of emancipation, Africans were seen as a social burden to the Colony, requiring prescribed remedies. A 1729 enactment addressed the issue:

> *"Forasmuch, as great charge, trouble and inconveniences have arisen to the inhabitants of diverse towns in this colony, by the manumitting and setting free mulatto and negro slaves: for remedying*

whereof, for the future. Be it enacted by the General Assembly of this colony, and by the authority of the same it is enacted, that no mulatto or negro slave, shall be hereafter manumitted, discharged or set free, or a liberty, until sufficient security by given to the town treasurer of the town or place where such person dwells, in a value sum of not less than 100 Pounds, to secure and indemnify the town or place from all charge for, or about such mulatto or negro, to be manumitted and set at liberty in case he or she by sickness, lameness or otherwise, be rendered incapable to support him or herself."[68]

American law enforcement has long treated allegations of sexual assault differently based on the race of the victim and the assailant.[69] By 1743, Rhode Island becomes an early American colony that enacts a directly racialized law punishing African-heritage men for the sexual assault on white women, declaring:

An ACT for the more effectual Punishment of Negroes that shall attempt to commit a Rape on any white woman. WHEREAS there have been Instances of Negroes attempting to commit Rapes on white women, and there being no particular Law subsisting to punish such Offenders.

BE IT THEREFORE ENACTED by the General Assembly of this Colony, and by the Authority thereof, it is Enacted,* That if any Negro shall hereafter attempt to force or to commit a Rape upon any White Woman, and be thereof lawfully convicted, he shall be branded on each Cheek with the Letter R, and shall be whipped in the most public Manner, at the Discretion of the Court of Assize and General Goal Delivery, where only such Offences shall be tried, and shall be sold by the Sheriff of the County of Newport (within thirty Days after Judgment pass against him) to any Purchaser who will transport or carry him out of this Colony, never to return into it again. And that the Conditions of the Sale of such Negro, shall be, that he shall be transported out of this Government as above said, and that said Sheriff have Two and a Half per Cent. As Commissions for his Trouble. AND be it further Enacted by the Authority aforesaid, That the Sheriff of the County of Newport, shall sell said Negro as before, and on the same Conditions of Sale, viz. to be transported out of said Colony; and for which he shall have the same Commissions as aforesaid.[70]

Scholar Joanne Pope Melish accurately interprets the interrelationship between early slavery and the follow-on conditions of racial prejudice. Beginning with enslavement and public laws designed to dehumanize the enslaved, racial prejudice directed towards African heritage people was directly borne from the slave system.[71] This is a legacy of racial prejudice that carries on into the present day in the forms of institutionalized racism.

Manacles, Rhode Island Black Heritage Society Archives

Between 1709 & 1807, Rhode Island merchants sponsored 934 documented slave voyages to West Africa and carried over 150,000 enslaved Africans to the West Indies and British North America.[72] A breakdown of the documented slaving voyages reveals an interesting pattern. Before the American Revolution, Newport dominated the transatlantic slave trade. After the war, Providence and Bristol became the leading slave trade centers, launching ships even when the trade was outlawed both by the newly established State of Rhode Island and the United States.

A MATTER OF TRUTH

> 672 ships sailed from Newport
>
> 167 ships sailed from Bristol
>
> 71 ships sailed from Providence
>
> 21 ships sailed from Warren
>
> 3 ships sailed from Tiverton, North Kingstown & Little Compton[73]

Finally, in 1787, the Rhode Island General Assembly *"made it illegal for any Rhode Islander to be involved in the African slave trade anywhere. This last law is noteworthy in that it was the first law in America prohibiting American citizens from involvement in the African slave trade,"* notes Rhode Island historian J. Stanley Lemons.[74]

While the Brown family has received much public attention for their infamous 1764 slaving voyage of the *Sally*, the Providence slave-trading sector was dominated by Cyprian Sterry and Company, led by family patriarch Cyprian Sterry.[75] Providence and Bristol merchants prospered in the trade through an innovative *"Intra-American"* slave trade route that transported enslaved Africans from the West Indies, mainly Cuba, directly to the busy American ports of Charleston and Savannah, feeding the insatiable demand for slave labor in the high-demand rice plantation economy of the American south. In a 1797 letter to his brother James, Rhode Island merchant Levi D'Wolf from Havana, Cuba, pointed to their tremendous sales in slaves.[76] An inventory of Providence slave merchants, ships, and destinations details the active trading between the West Indies and the American Atlantic southern coast:

DOCUMENTED PROVIDENCE BASED SLAVING SHIPS & VOYAGES
(Brigs, Sloops & Schooners)

Ship	Date	Captain	Owner(s)	Destination	Slaves
St. Mary	1736	Godfrey	James & Obadiah Brown	West Indies	
	1749	Wm. Brown	Elias Smith & Resolved Waterman	West Indies	
Wheel of Fortune	1759	Wm. Earl	Nicholas & Obadiah Brown	West Indies	
Sally	1764	Esek Hopkins	James, Nicholas & Moses Brown	Guinea Coast/ Antigua	178
Victory	1768	Benjamin Gorton			
William	1768	Jos. Kinnicut			
Victory	1769	Benjamin Gorton			
Sulton	1769	Silas Cook	John Brown & Hayward Smith	Barbados	
Neptune	1770	Esek Hopkins		Barbados	

Name	Year	Captain	Owners	Destination	#
Prudence	1784	Peleg Greene	Greene, Nicholas Power, Nightingale	African Coast/ GA	79
Eliza	1784	Joseph Russell			114
Providence	1785	Peter Wanton	John Brown	Hispaniola	83
Industry	1785	Benjamin Hicks		Charleston, SC	150
Enterprise	1785	D'Wolf		St. Eustacia	114
America	1786	Jos. Cooke	John Cooke		66
Providence	1786	James D'Wolf	Brown & Francis		88
	1786	Job Howland			114
Industry	1787	Benjamin Hicks	Cyprian Sterry & John Murray		66
Providence	1789	Oliver Bowen	Jos. Nightingale & John Clark	Havana, Cuba	87
	1789	John Tower			114
Union	1790	Batty			114
Sally	1791	Jeremiah Taber	James Graves & Wm. Valentine		53
Enterprise	1792	Nathan Sterry	Cyprian Sterry	Savannah, GA	177
Nancy	1793	Jos. Cooke	Zachariah & Phillip Allen	Africa	121
Susannah	1793	John Jenckes	Zachariah & Phillip Allen		112
General Greene	1793	Ross	Cyprian Sterry & Samuel Packard	Barbados	81
Susannah	1793	John Jenckes	Zachariah & Phillip Allen	Baltimore	114
Dolphin	1793	Gilbert Fuller		Savannah, GA	52
Louisa	1794	Nathan Sterry	Cyprian Sterry	Surinam	89
Rebecca	1794	Boss		West Indies	114
General Greene	1794	John Stanton	Cyprian Sterry & Samuel Packard	Savannah, GA	99
Susannah	1794	Wilson Jacobs		Surinam	149
Enterprise	1794	Nathan Sterry	Cyprian Sterry	Savannah, GA	167
James	1794	Edward Boss	Cyprian Sterry	Savannah, GA	110
Polly	1795	Isaac Gorham	Cyprian Sterry	Savannah, GA	40
Dolphin	1795	Alpert Fuller	Cyprian Sterry	Savannah, GA	53
Prudent	1795	Ebenezer Shearman	Ebenezer Jenckes, Jabez Bowen, Ben Brown, John Brown & Zachariah Allen	Savannah, GA	122
Nancy	1795	J.B. Cooke	Zachariah Allen	West Indies	121
Liberty	1795	Abijah Potter	Amassa Smith & Abijah Potter	Savannah, GA	104
Ann	1795	Samuel Packard	Cyprian Sterry & Samuel Packard		133
Abigail	1795	Caleb Greene	Ebenezer Macomber & Jos. Crawford	Savannah, GA	64
Hope	1795	Peleg Wood	John Brown & John Francis	Havana, Cuba	229
Mary	1795	Nathan Sterry	Cyprian Sterry	Savannah, GA	255
Betsey	1795	Peters			114
Polly	1795	Isaac Carr	Ebenezer Jenckes	Savannah, GA	67

Polly	1795	Joshua Smith	Cyprian Sterry	Savannah, Georgia	45
Louisa	1795	Elijah Briggs	Cyprian Sterry	Savannah, GA	89
Delight	1795	Jabez Gibbs	Benjamin Brown, John Brown & Sam Currie	Savannah, Georgia	81
Polly	1795	Lillibridge		Africa/Surinam	114
Betsey	1795	John Lippett	John Lippett & David Ballou		100
Delight	1796	Jabez Gibbs	Benjamin Brown, John Brown & Sam Currie	Savannah, GA	81
James	1796	Albert Fuller	Cyprian Sterry & Samuel Packard	Savannah, GA	87
Enterprise	1796	John Stanton	Cyprian Sterry & Samuel Packard	St. Thomas	145
Adventure	1796	Jeremiah Greenman	Ebenezer Jenckes	Turks Island	138
Agenoria	1796	Edward Boss	Amassa Smith, Benjamin Brown, John Adams, & John Brown		125
Minerva	1796	John Battle	Cyrus Butler		83
Louisa	1796	Elijah Briggs	Cyprian Sterry	Havana, Cuba	103
Abigail	1797	Nathaniel Packard	Ebenezer Macomber		64
Susannah	1799	Pearce Coggeshall	Wm. Church, Seth Clark, Oliver Brown, Pearce Coggeshall		39
Exchange	1799	John Pettis	Jos. Whiting & John Pettis		114
Chance	1799	Wm. Brown Jr.	Wm. Brown Jr.	Havana, Cuba	114
Caroline	1799	Gilbert Fuller	Sam Allen, Cyrus Allen, Edward Dickens & Benjamin Clifford	Havana, Cuba	79
Flying Fish	1799	Nathaniel Packard Jr.	Nathaniel Packard Jr.	Havana, Cuba	150
Flying Fish	1799	Nathaniel Packard Jr.	Nathaniel Packard Jr. & Sam McClellan	Havana, Cuba	91
Success	1800	Paul Brownell	Samuel W. Greene	Havana, Cuba	122
Ida	1800	Thomas Hudson	John C. Nightingale		162
Sally	1800	Thomas Baker	Edward Dickens, Thomas Baker, & George D'Wolf	Havana, Cuba	111
Betsey	1801	Nathaniel Packard	Benjamin Curtis		118
Eliza	1802				102
Resource	1805	Wm. Megee	Wm. Megee & Amos Jenckes	Montevideo	53
Columbia	1806	Thomas Hudson	James Bartell	Charleston, SC	178

Total Voyages (1736-1806) = 71
Enslaved Africans (1736-1806) = 6,795

Sources:
National Archives: U.S. Customs Service, Slave Manifests
Trans-Atlantic Slave Trade Database, Emory University
The Notorious Triangle, Jay Coughtry, Temple University Press, 1981

Molasses: The Essential Ingredient in American Independence

Most certainly, the principal driver of the Rhode Island Trans-Atlantic economy was rum. The Rhode Island merchants perfected the rum-for-slaves trade. Massachusetts and Connecticut participated, but Rhode Island surpassed them in proportion. Newport, growing rapidly in wealth and commerce, boasted twenty-two still-houses.[77]

The most important market for American rum was the Gold Coast, or what is present-day Ghana.[78] Rum was the most carried cargo to West Africa, and Rhode Island merchants so dominated the trade they were referred to as the "Rum Men." According to historian Randy Sparks, *"Rhode Island merchants carried about 150,00 slaves from Africa to the Caribbean and North America and controlled up to 90 percent of the American trade in slaves."*[79] Providence merchant Nicholas Tillinghast ordered rum for what he called the *"Guinea Trade."* And Nicholas Brown and Company told a potential Virginia slave buyer, *"We live in a place where we can procure a large quantity of rum distilled immediately."*[80]

18th Century Hogshead Rum Barrel, Rhode Island Black Heritage Society Archives

Rhode Island's dependence upon the rum-for-slave trade was critical to the economic prosperity of the Colony. When England enacted the Sugar Act of 1764 as a revenue-raising tax upon molasses from the West Indies and rum from the Americas, Governor Josias Lyndon, also a slave owner, sent a series of letters to the British Lord Commissioners for Trade & Plantations highlighting the following:[81]

- *The Colony of Rhode Island includes not much larger content of territory than about thirty miles square, and of this, a great part is of barren soil not worth the expense of cultivation.*

- *It is this quantity of molasses which serves as an engine in the hands of the merchant.*

- *Formerly the Negro upon the coast (Africa) were supplied with French Brandy, but in the year 1723, some merchants in this Colony introduced the use of rum.*

- *There are now upwards of 30 distilleries in the Colony.*

Colonial protests about the Sugar Act died out when the tax was lowered two years later. Still, it set the stage for Colonial American merchants, most notably in Rhode Island, who cast a disapproving eye on future efforts by England to promote "taxation without representation." Ironically, a few years later, a statement posted in the Newport Mercury newspaper called out the clear hypocrisy of Rhode Island merchants by reminding the soon-to-be patriots:

> *"If you say you have the right to enslave (Negroes) because it is for your interest, why do you dispute the legality of Great Britain's enslaving you?"*
>
> *– A True Son of Liberty, Newport Mercury, January 8, 1768*

Founding Father and second American President John Adams noted the role of rum in American independence in an August 11, 1818, letter to Judge William Tutor:

> "Witts may laugh at our fondness for Molasses & we ought all join in the laugh with as much good humour as General Lincoln did, General Washington however always asserted & proved that Virginians loved Molasses as well as New England men did. I know not why we should blush to confess that Molasses was an essential Ingredient in American Independence. Many great Events have proceeded from much smaller causes."[82]

Early Acts of Defiance: Runaways Ads

Enslaved Indigenous and African heritage people in Rhode Island did not passively accept forced servitude. As historian John Hope Franklin notes, day-to-day resistance was a powerful tool of defiance for the enslaved:

> Slaves pulled down fences, sabotaged farm equipment, broke implements, damaged boats, vandalized wagons, ruined clothing and committed various other destructive acts. They stole with impunity; sheep, hogs, cattle, poultry, money, watches, produce, liquor, tobacco, flour, cotton, indigo, corn, nearly anything that was not under lock and key, and they occasionally found the key.[83]

Providence Gazatte March 30, 1763

The open revolt was the most extreme form of resistance. This was one of the great fears for slave owners, particularly in the West Indies and southern American colonies, who retained significant numbers of enslaved laborers. This ultimate form of African resistance was rare in Colonial America outside of the 1712 New York City Slave Revolt.[84] Running away was another form of resistance. The maritime industry provided a ready path to freedom.

The peculiar institution of slavery had its start and evolution with the sea, through the Trans-Atlantic Slave Trade connecting vessels and crews with Europe, Africa, West Indies, and the Americas. And in colonial Rhode Island, one of the best paths for African freedom and prosperity led back to the sea. The early American maritime industry was also a meritocracy. Crews were hired based on their skill and ability, not on race. In his award-winning book on African heritage seamen, W. Jeffery Bolster points out that seafaring was one of the most significant occupations among enslaved and free African men in the eighteenth and nineteenth centuries.[85] In his ground-breaking study of the slave trade in Rhode Island, Jay Coughtry estimates that African heritage seamen comprised up to 21 percent of the Newport crews engaged in Caribbean, European, and African voyages.[86]

Many enslaved Africans who chose the path to freedom as runaways escaped to urban seaports, where they could sign onto vessels as crew-members. A review of runaway slave advertisements show they ran from one slave community in New England to *"hide in plain sight"* in other coastal urban centers. Enslaved Africans fled Boston to live relatively free lives in New Bedford, Newport, and Providence. Many slave runaway ads in the

Providence Gazette and Newport Mercury newspapers regularly included the statement, *"All Masters of Vessels and others, are cautioned against carrying off said Negro, on Penalty of the law."* Most importantly, ships offered a haven for runaways when no free states existed.[87]

Ironically, Rhode Island vessels in the Trans-Atlantic Slave Trade included African heritage crew members who played key roles in trading fellow Africans. African heritage crew members provided a disease-resistant workforce on African coasts. They also acted as translators aboard slave ships, and they had a keen knowledge of African coastal locations and logistics.[88]

African Governors

In Rhode Island, enslaved and free Africans reclaimed their African identity through African tribal election rituals. Beginning each spring as early as 1740, possibly in Newport, they would hold elaborate multiple-day ceremonies and elect a Tribal Leader or an African Governor on what was sometimes referred to as Negro Election Day—a ceremony common in Rhode Island, Connecticut, Massachusetts, and New Hampshire. By 1790 the practice had peaked, spreading to no fewer than eighteen towns in New England, among them Boston, Providence, South Kingstown, Portsmouth, New Hampshire, and New Haven, Connecticut.[89] In Providence, the African Governor rituals may have very well been the forerunner to African heritage civic and cultural organizations, followed by the establishment of the African Union Society, African Lodge, and African Meeting House.

Christian McBurney Collections

Negro Election Day presents one of the most striking examples of African creativity within the dominant slave society, combining African performance styles, artistic expression, and a measure of autonomy from daily life as someone's property.[90] These highly festive ceremonies, held in June of each year, reflected an important reconnection to Africa and its tribal customs. After the election votes were tallied, the new African Governor was honored in an inaugural parade that included food, games, socializing, and dancing in a celebration of the entire African community, enslaved and free.

The two most important facts about the African Governor ceremonies are that, first, they took place not only in Rhode Island and New England, but also across slave societies in the West Indies and Brazil;[91] and secondly, the ceremonies shared West African ritual and religious practices commonly found among the Ashanti people on the Gold Coast.[92] Despite the brutal and dehumanizing conditions of enslavement, African heritage people in Providence and across the African Diaspora survived and thrived through the preservation and reclamation of one of their most fundamental African traditions.

Gradual Emancipation Act of 1784 & Advent of Free African Union Societies

Through much of the 18th century, Rhode Island had the largest percentage of enslaved African heritage people in New England. Providence, Newport, and Bristol were leading slave ports.[93] By 1774, Rhode Island had enacted a law prohibiting the importation of new slaves into the colony. But it was silent on Rhode Island merchants' continued participation in slave trading in other countries and other American ports. Providence merchant and slave trader Cyprian Sterry was most active during the late 18th century. Sterry financed at least 18 voyages that transported more than 1,500 captives to the southern United States and the Caribbean during the 1790s.[94]

On February 25, 1784, the Rhode Island General Assembly enacted a law "authorizing the manumission of Negros, Mulattoes, and others, and for the gradual Abolition of Slavery," declaring:

> WHEREAS all Men are entitled to Life, Liberty and the Pursuit of Happiness, and the holding of Mankind in a State of Slavery, as property, which has gradually obtained by unrestrained Customs and the permission of the Laws, is repugnant to this Principle, and subversive of the Happiness of Mankind, the great End of all civil Government.[95]

While conveniently extracting the well-known phrase "Life, Liberty and the Pursuit of Happiness" from the United States Declaration of Independence, the law only provided for the gradual emancipation of the enslaved, and failed to fully grant to African and Indigenous people of Rhode Island their natural rights as free citizens. While slavery ended slowly in Rhode Island due to laws, disruptions from the American Revolution, and the waning economies of the transatlantic trade, free people of color faced new challenges. They might be free, but they were treated as inferior, second-class citizens based upon their race.[96]

As a graphic example, Rhode Island passed miscegenation laws barring people of different races from marrying or living together. The colonists worried about the weakening of "inheritable slavery laws," which said that children born to enslaved mothers were also slaves. This ensured free labor for the enslaver.[97] Under the law, children born to free (white) mothers could be placed into temporary indentured service, but not permanent slavery. This "new class" of temporary laborers would quickly diminish access to free slave labor. The second concern was based upon maintaining clear racial boundaries: free Blacks would compete for jobs and living space.[98]

In 1798, the Rhode Island General Assembly enacted a law that would strictly prohibit whites from marrying an African heritage or Indigenous person, asserting:

> That no person, by this act authorized to join persons in marriage, shall join in marriage a white person with any Negro, Indian or mulatto, on the penalty of two hundred dollars, to be recovered by action of debt, one money thereof to be paid to and for the use of the State, and the other money to and for the use of him who shall prosecute for the same; and all such marriages shall be absolutely null and void.[99]

These new challenges would require free African heritage people in Rhode Island to construct their own mutual aid organizations to promote and protect their inalienable rights. Immediately after the American Revolution and the gradual abolition of slavery in Rhode Island by 1784, free Africans in Newport and Providence and their counterparts in Boston and Philadelphia embraced their new identity as "Africans in America." One of their first acts as free men was the establishment of America's first Black civic institutions that would become the guiding light for all African heritage people moving from enslavement to freedom. On November 10, 1780, a group of African men assembled at the Newport home of Abraham Casey to organize and charter America's first mutual aid society for Africans and, later, African Americans. Known as the Free African Union Society, it predated slavery abolition in Massachusetts, Connecticut, New Hampshire, and Rhode Island. This new institution assertively embraced an African identity in its very name, and in 1787, its officers corresponded with their free African counterparts in Providence to form a similar organization:

> And, dear Brethren, we have established ourselves in the name of the Union Society, to be a subordinate part of the Society, as the officers that we have chosen are all inferior to your Officers in Newport, and, of course, we must be subordinate to your part of the Society in Newport. The officers that we have made choice of are as following: A Vice President, Moderator, Six Representatives, and one Treasurer and a Deputy Secretary, and a Sheriff to convene the Members at every Quarterly Meeting and Annual Meeting.
>
> And whereas, Brethren, we would wish for you to observe this Rule, that if any of our Members that belongs to Providence should by chance be in want of any sum of money, and our Treasury should not be sufficiently stored so as to supply his or our Necessary want, and we should make Application that they, or any of the Members so needful, shall have Resource to the Treasury in Newport for Relief of such Members, and the same Rule is to be observed and maintained in Providence by our part of the Society for the Relief of any member in Newport that should happen to come within the line of such Necessities.
>
> *By Order of the Society*
>
> | | |
> |---|---|
> | President Cato Coggeshall | Bristol Olney |
> | Moderator Bristol Yamma | Cudgo Brown |
> | Treasurer Bonner Brown | Cato Mumford |
> | Secretary James McKenzie | William Stober |
> | James McKenzie, Sec'ry | Felix Holbrook[100] |
> | London Spears | |

As noted by historian Richard S. Newman, after enslavement, *"Redeeming Africans and blackness could therefore occur anywhere in the Atlantic world, so long as people of color viewed themselves as a powerful collective entity."*[101] The Free African Societies of Newport, Providence, Boston, and Philadelphia all believed in the benefits of organizing around the shared values of African identity and justice. The importance of African identity can be seen in the ceremonial dress at public parades and gatherings, as recounted by William J. Brown in his memoirs:

> *The African Societies wore their regalia. The President of the societies, who was their commander, was dressed to represent an African chief, having on a red pointed cap, and carried an elephant's tusk in each hand; each end was tipped with gilt. The other officers carrying emblems, decked with lemons and oranges, representing the fruits of Africa, and other emblems.*[102]

An extraordinary group of men helped found the African Society of Providence. Felix Holbrook, originally from Boston, joined other Massachusetts Africans on a 1773 petition requesting emancipation for himself and others in the Commonwealth. Later, he would relocate to Providence and become a member of the 1st

Rhode Island Regiment during the American Revolution.[103] Cudjo Brown was enslaved in the Moses Brown household. He was a teamster by trade.[104] Bristol Yamma, who moved to Providence from Newport, achieved fame in 1774 when he and African John Quamino became the first African men to enter the College of New Jersey (Princeton University), where they were trained as Christian missionaries bound for West Africa.[105] James McKenzie endorsed a plan for Providence African heritage people to return to West Africa. In 1795, McKenzie—on behalf of the Providence Society and with support from Moses Brown —traveled to Sierra Leone to negotiate an emigration plan for Providence families to return to their African homeland.[106] Cato Coggeshall, another Newport African who relocated to Providence, was a friend of the African poet Phillis Wheatley.[107] Coggeshall was one of several free Africans who purchased as an original subscriber to Rev. Samuel Hopkins's important book on religious doctrine in 1793.[108] Coggeshall's son and namesake would later live within Providence's Hardscrabble neighborhood, surviving the 1824 race riot.

The founders and participants in the Providence African Society represented the first generation of African men (and later women) who would actively dissociate themselves from the slave society, setting the stage for future generations of "African" Americans who would pursue freedom, equality, and justice.

Dispossession & Native Land Sales

"That we cannot in no one place go to the salt water without passing through land now in possession of the English, and that upon the smallest affront we may expect nothing better than to be prosecuted and liable to be deprived of the privilege of fishing, which is the main branch of the support of the greater part of the Tribe."

- Tobias Shattock

As Africans would pursue those opportunities that would free them and provide a better life as unrestricted citizens, Indigenous people were simply trying to survive in late 18th century Rhode Island. From the end of King Philip's War until the beginning of the 19th century, Indigenous people endured a complicated relationship with the Rhode Island government, particularly with the use and preservation of native lands. The near annihilation of the Narragansett people before and after King Philip's War opened the door for considerable English expansion across Rhode Island. Baptist Minister John Callender described the impact this way: *"Their insufferable aversion to the English Industry, and way of life, the alteration from the Indian method of living, their laziness, and their love of strong drink, have swept them away, in a wonderful manner."*[109]

To his credit, Roger Williams believed Indigenous people rightfully owned their ancestral lands, though other English colonists strongly disagreed. The English believed that land ownership was defined by use. The colonists improved the land by growing crops, raising cattle, and erecting fences. In their view, the Indigenous people did none of these things; they left the land idle and unused.[110]

The colonists developed a shrewd and effective tactic for taking native land. Often, Indigenous people entered into a trade or purchase agreement with the English for various goods and services. In many cases, those goods were overpriced. When the native was unable to pay, the English sued and made them responsible for a debt. Since most natives did not have money or valuable possessions, the debt was resolved by taking the one item of value the natives owned—their land. This unsavory practice became so prevalent the Rhode Island

General Assembly passed a law as early as 1663 prohibiting it:

> *FOR AS MUCH as diverse Persons have made Purchases of Lands in this Colony of the Indians, without the consent or approbation of the General Assembly, which manifestly tends to the Defrauding, and Manifest Injury of such Native Indians, as well as defeating the just Rights of this Colony. BE it therefore Enacted by the General Assembly, and the Authority of the same, That no Person or Persons for the future, shall purchase any Lands or Islands within this Colony, of or from the Native Indians within the same, but such only as are so allowed to do by the General Assembly, upon Penalty of forfeiting all such Lands or Islands so purchased, to this Colony; And to pay for every such Purchase by them so made, the Sum of Twenty Pounds as a Fine, to and for the Use of the Colony; And all such Purchases shall be Esteemed and Adjudged Null, Void, and of none Effect.*[111]

The new law did not stop the debt suits against the natives. In 1730, the Rhode Island General Assembly enacted another law restricting the use of debt to place Indigenous people into indentured service, declaring:

> *WHEREAS several evil-minded Persons in this Colony, of a greedy and covetous Design, often draw Indians into their Debt, by selling them Goods at extravagant Rates, and get the said Indians to be bound to them for longer Time than is just and reasonable, to the great Hurt and Damage of the Indians, and to the Dishonor of the Government. For the Preventing whereof for the Future, BE IT ENACTED by the General Assembly of this Colony, That no Indian shall be bound an Apprentice or Servant to any of His Majesty's Subjects in this Colony, without the Consent, Allowance, and Approbation of two Justices of the Peace, or Wardens of this Colony, and for good Consideration therefor, and testified to under the Hands of such Justices or Wardens: Any Law, Custom, or Usage to the Contrary, in any wise notwithstanding.*[112]

The taking of Indigenous land took a disastrous turn for the Narragansett tribe in 1741 and again in 1746 with the selling of land to settle the supposed debts of the two Sachems, George Ninigret and Thomas Ninigret. In the case of George, the Rhode Island General Assembly stepped in to settle his personal debts, stating:

> *IT Is VOTED and ORDERED, That the said George Ninigret Sachem, be, and he is hereby fully empowered and enabled, by and with the Advice and Consent of his Trustees or the major Part of them, to sell and dispose of to the Highest Bidder, so much of his aforesaid Lands (that will least prejudice his Estate) as may be sufficient to pay his present Debts: And the Deed or Deeds by him given, and assented to by his Trustees, or the major Part of them as aforesaid, shall be good and valid in the Law. And that public Notice be given of the Sale of the aforesaid Lands, for the Space of one Month before the same is sold.*[113]

Thomas Ninigret would fare no better when several years later, he was forced to sell large tracts of native lands to settle his debts in 1746.[114] As a young man, he was sent to England to learn English customs. He returned to Rhode Island with newfound English appetites that drove him and his tribe into debt. It was during his reign—the English called him "King Tom"—that much of the remaining native land was sold off.[115] At the time of his death in 1769, the Boston Evening Post reported that all he had left was his title as Sachem.[116]

The actions taken by Rhode Island General Assembly freed up new land for white settlers. Tobias Shattock and his brother John attempted to circumvent Thomas Ninigret from selling the tribe's land in a powerful letter to the British Superintendent of Indian Affairs, Sir William Johnson:

> *May it pleas your Honour, with the deepest sense of Gratitude and thanks, we Approach you acknowledging your pious design and charitable Donation in assisting us in our Difficulty. and now we Humbly pray your Honour to Inform us By a Letter to Mr. Robinson whether you Have Received them orders from Home or not. moreover we would Inform your Honour that we Have used ye utmost of our skill, to Enlighten those of our Tribe that acted against us and have Been successful in a Good degree: for they have mainly seen their Error, and are Heartily united with us. We are all Harty and well, and Our Tribe in one sense Increases very fast, and in another Decrease for our Land is sold so that many of our young men are obliged to go to sea and so are Lost so that our most promising young men are often Laid in a watery Tomb to our Lamentation may it pleas your Honour we Esteem you as our Best friend and do always pray that you may Be assisted By our Dear Savior in all your proceeding[s] and finally Receive a crown of Glory that shall Never fade. We are Ever Bound to acknowledge ourselves your most obedient and very Humble servants until Death.*
>
> *Signed in Behalf of the Tribe pr Tobias Shadick*
> *Charlestown October*
> *ye 14th Day 1765*[117]

Leading Narragansett families added their names to a formal petition urging the return of their native land, including:

Elder Samuel Niles, Stephen Coheis, Ephraim Coyhies, Joseph Coyheis, Toby Coyheis, Roger Wampy, James Niles, Joseph Towhy, Thomas Lewis, Tobias Shaddock, John Wampy, David Seketor, Charles Anthony, Mercy Coyheis, Elizabeth Coheis, Mercy Reed, Hannah Coyheis, Elizabeth Niles, Peter Shaddock, William Coyhies, Thomas Coyheis, Sarah Niles, Hannah Shaddock. Hannah Towlly, Sarah Samson, Mercy James, Elizabeth Coyheis, Mercy Shaddock, Elizabeth Shesuek, Sarah Wampy, Samuel Niles, Jr., Samuel Wampy, Joseph Shaddock, Hannah Tomson, Tobias Hall. James Shaddock, Mary Rogers, and Simeon Niles.[118]

In a December 1767 follow-on letter to the General Assembly, Shattock continued to describe the circumstances the Rhode Island Colony had placed upon his native people: "*Send me to England for redress for the injuries, violations and frauds done to the Indians. By having our Land sold from us during a course of years.*"[119] Shattock continued. "*We are in great danger of losing our lands. We Indians have always kept our laws and customs among us. The great men of the government, who have been wanting to purchase our lands, have worked clandestinely and underhanded with us, who are ignorant people, being careless and not looking far enough into affairs have brought ourselves into this difficulty.*"[120]

While Indigenous people in 18th century Rhode Island struggled to maintain their ancestral land and personal freedom, the English colonists passed a 1729 law to curtail their tribal rituals and customs by policing tribal dances in 1729: enacting

> WHEREAS *it is very common in this Colony, and especially in Westerly and South-Kingston, for Indians to make Dances, which has been found, by Experience, to be very prejudicial to the adjacent*

Inhabitants, by their excessive Drinking, and Fighting, and Wounding each other; and many Servants are enticed to out-stay their Time at such Dances, and then run away from their Masters.

BE IT THEREFORE ENACTED by the General Assembly, and by the Authority of the same it is Enacted and Declared, That the Town Councils of each Town in this Colony, have full Power to make such Laws and Orders, for the better regulation of such Indian Dances in their respective Towns, as they shall think needful and necessary; and to Fine all such Persons, either English, Indians, or others, that shall sell or give any Strong Liquors at any such Dances, not exceeding Forty Shillings.

The Indigenous people of Rhode Island, particularly the Narragansett tribe, endured much in a century: war, slavery, banishment, loss of land, and control of their cultural expression. The newly established State of Rhode Island would move to formally abolish the position of the Sachem, the traditional tribal leader, in a 1792 act that would establish a state-appointed Tribal Council:

It is further voted and resolved that all the males of said tribe, of twenty-one years of age, shall and may meet together at the school house, their accustomed place of meeting, on the last Tuesday in march, A.D. 1792, and annually, and every year on that day, for the purpose of electing their Council, which shall be chosen by a majority of votes, and that in such meetings, and all others, and upon occasions, every male person of twenty-one years, born of an Indian woman belonging to said tribe, or begotten by an Indian man belonging thereto, of any other than a negro woman, shall be entitled to vote. :[121]

While the Rhode Island government may not have wanted to see the Narragansetts flourish, they also did not want the remaining natives to become paupers and social burdens in the new state.[122] These concerted actions—beginning with the taking of native lands through the 1792 law replacing the tribe's Sachem with a Council—initiated the process of Narragansett detribalization that would only accelerate through the 19th century. The documents provide a new perspective on the state's past. Rhode Island's early success—its founding, settlement, and growth— is firmly rooted in the enslavement of African people and the dispossession of native lands.

PART 2: SEPARATE & UNEQUAL IN 19th CENTURY PROVIDENCE (1800-1899)

Evolution of Free African Heritage Community in Providence

On July 4, 1776, members of the Continental Congress signed the Declaration of Independence in Philadelphia. The following year, Vermont became the first of the thirteen colonies to abolish slavery. Over the course of the next few years, Massachusetts, Pennsylvania, Rhode Island, New Hampshire, Connecticut, and New York all passed slavery abolition laws. This "First Emancipation" not only set African enslavement on a course towards extinction in America but would also create a new large population of free Africans in America.

At the end of the 18th century in Rhode Island and particularly in Providence, a new class of people emerged: the free African heritage resident. According to the first federal Census of 1790, 475 African heritage people lived in Providence, with 427 listed as free people and 48 enslaved.[123] The majority settled in two census districts on the East Side, including the present-day College Hill neighborhood and the northern outskirts of town between North Main Street and the Great Basin. Names of heads of households at that time included:

Newport Arrow	Peter Barras	Disimbo Bay
Bonner Brown	Liverpool Brown	London Brown
Primus Brown	Providence Brown	Waitstill Brown
Peter Browning	Quaco Butler	William Cesar
York Champlin	Deborah Church	Cato Coggeshall
Isaac Cooper	Dick Cozzens	Prime Cushing
Cudge Earl	Cuff Easterbrooks	Comfort Ephraim
Yockey Fenner	Cato Freeman	Jacob Freeman
Cato Gardner	Patience Gardner	Primus George
Tobey Harris	York Hanover	Sampson Hazzard
Pleasant Hicks	Ebar Hopkins	Pamp Hopkins
Primus Hopkins	Sant Hopkins	Bazil Human
Prince Jencks	Cato Johnston	Quaco Johnston
Medford Keen	James Lippitt	Cesar Lyndon
Lewis Manning	James MacKenzie	Plato M'Leannen
Member Nava	Mary Newfield	Quam Nightingale
Bristol Onley	Freelove Parker	Thomas Pegan
Abijah Read	Baston Ruggles	Brittan Saltonston
Samuel Sharp	Ebin Sico	Mode Siscoe
Quam Simmons	Jack Smith	London Spear
Fortune Stanford	Patience Sterry	William Stoves
Henry Tabor	Newport Tew	Cesar Waterman
Robert Wainwood	Bristol Yamma	

The African heritage community in Providence faced new challenges in the early 19th century. As historian Robert J. Cottrol notes, *"For the black people of Providence, the decades following emancipation were to be a time of burgeoning consciousness and organization."*[124] During the era, the City of Providence experienced explosive economic growth, replacing Newport as one of America's leading ports and also driving the nation's economy from maritime ventures to industrial manufacturing. These dramatic changes in population and commerce created a rapidly urbanized Providence—and new levels of racial prejudice.

The 19th century would bring new challenges and discrimination to overcome for Providence's small but dynamic free community of color, including surviving race riots, equal access to public education, voting rights, and general civil rights. One of their first acts as free people was joining fellow free African heritage people in Newport, Boston, and Philadelphia to establish America's earliest Black benevolent institutions. These organizations would quickly become the guiding light for all African heritage people from enslavement to freedom and would embrace an African identity in their very names, including the African Society, African Church, African Lodge, and African School. The Providence Free African Society was organized in 1789. At least seven men who lived on College Hill—London Spear, William Stoves, Bonner Brown, Cudge Brown, Cato Coggeshall, James Mackenzie, and Bristol Olney were founding members. As similar to their Newport counterparts, the Providence African Society would organize their society to advance a common good for all free Africans in Providence as stated in a July 27, 1789 letter from the Newport Society to London Spear and Cato Gardner in Providence stating:

> *Therefore, our sincere desire is that you join us in this Society so that we all may promote one common good. We have agreed upon certain regulations to be maintained in the Society, which you may see, and if you should fully comply and join us, you shall have a part of the Officers at Providence.* [125]

Achieving freedom and establishing a physical presence in early 19th-century Providence was a crucial first step for the African heritage community. The formation of the African Society would set the stage for significant Black institutions in Providence, with soon-to-follow religious, civic, and educational organizations, highlighted by the founding of the third African Masonic Lodge in America, the Hiram Lodge No. 3 on September 27, 1797. [126]

A Return to Africa

As early as 1787, the Free African Union Society of Newport pursued a plan to return to Africa. In a January 24, 1787 letter to abolitionist Dr. William Thornton, Society President Anthony Taylor outlined the group's desires:

> *Our Earnest desire of returning to Africa and settling there has induced us further to trouble you with these lines, in order to convey to your mind a more particular and full idea of our proposal..We want to know by what right or tenor we shall possess said Lands, when we settle upon them, for we should think it not safe, and unwise for us to go and settle on Lands in Africa unless the right and fee of the Land is first firmly and in proper form, made over to us, and to our Heirs or Children.* [127]

The Newport plan did not gain much traction, but in 1794 the African Society of Providence sent one of their members to Sierra Leone to establish a new settlement. With his passage supported and underwritten by Moses Brown, Society secretary James Mackenzie met with the Governor of British-occupied Sierra Leone and negotiated an agreement to send twelve Providence families to Sierra Leone and provide each family with ten acres of land.[128] Mackenzie carried a formal letter on behalf of the Providence Society cosigned by fellow members London Spears, Bonner Brown, and William Olney asserting:

> *We, the undersigned, having embraced this opportunity of informing you of our wishes to emigrate. Therefore, for the full investigations to the Rules & Regulations of the Colony, we have appointed Mr. James Mackenzie & sent him as our Representative with full power to transact, bargain & agree to anything respecting our Emigration.* [129]

But there was a problem. Each of the future emigres needed an endorsement of their moral character from two respectable white clergies. For an unknown reason, Reverend Samuel Hopkins of Newport, a Moses Brown friend and fellow abolitionist, would not endorse the Providence group. The next successful emigration to Africa would not occur until 1826, when a group of 32 African heritage men, women, and children, mainly from Newport, would emigrate to Liberia. Tragically, soon after arriving in Monrovia on February 26, 1826,[130] most of the party succumbed to coastal fever and died within a year of their arrival. But even in death, they were able to die as free people in a free land.

African-Self Determination: Meeting & School Houses

The African Union Society and Hiram African Lodge organizations provided a place for Black civic engagement. But what about their spiritual and educational needs?

The First Baptist Church of Providence, the oldest Baptist church congregation in the United States, met some of those needs. Roger Williams and his followers started the church in 1638. A later congregation erected the present church in 1774–75 and held its first meetings in May 1775. Two years later, the "Great Awakening," a Christian revitalization movement that swept Protestant America in the mid-18th century, encouraged African-heritage people, initially enslaved, to become a part of the congregation.[131] A review of African heritage membership in the First Baptist Church before the American Revolution included a large number of women. (*see image p.39*)

19th Century Providence Couple, Rhode Island Black Heritage Society Archives

While Providence prided itself on being founded under the principles of religious toleration and freedom, African-heritage Christians were limited in where and how they might worship. In his autobiography, William J. Brown explains the situation: *"Many attended no church at all because they said they were opposed to going to churches and sitting in pigeonholes as all the churches at that time had some obscure place for the colored to sit in."*[132]

As Brown notes, African heritage people were segregated, second-class worshipers. *"I went to the First Baptist Church in company of Miss Wescott, climbing up three or four pair of stairs to where the colored people sat."* [133]

On March 19, 1819, a group of African heritage members met at the First Baptist Church to organize a plan to raise funds for their own meeting house.[134] The founding committee included leading African heritage men, many of them accomplished tradesmen: George McCarty, Warwick Sweetland, Abraham Gibbs, George

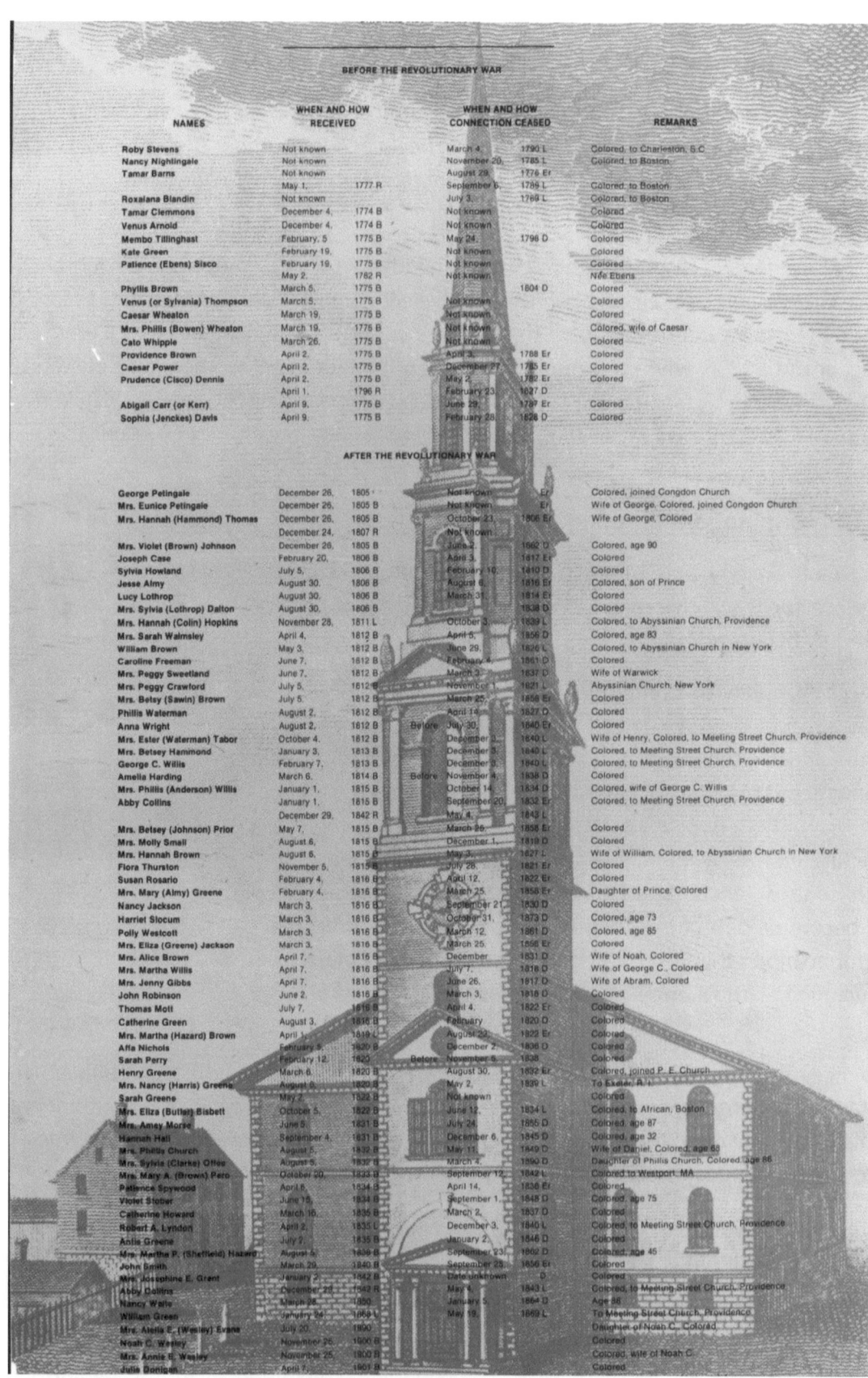

List of African heritage members of First Baptist Church, Rhode Island
Black Heritage Society Archives

Smith, George Willis, Joshua Weeks, Derry Williams, Hodge Congdon, Nathaniel Paul, Henry Taber, Peter Waters, Thomas Graham, James Harris, Thomas Thompson, George Barrett, Henry Greene, Stephen Walmsley, and Asa Goldsbury.[135] Moses Brown transferred his land along Meeting Street to the African Society with the specific requirement that *"the Meeting House is to be open and free for all denominations of Christianity."*[136] On August 21, 1821, the African Meeting and Schoolhouse was completed. A town-wide celebration and parade — organized by the African heritage community of Providence and led by Hodge Congdon—marked the event. As described by William J. Brown, the celebration was a highly festive occasion:

> *The young men formed a military company called the African Greys to escort the African societies to their new house of worship. The procession line of march was to pass Meeting Street by the Friend's Meeting House. There, the Friends were to join the society, and the procession moved up to Meeting Street church, where the service of dedication was to be performed.* [137]

Despite the challenges of living in Antebellum America, Providence's African heritage community, although small, built livelihoods through their African meeting house and school. These places of ownership and pride would serve as platforms from which productive Black life launched in Providence.[138] Only a few days after the completion of the meeting house in 1821, an anonymous writer in the Providence Journal complained about the growing number of fugitive Blacks from other locations who were coming to Providence. The writer suggested a general register of all Blacks in town to regulate and remove a transient Black population.[139] Coincidentally, the following year, in 1822, male African voters were legally disenfranchised as qualified voters in Rhode Island.[140] The loss of suffrage rights, the growing concern with Black emigration, and the appearance of Black organizations within a rapidly growing industrial city would set the stage for a series of devastating race riots.

Racialized Riots: Hardscrabble & Snowtown

Hardscrabble

While emancipation brought about the end of slavery, life for many African heritage people in antebellum Providence was undoubtedly a "hardscrabble" existence. The meaning of the word may have been first defined by the explorers Lewis and Clark in their journals. They referred to an imaginary place marked by hard work and struggle.[141] Providence's people of color faced clear hardships. Thanks to the legacies of enslavement, men mostly worked at menial jobs. Women had even fewer opportunities. Living choices were minimal. Nearly all of the African heritage working poor lived in substandard housing east of the Providence River on the northwestern edge of town.[142] By the 1820s, it was referred to formally as Addison Hollow. Others called it Hardscrabble. William J. Brown provided a snapshot of the community:

> *In the northwest part of the city was a place called Addison Hollow, but was nicked named Hardscrabble. A great many-colored people purchased land there because it was some distance from the town, and hence quite cheap. They put up small houses for themselves and earned their living in various ways.* [143]

Additionally, they faced an unrelenting and legalized effort to label them "outsiders" and settle them elsewhere.[144]

The Hardscrabble riot of October 1824 had its roots in the growing pains of a rapidly expanding and industrialized town, attracting immigrants looking for work. But the open resentment of African heritage people relocating to Providence became the match that lit the flame of violence that would soon engulf the Hardscrabble neighborhood. Providence's African heritage residents routinely fought against unruly white sailors and young belligerents. People of color in early 19th century Providence could not banish the city's rowdier elements from their midst; they often found themselves in conflict with the more boisterous denizens of the waterfront communities that they inhabited. Harassment by rowdies was a constant problem for the Black people in Providence. Whole neighborhoods became gauntlets for Blacks in Providence, areas where there was an ever-present fear of being set upon by criminals. Little protection was offered to Black people by the authorities.[145]

HARDSCRABBLE RESIDENTS

Name	Year	Location/Description
Thomas Gardner	1844	Hardscrabble, Laborer
Nathan Gilbert	1841	N. Shore Cove, widower
Mary Goulding	1830-41	Smith St., widow, female nurse
Jane Greene	1836-41	N. Shore Cove
William A Grose	1842-44	Hardscrabble, Laborer
Joseph Hagard	1841	Hardscrabble, Laborer
Violet Howland	1844	N. Shore Cove
William Hull	1841	Hardscrabble, Laborer
	1844	Hardscrabble, Laborer
John Jackson	1841	Hardscrabble, Laborer
	1844	Hardscrabble, Laborer
William Jackson	1841	N. Shore Cove, Laborer
	1844	N. Shore Cove, Laborer
Judith Johnson	1844	N. Shore Cove
Harriet Lippett	1832-9	N. Shore Cove
Patience Lippett	1838-9	N. Shore Cove
Simon Lippett	1836-44	N. Shore Cove, Laborer
John M'Leary	1838-41	N. Shore Cove, Laborer
Amos M. Malbone	1844	N. Shore Cove, Mariner
Mrs. Lucy Malbone	1844	N. Shore Cove
Eleanor Olney	1844	Hardscrabble
Abraham Padelford	1841	N. Shore Cove
	1844	Cove (not listed black)
John Phenix	1832-9	N. Shore Cove, Laborer
Congdon M. Potter	1844	Hardscrabble, wagoner
John R. Potter	1841	Smith St., Laborer
	1844	Hardscrabble, laborer

Antebellum Residents of Hardscrabble Neighborhood, Rhode Island Black Heritage Society Archives

The Hardscrabble riot commenced on the evening of October 24 when several Black men refused to give way on a sidewalk to a group of white men. According to various accounts, a mob of nearly fifty whites armed with clubs marched to the Hardscrabble neighborhood and gathered at Henry T. Wheeler's home. While Wheeler lived on the second floor of the house, above a popular dance hall on the first floor. The mob began destroying Wheeler's house and would later destroy another twenty homes and businesses.[146] What stood out during the rampage was the organized and methodical destruction of a Black neighborhood sparked by a single, isolated altercation.

The riot did not occur in a vacuum. In the months leading up to the event, newspaper articles and letters from "anonymous" citizens openly disparaged African heritage people in Providence, frequently linking them to the town's rising crime, poverty, and general moral decay. One letter, penned by a well-educated author, under the title "An Increase of Blacks," appeared on July 7, 1824, in Providence Gazette, a few months in advance of the riot. The author called on residents to act against a recent surge of "evil" and "worthless" Black visitors and immigrants:

There seems to have been an unusual augmentation of our coloured population within a few weeks, and the number of blacks now in this town, probably bears much greater proportion to the white population than it does in any other town, except in the slave-holding states. At this season of the year there has generally been a migration of blacks to this town from various other parts of this state, and from places more remote, there being at this time great facilities offered to them to live on the labors and earnings of others, to riot in dissipation and idleness. The more than ordinary increase of these emigrants at the present season, may be attributed to rigorous measures that have recently been taken by the city authority of Boston to rid that place of such worthless black population, as have not obtained a legal settlement there, and have disturbed the city with noise, riot and thefts. Many of these dissolute vagabonds have undergone an examination before the Town Council of this town, and ordered to depart, and should they neglect to comply with such orders, they will undoubtedly experience the severity of the law in force against such characters. But while our municipal authority is thus manifesting a disposition, and exerting its lawful powers, it may be reasonable to call for the cooperation of all citizens to aid them in their exertions to apply the axe to the root of an evil which is alarming in its extent. This aid may be effectually given by information communicated to the Overseers of the Poor, in all cases, where a suspicious person, whether coloured or white, having no settlement in this town, is not at service in any respectable family, nor has any ostensible means of obtaining a livelihood. This is the duty of every citizen, and if this duty be performed faithfully, the number of these locusts who consume the fruits of industry and labours of our citizens, may be easily ascertained, and they will be driven from our confines. [147]

This incendiary letter helped set the stage for an attack now grown to several hundred white people on Hardscrabble. As William J. Brown remembered, the rioters *"drove many from their houses, then tore them down, took their furniture, what little they had, carried it to Pawtucket, and sold it at auction."* [148]

Snowtown

A second race riot took place seven years later in Snowtown, a surviving neighborhood comprised of Black, white, and Indigenous people. Lying west of the cove and situated on the town's northern edge, the mixed-race community occupied a spot near the present-day State House. Like Hardscrabble, many of the residents were poor and working-class people. Census and town records reveal an interesting demographic within the Snowtown neighborhood before, during, and after the riot. Between 1830 and 1840, most of the household wage earners on Olney Lane worked as day laborers and mariners. Of the 13 female household heads, 8 are listed as widows. The work options for African heritage women of the day were even more circumscribed than for men. The fast-growing textile jobs that attracted white women were out of bounds for women of color.[149] One exception is the story of Ellenor Eldridge, a woman of mixed African and Indigenous background. Born in 18th century Warwick and trained as a seamstress, she designed and wore her own dress to a Negro Election Day ceremony that resulted in the installation of her brother George as an African Governor in the Apponaug section of town.[150] A self-supporting entrepreneur in Providence, she ran a laundry business and owned property.[151]

Olney Lane Inhabitants

Henry Bannister, Waiter	Edward Barnes, Mariner/Gardner
William Barnes, Laborer	Bonner Brown, Widow
George Brown, Laborer	Jane Brown, Widow
Noah Brown, Laborer	Stephen Brown, Laborer
Prosper Burden, Laborer	Stephen Burgess, Waiter
William Caesar Laborer	Elizabeth Chambers widow
James Chambers, Laborer	Sylinda Chambers, Widow
Robert Crummell, Laborer	Howland Freeelove
Charles Gardner, Laborer	Francis Guant, Mariner
John Gaunt, Mariner/Cook	Rev. Eli Hall (Bethel AME Church)
Elijah Hall, Laborer	Isaac Hazard, Mariner
William Hull, Laborer	Alfred Jackson, Laborer
Francis Jackson, Laborer	Sarah Jackson, Widow
Antonio John, Mariner	Richard Kyon, Laborer
Pero Martin, Laborer	Menta Payne, Widow
Cynthia Sampson, Widow	Hannah Sampson, Widow
Henry Sampson, Mariner	James Sampson, Laborer
Celia Sands, Widow	Judith Sands, Widow
Porter Sands, Laborer	Rev. Peter Schuyler
John Smith, Mariner	Levens Smith, Laborer
Mrs. Phebe Smith	Elizabeth Wamsley Widow
George Wamsley, Laborer	Alexander Williams, Mariner
John Willis, Laborer	William Wright, Laborer

A dispute between a group of white sailors and a Black man on Olney Lane may have sparked the Snowtown Riot in September 1831. Racial animosity ignited both the earlier Hardscrabble and Snowtown riots. According to some, the "Black" Snowtown neighborhood included poor and unsafe structures and prostitution, and other illicit activities. Race relations in Providence remained tense in the years between the Hardscrabble and Snowtown disturbances. As William J. Brown noted, *"The feeling against the colored people was very bitter. Mobs were the order of the day, and poor colored people were the suffers."*[152] *Ironically, many of the vandalized dwellings within Olney Lane were owned by white elites and their families, including Nicholas Brown, whose property sustained considerable damage."*[153]

The rioting in Snowtown lasted five nights. On the first night, rock-throwing seamen advance on the Olney Lane home of Richard Johnson. Defending his house, Johnson fired on the crowd and killed one sailor.[154] Newspapers provided a vivid account of the mobs descending upon Snowtown as homeowners and others fought to defend their lives and property. An October 11, 1832 account in the Rhode Island American started this way:

Outrage. On Wednesday evening between 7 and 8 o'clock, some persons belonging in a neighboring town, endeavored to force their way into the house of a man named Morse, at a place called Snowtown, near Smith Bridge, near the northern extremity of the city against his consent. A battle was commenced by the visitors, and they availed themselves of bricks, stones, and such other missiles as came to hand. A crowd collected, and in the course of affray, a man be the name of Ormsbee was killed.[155]

"Creative Survival Exhibit,"
Rhode Island Black Heritage Society Archives

The Providence Patriot provided this account: *"On Wednesday evening, a party of sailors, on a frolic, proceeded to some houses of ill fame, on Olney's lane, occupied by blacks, an altercation ensued, stones were thrown, three muskets discharged at the assailants by persons occupying the houses, whereby a sailor was killed on the spot, and two others wounded."*[156]

Many blamed the town's social ills on "Black" neighborhoods like Hardscrabble and Snowtown, communities that included brothels, gambling houses, and other underground enterprises. Joseph Tillinghast, a Trustee of Brown University, state representative, and defense attorney in the "Hard Scrabble Riot" trial, argued the white rioters were protecting "the morals of the community." Tillinghast, representing one of the rioters, offered a sarcastic, race-tinged defense before the jury on December 30, 1824. The Independent Inquirer provided a transcript of his testimony:

Gentlemen of the jury. The renowned city of Hardscrabble lies buried in its magnificent ruins! Like the ancient Babylon, it has fallen with all it graven images, its tables of impure oblation, its idolatrous rights and sacrifices, and my client stands here charged with having invaded this classic ground and torn down its alters and its beautiful temples! I might, gentlemen, be pathetic on this subject, but I spare your feelings. The name of this celebrated city must give you some idea of its character if you have not been sufficiently conversant with history to have become acquainted with it, Hardscrabble!! The origin of the name I cannot pretend to trace. It must hereafter remain for the researchers of antiquity. Whether it is because you have to scrabble hard to get there, or scrabble hard when you are there, or to scrabble hard to get safe away, I cannot take upon me to determine. It is much to be regretted that among the thirty or forty witnesses the Attorney General has examined, some of them have not explained the etymology of this name. Perhaps, after all, it is only meant as descriptive of the Shuffling, which is there practiced in the graceful evolutions of the dance, or the zig-zag movements of Pomp and Phillis, when engaged in treading the minuet de la cour! But be that as it may, we must all agree the destruction of this place is a benefit to the morals of the community.[157]

The race riots directed at Hardscrabble and Snowtown were not limited to Providence. Riots occurred in many urban cities, most notably Boston, Philadelphia, and New York, where African-heritage men, women, and families dared to build a life for themselves as equal Americans. This racist rationale for razing "coloured" neighborhoods (places including blight, poverty, and crime) would reoccur during the "urban renewal" wave of the mid-20th century. In Providence, urban renewal—coupled with gentrification—dislodged Black and Cape Verdean populations in College Hill, Lippitt Hill, Fox Point, and Upper South Providence.

Encouragement of Domestic Service

As noted previously, antebellum Providence was a time of rapid economic and population growth, much of it fueled by new industries and immigrants—Irish, French-Canadians, Germans, and Jews among them—looking for work. During the first quarter of the 19th century, Rhode Island, and Providence in particular, became the center of textile production in America.[158] While employment options were limited for African heritage

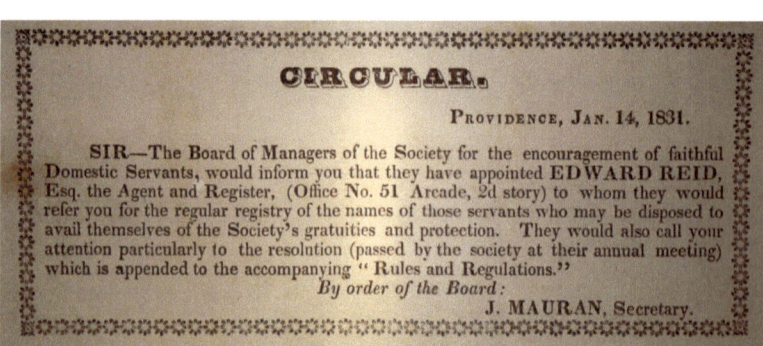

"Creative Survival Exhibit," Rhode Island Black Heritage Society Archives

women in Providence, a few entrepreneurs like the aforementioned Ellenor Eldridge prospered. Lucy Mackenzie, James Mackenzie's wife, an African Union Society member and emissary to Sierra Leone, was a seamstress along with her daughter Sally. Susan Garrison worked as a dressmaker at a shop at 95 Benefit Street. And Hager Bintum, originally from Connecticut, sewed for a living after moving to Providence in the mid-1820s.[159]

People of color had few job opportunities. The textile mills hired mostly white women. The rush to work at the mills created an acute shortage of domestic workers within Providence's upper-class families. Town leaders looked to African heritage women to fill those jobs by establishing the *"Providence Society for the Encouragement of Faithful Domestic Servants"* in 1831, an agency headed by the soon-to-be first mayor, Samuel Bridgham.[160] As described by scholar Jane Lancaster:

> *With white, native-born servants in short supply in Providence, employers increasingly recruited from among the free black population. This made the servant problem very complex, since it now involved control and racial issues: the upper and middle classes were seeking reliable servants from a racial group that was increasingly seen as deviant.*[161]

The use of African-heritage women as domestic servants was short-lived in Providence. Independent-minded Black women who were no longer required to labor under compulsion (slavery) would actively bargain with their employers in the free labor market.[162] The large-scale immigration of Irish women beginning in the 1840s—the women were called "Bridget" — filled the demand for live-in domestic servants in Providence and across northeastern America.[163]

Antebellum Providence
African Heritage Entrepreneurs

1- Atwells Ave - Enoch Freeman, Barber
2- High St. - 87 - Alfred Niger, Barber
3- 132/134 - Samuel T. Mason, Barber
4- Broad St. - Cornelius Maxwell, Barber
5- 50-Gilbert D. Gardner, Hairdresser
6- 57 Westminster - Alexander G. Sweet, Barber
   Moses H. Jackson, Barber
   A. M. Narr, Hairdresser
7.- 75 Weybosset - James E. Elless, Barber
8- Old Market - Simon Manuel, Butcher
9- 63 Canal - John Freeman, Engineer
10- South Water St. - 124 - Moses Potter, Barber
11- 125 - Thomas Howland, Victualing Seller/
    Grocer Market
12- South Main St. - 19 - George Head, Clerk
13- 27 Joseph Narr, Confectioner
14- 49 - James Hazard, Clothier
15- 78 - Leonard Brown, Clothing Store
16- 152 - William Congdon, Shoemaker
17- 190 - Samuel Darrell, Confectioner
18- 225 - David Ballou, Cigar Maker
    Charles Johnson, Shoemaker
19- Wickenden St. - Philip Lewis, Barber
20- 95 Benefit - Susan Garrison, Dress Maker
21- Power St. - Nathaniel Head, Pilot
22- Benevolent St - George C. Willis, Sexton
    William J. Brown, Shoemaker
    45-Charles B. Burill, Keeper City Baths
23- 5 George St. - John Mason, Carpenter
24- Colllege St. - Charles G. Brown, Bathhouse
25- North Main - 106 Lewis Figurado, Barber
26-38 - James Scott, Barber
    38 - Henry Lewis, Clothes Cleaner
27- 77 - Manuel Fenner, Hostler
28- 78 - W.G. Kinnicut , Barber
29- 80 ½ - Robert Lind, 2nd Hand Clothing
30- Meeting St. - George McCarty, Trader
31- N.Main cont. -105 - Charles Gray, Barber
32- 179 - James Crawford, Barber
33- 190 - Henry N. Gaskin, Oil Stone Manufacturer
34- 192 - William Howard, Hairdresser
35- 323 - Oliver Smith Soap Boiler

Map of Town of Providence from survey by Daniel Anthony 1823
(Rhode Island Historical Society)

Warning Out, Settlement Laws

In the 1800s, African heritage and Indigenous people fought against racism and mob violence, but one of the greatest threats they faced came not from rioters but from laws promulgated by towns, cities, and states. During the colonial years, officials resorted to "warning out" individuals, an old English law used to force religious nonconformists, the poor, the unproductive, and other troublemakers to settle elsewhere. In 18th century America, a central system of welfare support did not exist. Local officials had the power to differentiate between drifters and the indigent—outsiders—and those rightfully settled in the town. A constable could remove the offenders.[164] Town officials needed to distinguish between those poor with the rightful and legal settlement and those who would be deemed as an outsider. As historian Christy Clark-Pujara points out:

> *"The poor, especially people of color, were heavily regulated in the new nation. The poor were effectively barred from moving out of the communities in which they were born or bound, because receiving assistance; food, clothing, shelters, and burials; required that one be a legal resident of the town, city, or county. And legal residency required that an individual be born, be bound, or own property within town limits."* [165]

These municipal "warning-out" laws were enacted to determine who was a lawful inhabitant of a town and who the town would officially examine as a candidate for expulsion. The combination of dramatic population growth during the first part of the 19th century and the rise in crimes, particularly those associated with public disorderly conduct, alcohol abuse, and prostitution, propelled the Providence Town Council to accelerate its warning-out examinations. Examinations would particularly quicken as an aftermath of the Hardscrabble and Snowtown riots, *"as the council associated disorder less with individual actions and more with membership in a group: a race, a social class, a gender, or residence in a particular neighborhood."*[166] As pointed out by historian Billy Smith, "Between 1750 and 1800, Providence officials warned out 682 people, five times the number for any other town; thus, Providence's councilmen were five times as busy at this task as any of the other six councils throughout the state."[167] And for people of African heritage, warning out examinations with the follow-on removal from the town of Providence became a common occurrence even at the start of the 19th century, as reported:

> *"When Boston Nance came before the Providence councilmen in 1800, people of color constituted half of all transients warned out of Rhode Island that year; an astounding statistic in light of the fact that "Negroes" represented only 6.3 percent of the population of Rhode Island in 1790 and that figure had decreased to 5.3 percent ten years later."* [168]

African heritage women ran afoul of the law during the early 19th century because they operated what the town authorities called "disorderly houses." While some operations were illicit, such as houses of prostitution, many were simply unlicensed boarding and drinking establishments that were in great demand by the many sailors and mariners on Providence's busy waterfront. Widows with children were placed in impossible circumstances when officials refused to issue them entertainment licenses. Such denials turned their businesses into illegal activities. In reality, they were businesses run by poor women of color trying to keep their heads above water and feed their families.[169]

Betsey Taylor, an African-heritage woman who moved to Providence in the early 19th century, was ordered to leave many times. Initially, she lived in a boarding house that catered to sailors. Officials deemed the house a public nuisance, and the town council expelled Taylor in 1809. She returned to Providence in 1822 with a daughter, Eliza, and lived on Olney's Lane. Taylor was examined and ordered to leave on seven separate occasions between 1822 and 1830.[170]

At least one inhabitant of color offered some level of assistance to those facing removal because of poverty. Michael Tillinghast, an African heritage man of some financial means, left assets in his will "for the relief of destitute colored people residing in Providence." He directed his trustees to sell his property at 25-27 Beacon Avenue and Pine Street, invest the proceeds, and use the interest to help the poor.[171]

Phillis Wanton's "warning out" represents the constant challenges faced by those African heritage women who had survived enslavement only to live as marginalized free women. She met exclusion from multiple towns because, in the eyes of New England's dominant white government, she was, "after all, a Black person without a master and a woman without a husband."[172]

An African heritage woman born enslaved in Attleboro, Massachusetts, she moved to Boston and then Providence, where she lived in Moses Brown's household. She married a man named Jack Wanton of Newport. Wanton was born in Africa and had been manumitted by John Wanton in 1791. At some point, Phillis left her husband in Newport—she said he was insane— and fled with her young children back to Providence.

Both Jack and Phillis faced warning out reviews during the late 18th century and later. One warning out examination of Jack Wanton took place on December 17, 1792. *"Jack Wanton, a Negro man...saith that he was an African born; that he came to Newport with Capt. John Goddard, who sold him to John Wanton of said Newport, with whom he lived about 15 years; that about a year since his master gave him his freedom; that he has a wife named Phillis."*[173] Phillis was called before the Providence Town Council in October of 1800, and she stated that her husband was "at times insane." Two of her children, Squire and Mariane, were "bound out" in Foster and the youngest, Vina, lived with Phillis. The Town Council twice rejected her pleas to live in Providence. Officials judged Newport to be her legal settlement and ordered her removed to Newport on October 7, 1800.[174]

The story of Jack and particularly Phillis Wanton was emblematic of the ways that municipal and state laws were employed to exert power over the lives of African heritage people in Providence and across New England. Their painful experience—struggling to find a permanent home and community, largely due to their race and previous condition of servitude—was recognized by the Newport African Union Society in a poignant July 27, 1789 letter:

> *We, the members of the Union Society in Newport, taking into consideration the calamitous state into which we are brought by the righteous hand of GOD, being strangers and outcasts in a strange land, attended with many disadvantages and evils, with respect to living, which are like to continue us and on our children while we and they live in this Country.*[175]

Indian Indentured Servitude

While African heritage people struggled to maintain a livelihood in the face of mob violence and oppressive settlement laws, Indigenous people, particularly through their children, faced an insidious legal practice called "pauper apprenticeship." Children determined by government authorities to be poor, bastards, and suffering were removed from their parents and placed into indentured service within a white family until adulthood. Historians Ruth Wallis Herndon and Ella Wilcox Sekatau describe this practice:

> RAN away from the Subscriber, on the Morning of the 20th Inst. an indented Apprentice, by the name of Isaac How, about 14 Years of Age, slim built, and has a Nose uncommonly prominent; had on when he went away, a short blue outside Jacket, and blue and white striped Linen Trowsers. Whoever will return said Runaway shall receive the above Reward, but no Charges.
> C. C. OLNEY.
> N. B. All Persons are forbid harbouring said Runaway on Penalty of the Law.

Providence Gazette, June 7, 1806

> *"This coerced servitude, rooted in English poor law, effectively secured the labor of particular youngsters to serve the needs of the community in general and larger property owners in particular. The system also enabled local officials and "respectable" inhabitants to impose their ideal of family organization on others by removing children from "improper" situations and placing them in "proper" households, where they would be maintained during their youth and trained for adulthood in ways deemed appropriate for their race, sex, and class."* [176]

Authorities targeted Indigenous and African heritage children—especially girls—and placed them in what they deemed to be their appropriate "station" in life. Children of color were highly overrepresented in pauper apprenticeships, constituting some 25 percent of these young laborers at a time when all people of color probably constituted around 10 percent of the region's general population.[177]

The self-fulfilling prophecy that Indigenous people could not maintain their lives and support their children in 18th- and 19th-century Rhode Island had its roots in the destruction of native people through English-born disease and the near-genocidal aftermath of King Philip's War. These conditions made most surviving natives dependent on their white colonizers for employment and basic living. As early as 1731, Bishop George Berkeley, a philosopher, and slaveholder, in a sermon before the Society for the Propagation of the Gospel, asserted, *"that nearly all the Rhode Island Indians were servants or labourers for the English."*[178]

While indentured servitude was not inheritable enslavement, it did succeed in removing Indigenous children from their parent or parents and placed them within a white household that separated them from their native culture. In many cases, when indentured native women died, their children were not set free, but placed into a new servitude. That happened to Hannah, a half-Indian, half-Black girl who was forced to live with a white master after her native mother died.[179]

As early as the Colonial Era, African and Indigenous people lived and worked together on the plantations of Narragansett County (today's South County) and in the urban seaports of Newport and Providence. As pointed out by Brown historian Rhett Jones, Africans and natives were common victims of oppression and they naturally drew together.[180] Jones notes one such union: Thomas J. Walmsely (the name is variously spelled in the eighteenth-century records), described as a "mustee or at least an octoroon," married an Indian woman. He had a small holding of his own and a slave but did odd jobs for the planter aristocracy.[181] "Creative Survival" enabled both African and native people to survive despite living within the oppressive system of human bondage and indentured servitude brutal and dehumanizing system that extended well into Rhode Island's next centuries.

Law, Order & The Public Execution of Amasa Walmsley

Providence's African heritage community grew rapidly from 475 inhabitants in 1790 to 975 in 1820. Most lived on the east side of the river. About a quarter lived on the west side.[182]

While free of bondage, most scraped by on society's margins, largely living on the outskirts of town in lower working-class neighborhoods. In the direct aftermath of the 1824 and 1831 race riots in Hardscrabble and Snowtown, town business and government leaders called for law and order. As detailed by historians Howard Chudacoff and Theodore Hirt, *"These events blended race and vice issues to produce heightened concern over public order, concern made by acute urbanization. Thus, the disorder had a significant role in stimulating the reform of Providence's government and forcing citizens to acknowledge problems that a once small town never had faced."* [183]

In the wake of the riots, Providence's leaders created a formal city government in January 1832. They elected city officers on the fourth Monday in April. Samuel W. Bridgham was elected mayor, an office to which he was successively re-elected without opposition until his death in December 1839.[184] Samuel Bridgham was also a leading voice in the Providence Society for the Encouragement of Faithful Domestic Servants, a short-lived association that looked to encourage "law and order" among domestic servants, mainly African heritage women.[185] In his June 4, 1832, inaugural address to the city council, Bridgham evoked Roger Williams's spirit, declaring that the new form of government and its laws would be "truly republican in all its principles. It is founded upon the Roger Williams platform and breathes as pure a spirit of freedom as any of the free and liberal institutions of our country."[186]

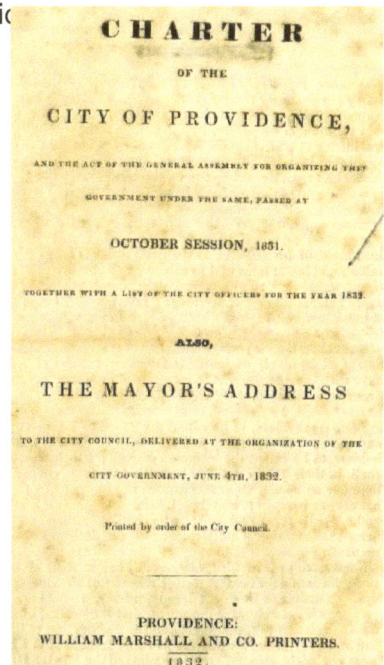

Mayor's Address to the City Council, June 4, 1832, Printed by the Order of the City Council, William Marshall and Company Printers, 1832, City of Providence Archives

The mayor talked about how to best organize a government to protect the health and welfare of businesses and citizens. The newly established city council, he said, would be given broad powers to promote and protect the city's health. A new health officer could *"adjudge and determine as to the settlement of paupers, and to remove all such as are not legally settled in the city, or who have become or are likely to become chargeable to the city and also to remove persons of bad fame and reputation and such as shall be adjudged unsuitable to become inhabitants of the city."*[187] These powers targeted African heritage people and gave white officials the power *"to bind out the children of poor colored persons, also disorderly black or colored persons."*[188] To be clear, "black" described African heritage people. The term "colored persons" was used to describe Indigenous or mixed-heritage people. Still, the targeting of citizens of color must have sent a chilling message to those Providence inhabitants struggling to survive in the city's poorest neighborhoods.

A town marshall was established in 1833 to keep the peace. The marshall's job was to run a department of twenty-four who worked a day and evening shift. A formal police force—complete with badges—began patrolling the city by 1848.[189] With the mayor's newly granted police powers, the old town watch evolved into an armed police department in response to the Snowtown riot and north-end disturbances.[190] The City of Providence was now ready and able to protect its citizens and property and, most importantly, enforce the laws against disorderly inhabitants and those deemed as noncitizens.

On June 1, 1832, three days before the mayor's inaugural address, Amasa Walmsley, an Indigenous man charged with murder, was hanged before an estimated crowd of 10,000 spectators in Providence. He was reported to be executed at Squaw Hollow, the name given to a district between Orms and Martin Streets, adjacent to Bull-dog Hill. *"It was formerly inhabited almost wholly by Negroes and a low class of white people."*[191]

Walmsley's hanging— the first public execution in Rhode Island in over thirty years—clearly demonstrated the City of Providence's commitment to law and order. As described in newspapers across the country, the execution turned into a public spectacle marked by "beastly intoxication" and public disorder:

> *"Before night, on the proceeding day, persons from all directions were seen flocking into town. By four in the morning of Friday, the mass began to thicken, by seven, the streets were thronged and so continued till after dark, and it is probable that more than ten thousand people had collected to witness the execution besides the inhabitants of the town themselves. And to their everlasting disgrace, there were not wanting a considerable number of females, who could so far set aside the native delicacy and refined feelings that generally characterize their sex, as to mingle in the motley throng, and eagerly force their way to the fatal spot, to satiate their curiosity by gazing on a fellow human being, writhing in the last agonies of a violent death. But the scene in the afternoon gave finish to the picture. Thousands of persons returned from the scene of death, were collected in the streets and public squares. Bar rooms tippling shops, and victualing cellars, were filled to overflowing. The jest and joke went round in allusion to what the thoughtless multitude denominated the "hanging match;" and from our windows we noticed within twenty rods, many instances of beastly intoxication, and some ten or twelve quarrels and fights."*[192]

Walmsley was born around 1807 to Thomas J. Walmsley, listed in various records as a mixed person of Narragansett ancestry.[193] The senior Walmsley was originally from Narragansett County but relocated to Smithfield, according to the 1790 Census.[194] Amasa and a brother Thomas were born and raised in the adjacent small town of Burrillville.

There is little doubt that Amasa and his brother Thomas[195] murdered two people on September 11, 1831, only a few weeks before the Snowtown riots. His trial, execution, and native ancestry all exacerbated the community's fears of outsiders. As part of Amasa's confession, he lamented that as the son of a "half-breed Indian of Narragansett Tribe," he was *"shut out by my complexion, and the ignominy [sic] which the world has cast upon the tribe to which I belong, and from which I was lineally descended, from all the benefits of education, and from the opportunities for moral improvement."*[196] Amasa's execution, coming on the heels of the tragic Snowtown riots, reinforced the white public's commonly-held beliefs in the inferiority of Indians and African heritage people. It also demonstrated the tragic consequences of associating crime with race and class, a belief that would continue to shape Providence's policing policies for many years to come.

Negro Cloth & Continued Rhode Island Complicity

Providence's transformation from a small New England settlement into a major industrial city was dramatic. The establishment of water-powered mills along the Blackstone River made Rhode Island a world leader in the emerging textile manufacturing industry. Moses Brown, working with the English factory expert Samuel Slater, built spinning machines powered by the Blackstone River. By the first decade of the 19th century, twenty-seven spinning mills operated in Rhode Island. Providence merchants, such as Brown and Ives, invested in cotton-spinning mills across the state where water-power was cheap and available.[197] Ironically, Moses Brown, the great abolitionist, would help launch the textile business that would produce cotton fabric to clothe slaves.

"Negro Cloth" was cheap but strong coarse cloth used in making clothes for slaves in the American South. During the early 19th century, Rhode Island textile manufacturers specialized in Negro cloth production. At least 84 Rhode Island mills produced the material during that era, the highest concentration in New England.[198]

Rhode Island's economic makeover from a maritime-based slave system to a textile-based slave system was a remarkably fast and convenient transformation. As the operator of most of the 19th century America's textile mills, Rhode Island—aided by favorable federal tariffs—was well-positioned to enter the slave cloth market.[199] Many of the leading families of commerce in Providence, Newport, and Narragansett County who profited from the Trans-Atlantic Slave Trade would also dominate the textile market. The Hazard, Rodman, Babcock, Aldrich, Nichols, Brown, and Slater families were all tied to the production of Negro Cloth. While most of the mills operated in Narragansett County and Blackstone Valley, the Elisha A. Durfee Mill and Elm Street Mill in Providence also produced slave cloth.

Advertisements for Negro Cloth appear frequently in Providence-based newspapers throughout the early 19th century. On June 19, 1822, the Providence Patriot announced to American Manufactures:

> *It is nearly a year since a new description of cheapo goods, made of cotton and wool, and intended as a substitute for the coarse imported planes (planes?) hitherto used for clothing the slaves in the southern States, was first manufactured in this section of the country. At that time we took occasion to address a few observations upon the subject to the southern planters and to express our conviction that they would find it for their interest to introduce the home manufacture in preference to the more costly, less durable, and clumsy foreign fabric, in general use as clothing for slaves. The substitute has acquired the name of Negro Cloth, and we are very glad to find that it is considered by the planters themselves decidedly preferable to the foreign fabric, which it is well known is made up of the bits, scraps.*[200]

Some condemned the state's textile trade with the South. Providence industrialists worried that the activities

Rhode Island Negro Cloth Manufactories: Wrap & Cloth Mills

Courtesy of the Rhode Island Black Heritage Society Archives

1. Thomas R. Hazard Mill, Rocky Brook, South Kingstown
2. Rodman Mill, Samuel Rodman, Rocky Brook, South Kingstown
3. Williams Mill, T.R. Williams, Rocky Broon, South Kingstown
4. Rocky Brook Mill, Samuel Rodman, Rocky Brook, South Kingstown
5. Durfee Mill, N.B. Durfee, Rocky Brook, South Kingstown
6. Satinet Mill, J.B. Hazard, Rocky Brook, South Kingstown
7. Peace Dale Mill, J.P. and R. G. Hazard, Peace Dale South Kingstown
8. Wakefield Mill, W. A. Robinson, Wakefield, South Kingstown
9. Daniel Rodman Mill, Mooresfield, South Kingstown
10. Carmichael & Schofield Co. Mill, Burnside, South Kingstown
11. W.G. Holburton Mill, near Perryville, South Kingstown
12. Glen Rock Mill, Daniel B. Rodman, Glen Rock, South Kingstown
13. Narragansett Mill, Wm. E. Pierce & Co., Belleville, North Kingstown
14. Annaquatucket Mill, Ezbon Sanford, North Kingstown
15. Davis Mill, Davis Reynolds & Co., Davisville, North Kingstown
16. Reynolds Mill, G.W. Reynolds & Co., Davisville, North Kingstown
17. Silver Spring Mill, Wilcox & Pierce, North Kingstown
18. Shady Lea Mill, Charles Allen, North Kingstown
19. Lafayette Mill, Robert Rodman, Lafayette, North Kingstown
20. Sodman Mill, Charles Allen, Hallville, Exeter
21. Fisherville Mill, Schuyler Fisher, Fisherville, Exeter
22. Hallville Mill, Dutee J. Hall, Hallville, Exeter
23. Dawley Mill, Dutee J. Hall, Hallville, Exeter
24. Lawton Mill, Thomas A. Lawton, Lawtonville, Exter
25. Greene Mill, Christopher C. Greene, Exeter Hollow, Exeter
26. James S. Harris Mill, Millville, Exeter
27. E.& H. Babcock Mill, Yawgoo, Exeter
28. Ezra Pollard Mill, East Greenwich
29. Hill, Baker & Benson Mill, Millville, Kent Co.
30. Green Mill, Brown & Aldrich, Centerville, Warwick
31. Wakefield Mill, R. Wakefield, Artic, Warwick
32. Christopher Allen Mill, Warwick
33. Festus L. Thompson Mill, Warwick
34. C & S Harris Mill, Warwick
35. J. Rhodes & Sons Mill, Warwick
36. Arnold Mill, Anthony, Coventry
37. Shannock Mills, John T. Knowles, Shannock, Richmond
38. Clark's Mills, J.T. & J. Knowles, Clark's Mills, Charlestown
39. Tug Hollow Mill, Sheldon & Hoxsie, Tug Hollow, Richmond
40. Hillsdale Mill, Kenyon & Lillibridge, Hillsdale, Richmond
41. Independence Mill, J.B.M. Potter, Usquebaugh, Richmond
42. David L/ Aldrich Mill, Hope Valley, Richmond
43. Kenyon Mills, A & S. E. Kenyon, Kenyon, Richmond
44. Carolina Mill, R. G. Hazard, Carolina, Richmond
45. King's Mill, Daniel King, Charlestown
46. Hazard Mill, J.P. & Jonathan Hazard, Locustville, Hopkinton
47. Smith & Campbell Mill, S. Smith & D. Campbell, Ashaway, Hopkinton
48. Moscow Mill, T.R. Wells & Co., Moscow, Hopkinton
49. Laurel Dale Mill, L.C. Carr & Co., Ashaway, Hopkinton
50. Bethel Mill, A. Babcock & W. Stillman, Hopkinton
51. O. Langworthy Mill, Burdickville, Hopkinton
52. Joh E. Weeden Mill, Bradford, Hopkinton
53. Oakland Co. Mill, Hopkinton
54. Briggs & Wilcox Mill, Hopkinton
55. Sea Island Manufactory, T.R. Hazard, Newport
56. Enterprise Factory, Edward W. Lawton, Melville, Portsmouth
57. Clarke's Mill, Andrew W. Gilmore, Glen-anna, Portsmouth
58. Daniel Paine Mill, Hathaway, Paine & Co., Cumberland
59. Merino Mill, H.P. Franklin, Merino Village, Johnston
60. Appleby Smith Mill, Smithfield
61. Pooke Mill, Pooke & Steere, Smithfield
62. Slater & Co. No. 3 Mill, S&J Slater, Slaterville, North Smithfield
63. Elm Street Manufacturing Co., Providence
64. Elisha A. Durfee Mill, Providence
65. Bowen & Bailey Mill, Cranston
66. Lenard Nason Factory, Nasonville, Burrillville
67. George W. Marsh Mill, Bridgeton, Burrillville
68. Whipple Mill, Daniel S. Whipple, Gazzaville, Burrillville
69. Tar Kiln Mill, Joseph D. Nichols, Oak Valley, Burrillville
70. Sayles Mill, Union Manufacturing Co., Pascoag, Burrivlle
71. Moses Albridge Factory, Burrillville
72. Harrisville Mill, Steere & Tinkham, Mapleville, Burrillville
73. Peter Place Mill, Burrillville
74. John T. Phillips Mill, Burrillville
75. Sales & Shumway Mill, Burrillville
76. John L. Barbour Mill, Burrillville
77. John Waterman Mill, Burrillville
78. B.I. Lawton Mill, North Scituate
79. Gideon Bradford Mill, Woonsocket
80. E.& H. Bradford Mill, Potter Hill, Westerly
81. White Rock Manufacturing Co., Babcock & Moss, White Rock, Westerly
82. W. P. Arnold Mill, Niantic, Westerly
83. O.M. Stillman, Stillmanville, Westerly
84. Happy Hollow Mill, Allen Haskill, Cumberland

of abolitionists and others would disrupt commerce and the steady flow of profits. The state's abolition movement started early. Led by Moses Brown and Newport Reverend Samuel Hopkins, the Rhode Island General Assembly in 1790 enacted a law establishing the "Providence Society for Promoting the Abolition of Slavery, for the Relief of Persons Unlawfully Held in Bondage, and for Improving the Conditions of the African Race."[201] In response to Rhode Island and other New England states calling for the end of slavery and the slave trade, the United States Congress passed its first law against the African slave trade in 1794 and outlawed it completely in 1808.[202]

In 1835, a group of prominent Providence business and civic leaders came together to express their concerns with local and national anti-slavery societies, a movement that threatened Negro cloth production. As reported in the November 4, 1835 edition of the Providence Daily Journal, the meeting included numerous resolutions that warned against the social and economic agitation caused by "reckless fanatics:"

Slave Doll, c. 1830, Clothing Made From Negro Cloth, Stokes Family Collection

> *Whereas numerous Anti-Slavery Societies have recently been established in the several States where Slavery has ceased to exist, and whereas the designs and the proceedings of such Societies are, in the judgment of a large majority of this community, considered not only to be dangerous to the existing relations of friendship and of business between different sections of our country, but to menace with the destruction the rights, privileges and blessings, enjoyed under the Union, and secured by the Constitution, We, the People of Providence, deem it to be a solemn duty to our fellow-citizens and ourselves, explicitly to declare our sentiments upon this vitally important subject.*[203]

Providence's businessmen, politicians, and civic leaders endorsed this view, including Nicholas Brown, James Fenner, Resolved Waterman, Samuel Dexter, William Blodget, Moses Ives, Joseph Manton, John Slater 2nd, Benjamin Hopping, Edward Carrington, Luther Pearson, Wilbur Kelly, Benjamin Clifford, Carlo Mauran, Elisha Dyer, Orray Taft, Nehemiah Dodge, Shubael Hutchins, William Church, Salma Olney, Jessie Olney, Walter Danforth, Horatio Rogers, Amos Smith, George S. Wardwell, William G. Goddard, Amasa Manton, Benjamin Cozzens, Burton Anthony, Henry P. Franklin, and John H. Clark.[204] The list of names included a majority of the city's leading citizens united in endorsing economic prosperity over human bondage and suffering. As noted by historian Christy Clark-Pujara, *"And while Rhode Islanders were willing to accept the elimination of slaveholding in their midst, they remained complicit in slaveholding outside their state."*[205]

Black Suffrage & The Dorr Rebellion

Alfred Niger and George C. Willis were African heritage renaissance men of early 19th century Providence. Niger moved from Connecticut to Providence around 1820. He operated a successful barbershop at 87 High Street. A leader within Providence's small African heritage community, he helped found the Harmony (Prince Hall Affiliated) Masonic Lodge in 1826[206] and served as a Providence delegate to the National Colored Convention in Philadelphia in 1830.[207] George Willis, also Connecticut born, arrived as a young man in Providence around 1810, and by 1813, was married, living on Benevolent Street, and an active member of Providence's First Baptist Church. Like many African heritage members forced to pray at the back of Providence's white churches, he grew frustrated with the separate and unequal treatment and helped found the African Meeting and School House.[208] He later became sexton of the meeting house, in charge of operations and maintenance. Willis also became a founding member of the Harmony Lodge and joined Niger as a delegate to the National Colored Convention. Legally disenfranchised in 1822, both Niger and Willis later became voting rights activists.

They owned property and fought in the American Revolution, yet their right to vote—a basic foundation of American democracy—was stripped away. This highly targeted act became yet another socio-political obstacle that African heritage people faced in Providence. As detailed by Robert Cottrol, *"the heightened racial regulation that free Negroes encountered in the 1820s and throughout the nation, and the erection of barriers set the free Negro apart from the rest of the population."*[209]

Beset by political disenfranchisement, economic discrimination, and even violent mob attacks, the African heritage community of antebellum Providence struggled to remain resilient. But the challenges continued. Soon after the Snowtown riots, city and state officials joined together to levy a tax on African heritage inhabitants' property. A group of men met at the African Meeting House to discuss the issue. The American Revolution had been fought and won under the banner of *"no taxation without representation."* Now, officials wanted to tax Black men who had been stripped of their right to vote. Led by Niger and Willis, the committee included George McCarty, Edward Barnes, Ichabod Northrup, and James Harris. On July 11, 1831, they delivered a petition to the Rhode Island General Assembly seeking relief from taxes because they had no standing in a representative government.[210] William J. Brown would candidly point out the white opposition to Black voters:

> *"The committee believed that taxation and representation went together; they were unwilling to be taxed and not allowed to be represented. Some of the members of the house said it was perfectly alright; if the colored people were to be taxed, they should be represented. But the members of the house from Newport were bitterly opposed to colored people being represented, saying:* "Shall a Nigger be allowed to go to the polls and tie my vote? No, Mr. Speaker, it can't be. The taxes don't amount to more than forty or fifty dollars; let them be taken off."[211]

The idea of taxing the men was abandoned. But any request for voting rights was ignored. Meanwhile, both Willis and Niger became Rhode Island delegates to the National Convention for the Improvement of Free People of Color in the United States, where they advanced their support for African heritage enfranchisement on a national level.[212]

The fight for the right to vote resurfaced during the Dorr Rebellion in 1841. The four-year uproar occurred when working-class white inhabitants sought a voice in the government. The Industrial Revolution brought waves of newcomers to the state and Providence, including Catholic immigrants from Ireland. Most were not landowners. Voting right laws dating back to Rhode Island's Charter of 1663 restricted the right to vote to white men who owned $134 in property or paid $7 in rent.[213] The outdated law created a constitutional crisis. Thomas Wilson Dorr, a Providence lawyer and state representative, was elected as the "People's Governor" under a so-called People's Constitution.[214] He helped form the Suffrage Association to address the limitations of current voting rights.

African heritage men in Providence seized the opportunity to advance their re-enfranchisement cause by attempting to join the association. At a September 24, 1841, meeting of the Suffrage Association, Alfred Niger placed his name for nomination on the executive committee. White members strongly objected to the nomination of an African heritage man to such an important position.[215]

The following month, Reverend Alexander Crummell, who had recently been invited to Providence to organize an African Episcopal church,[216] presented a petition through Dorr at the October 8 suffrage meeting. Signed by many leaders within the Providence African heritage community, it stated:

> GENTLEMEN: The remonstrance of the undersigned colored citizens of Rhode Island, respectfully represent, that, in the constitution that is proposed to be sent forth by your respected body for adoption, there is one measure inserted, upon which we as an interested party, beg leave, with deference, to make known our views, and give an expression of our sentiments. We have reference to that proposed article which, in inserting the word "white," denies all persons of color the use and exercise of the elective franchise. It is justification of our disfranchisement sought in our want of Christian character. We point to our churches as our reputation. (Is?) In our want of intelligence? We refer not merely to the schools supported by the State, for our advantage; but to the private schools, well filled and sustained, and taught by competent teachers of our own people. Is our industry questioned? This day, where there are no complexional hindrance, we could present a more proportionate number of our people, who might immediately, according to freeholder's qualifications, become voters.[217]

As later reported in the October 24 edition of the New Age and Constitutional Advocate newspaper, "Mr. T.W. Dorr, one of the most efficient members of the Convention, known to be friendly to freedom, education, and encouragement of the colored race, stated that, just an hour of the meeting, a respectable colored man of this city called at his office and handed him a memorial signed by a Committee of colored men, who requested him to communicate it to the Convention."[218] While Dorr himself called the exclusion of African heritage suffrage unjust, the exclusion was upheld by a vote of 46 to 18.[219]

By 1842, Dorr and his Suffrage Party were in open rebellion against the Rhode Island government, a government led by landowners who represented the newly formed Law and Order party, a coalition of Whigs and conservative Democrats seeking to put down the rebellion.[220] When armed conflict became an almost certainty, the Providence African heritage community seized the opportunity for advancement and, akin to the American Revolution, came forward to defend the state and place themselves in the best position to be recognized as free inhabitants. Nearly two hundred men of color organized a state-supported militia under the

Reverend Alexander Crummell, "Creative Survival Exhibit," Rhode Island Black Heritage Society Collections

banner of the "African Grays"—a group formed in 1821 to lead the procession for the opening of the African Meeting House. Now, in 1842, the Black militia would be armed and prepared to defend the state against insurrectionists as part of a City of Providence Home Guard.[221]

The Dorr Rebellion was crushed, and the Law and Order party held a new state convention in September 1842 to determine state voting requirements. The Rhode Island Constitutional Convention gave all native-born males, white and Black, the right to vote. As noted by William J. Brown, the Law and Order party eventually broke up, and Providence voters of color would follow the Whig party until the Civil War.[222] African heritage people in Providence and Rhode Island had accomplished something no other free Black residents across the North would achieve before the Civil War—they fought for and won their rights to vote.[223] Ironically, that right was denied to Rhode Island's Indigenous people in their native land.

Struggle for Public School Integration

Since the early 19th century, the education of children within Rhode Island's African heritage community was the responsibility of the African Societies. Before the Societies, their education largely fell to their relationships within white households, an extension of enslavement.[224] Newport's African Union Society organized the first Black-owned and operated school in America in 1808. From its inception, the 1819 African Meeting House in Providence included a school. By 1837, the Second Free-Will Baptist Church opened a school in Providence, and the following year, the first public school for children of color was opened in the Old Brick Schoolhouse at 24 Meeting Street.[225] As early as 1853, African heritage leaders in Providence and Newport raised serious concerns about the exclusion of their children from attending public schools. As reported in the April 11, 1865 edition of the Anglo-African Newspaper:

> *"The battle raged here in Rhode Island for almost five years. It commenced in public in the month of October in Newport, in 1853, at a public meeting held by the colored people in the Union Congregational Church. The meeting was a large and spirited one. The condition of their schools, the education of their children in the school established by law and supported by taxes, and the best mode of securing their rights, were ably discussed in this meeting, and a series of resolutions, introduced by Mr. Downing, was unanimously adopted, and a mode of action agreed upon."*[226]

*George T. Downing
Rhode Island Black Heritage Society*

In December 1857, a remarkable group of men joined together to protest school segregation. They included George T. Downing, one of America's most successful hospitality entrepreneurs, the owner of hotels and restaurants along Bellevue Avenue in Newport and a catering business on Benevolent Street in Providence; Ichabod Northrup, whose father had fought in the American Revolution with the famous First Rhode Island Regiment; and the Providence leaders James Jefferson, Henry Brown, and George Henry. They and others presented their case for equal public education to the Rhode Island General Assembly in a resolution titled, *"Will the General Assembly Put Down Caste Schools?"* Their argument for ending segregated public schools was directly aligned with their advocacy for the right to vote. People of color in Providence and across the state paid their fair share of taxes; therefore, local and state governments had an obligation to provide public services equally for all citizens. At the time, segregated Black schools were grossly underfunded and lacking in the most basic educational resources. As clearly detailed in the resolution to the General Assembly:

> *Respected Sir: The Colored people of the cities of Providence and Newport, and the town of Bristol, feel that they are unjustly denied a portion of their just right, and APPEAL to you, dear Sir: they respectfully ask that you enquire into their case and defend them if you think their request is a just one; they appeal to you as a member of the General Assembly, knowing that you can, as such, defend them. We feel that we stand, before Rhode Island laws equal; that which is right of any other citizen of the State as such, is our right, and that we should enjoy the same without proscription; that this is the spirit of the laws. Our grievance is that the local school powers of the three places above mentioned have given us indifferent schoolhouses; with but partial accommodations as compared with the other schoolhouses; that they have given us indifferent teachers…*[227]

George Henry, one of the most active Providence leaders in the cause for public school equality, wrote in his autobiography: *"In the year of our Lord 1855, I turn my attention to the subject of public-school rights. I find myself paying a heavy tax, and my children debarred from attending the schools for which I was taxed. So, a few of us got together and resolved to defend ourselves against such an outrage. Mr. George T. Downing was the leading man in the first part of the campaign."*[228] Concerns about unequal education were well documented in an 1854 auditors report for the Providence School Committee, which revealed that the annual pay for white schoolteachers was nearly twice that of the three Black teachers.[229] An 1862 petition to the General Assembly vividly described the hardships faced by children of color, *"who are forced to walk long distances to reach the schools that are assigned them, and are deprived of the advantages of the High School altogether."*[230] A later case put a human face on the issue of racial segregation in public schools. In 1865, 16-year-old Maritcha Remond Lyons was refused entry to Providence's high school simply because of her race. Her family successfully sued the State of Rhode Island, which publicly accelerated the campaign to bring an end to segregated schools. Lyons would soon become the first African heritage student to attend and graduate from Providence High School.[231]

As the country became mired in the Civil War, public opinion—influenced by pressure from the African heritage community—began to shift from political resistance to educational equality. In Providence, the Committee on Education held hearings on the calls for equal education. As described by historians Erik Chaput & Russell J. DeSimone:

> *"Recognizing the monumental changes that had been brought about by the Civil War and the civil rights bills being debated in the U.S. Congress, a minority report from the Committee declared that the "great events of the time" are all "in favor of the elevation of the colored man." They are all "tending to merge the distinctions of race and of class in the common brotherhood of humanity. They have already declared the negro and the white man to be equal before the law, and the privileges here asked for by these petitioners are simply a necessary result of this recognized equality."*[232]

Nearly one year after the end of the Civil War, the Rhode Island General Assembly, on March 7, 1866, enacted a law that stated, *"no distinction be made on account of the applicant's race or color."* African heritage residents had achieved a major civil right, one that would remain elusive for other Americans of African heritage until well into the 20th century.

The Negro In Rhode Island – Representative Mahlon Van Horne

Securing the right to vote and equal access to public education were major first steps for African-heritage people in Providence and across Rhode Island. To ensure these hard-fought rights continued for generations to come, Rhode Island's Blacks sought political and municipal posts. George Henry of Providence became the first African-heritage person to serve on a jury.[233] The first person of color to obtain elected office in antebellum Rhode Island was Providence entrepreneur Thomas Howland. He was listed as a tavern keeper on Market Square as early as 1832 and later as a grocer at 125 South Main Street.[234] Howland served as a City Warden, supervising local elections within the city's Third Ward.[235] (His election may have been an unintended action by Democratic Party members who jokingly persuaded their members to vote for the Black Republican.)[236] Surprisingly, Howland emigrated with his family to Liberia at the end of 1857 to pursue sugar or cotton cultivation. In a November letter from Howland to Rev John Orcutt, a leader in the American Colonization movement,

Thomas Howland
Rhode Island Historical Society

he would include a sample of unprocessed cotton that he would grow on his farm near St. Paul's river, some fifteen miles from the capitol at Monrovia.[237]

Two decades later, an African heritage man and a man of the cloth won a popular election to serve at local and state levels. Reverend Mahlon Van Horne was a protégé of two of America's most active civil rights leaders, George T. Downing and Col. Thomas Wentworth Higginson. Reverend Van Horne was pastor of the Union Colored Congregational Church in Newport for thirty years, from 1869 to 1898. His church was the second African heritage church in Rhode Island after Providence's Congdon Street Baptist Church. The importance of the Black church during the years after the Civil War cannot be understated. At the time, the center of the African heritage community was the church, which attended to the religious, civic, social, and political needs of the people. According to the Providence City Directory of 1889, active Black churches included Congdon Street Baptist Church, Ebenezer Baptist Church, Christ Church, Second Free Baptist Church, African Union Methodist Episcopal, Bethel Methodist Episcopal, Lilac Street Methodist Episcopal, Sheldon Street Mission, Union African Methodist Episcopal, Zion Church, and Mount Zion.[238] These historic religious congregations would form the basis of leadership roles within the American Civil Rights Movement well into the 20th century.

Van Horne topped his stellar career as a religious, civil rights, and political leader by becoming the first member of color elected to a public School Board in 1871 and the first Black man to serve in the Rhode Island General Assembly in 1885. He helped to lead the passage of the state's first Civil Rights bill that declared,[239] *"No person within the State shall be debarred from the full and equal enjoyment of the accommodations, advantages, facilities, and privileges of any licensed inn, public conveyance, on land or water or from any licensed places of public amusement on account of race, color, or previous condition of servitude."* One of his proudest contributions would be in joining Christina Bannister at Transit Street for the April 1890 dedication of the Home for Aged **Colored Women**.[240]

Van Horne was also a public historian who collected and preserved the history of African heritage people in Rhode Island and across America. In 1887 he composed a sermon entitled *"The Negro in Rhode Island: His Past, Present, and Future."* His introduction captured the bitter irony of the often-touted religious freedom established in early Rhode Island, a state that condoned the enslavement of Africans:

Reverend Mahlon Van Horne
Rhode Island Black Heritage Society

> *The Negro was landed in America not to catch the spirit of liberty and religious freedom which the Puritans expected. His was to be an entirely different experience. The Puritan would be schooled in the things that would draw out his self-reliant individuality in all matters pertaining to manhood. The Negro was to live in the Christian home and upon the rich plantation of the now favored pilgrim, yet the Negro is impressed with the fact by teachers in the schools, the pulpit, and the press that his destiny was to be a hero of wood and drawer of water. That his individuality was to be the personality of his master.[241]*

By the close of the 19th century, African heritage citizens in Rhode Island had fought for and won new civil rights. But Plessy v. Ferguson, a landmark U.S. Supreme Court decision, challenged those advances. The high court's decision upheld the constitutionality of racial segregation under the "separate but equal" doctrine. The ruling gave new life and legal sanction to Jim Crow segregation laws. In the years ahead, Providence's African heritage leadership would combat Jim Crow laws in Rhode Island, redefining their fight for civil rights to include fair employment and fair housing practices.

Detribalization, Emigration & Notion of "Pure Indian Blood"

The 19th century presented a point in time when African-heritage people in Rhode Island defined and defended their rights and freedoms as equal citizens. For the Indigenous people, mostly represented by the surviving Narragansett tribe, the 19th century was a time of great struggle. Unlike their African heritage counterparts, the Indians battled a widespread narrative that argued they had all but disappeared:

> *This myth describes how Roger Williams first befriended the Narragansetts, how the Indians, in turn, displayed an undying friendship for early Rhode Island settlers. Then, according to the myth, the noble savages came to resent white encroachments on their land and loss of their autonomy. Finally, in 1675, the Narragansetts became allies of King Philip, the great Wampanoag Sachem, and fought a desperate war to preserve their way of life. But all the odds were against them. At the Great Swamp Fight that took place in present-day South Kingstown on December 1675, a military force of Puritans from Plymouth, Massachusetts Bay, and Connecticut surprised the Narragansetts and exterminated nearly the entire population. By the Summer of 1676, so says the myth, the Narragansetts were no more, they had been wiped off the face of New England.[242]*

As the 19th century former congressman for the Confederate States of America, George Graham Vest, once wrote: *"History is written by the victors and framed according to the prejudices and bias existing on their side."*[243] The Narragansetts and other Indigenous people of 19th century Rhode Island would face the heavy weight of the myth of extinction that would accelerate the loss of native land, sovereign rights, and even their very existence as uniquely Indigenous people based upon the mythical prejudices of the white victors. The Indigenous people who survived the early European diseases and who were not killed by war or sold into West Indian enslavement fought to maintain their native identities throughout the 19th century in Rhode Island. One group, led by a Moses Stanton, moved to the frontiers of the West.

As white expansionism accelerated in Rhode Island well into the 19th century, native land acquisitions continued at a breakneck pace. As early as 1832, the Narragansetts, led by Chief Daniel Sekater, would resist the General Assembly's actions to negate native sovereignty and rightful ownership of their lands.[244] Around the same time, a group of Indigenous people from southern New England formed a tribal alliance that included Narragansett, Mohegan, Montaukett, Niantic, Pequot, and Tunxis peoples. Organized as the Brotherhood Nation, they moved to Wisconsin in search of autonomy and freedom.[245]

Moses Stanton, a Narragansett tribal elder, and converted Christian preacher, joined other tribal members who sold their land in Charlestown and joined the Brothertown Nation in Wisconsin.[246] [247] On August 19, 1843, Newport Mercury newspaper reported on the debate on relocating to Wisconsin:

> *"Our Narragansett Indians yesterday held one of their religious meetings in that town (Charlestown), which as usual at this time of year, was very fully attended. Many Indians from Long Island were there, and great numbers of white people were present. One of the preachers was from Long Island, and another from Newport. The General Assembly had been informed that a number of the tribe wished to have liberty to sell their lands and emigrate. Elder Moses Stanton, who had lately returned from Green Bay, then gave an account of the situation of their brethren there. Tobias S. Ross and Deacon Sekatur then made some remarks in opposition to emigrating. The meeting was a very interesting one."*[248]

Moses Stanton and his family settled east of Lake Winnebago and built a sawmill and gristmill by 1845. The Stantonville settlement later became Chilton, Wisconsin.[249] The urge to emigrate to a more welcoming place mirrored the desire among some Providence Blacks to follow James McKenzie to Africa. The unbroken belief in freedom and self-determination within African heritage and Indigenous people in 19th century Rhode Island was a culmination of their shared experiences of enslavement, religious conversions, and disenfranchisement. As nonwhites, they were singled out for discrimination, and it would be the institution of a targeted racial classification that would prove particularly devastating to Narragansett sovereignty well into the 20th century.

As enslaved Africans arrived at Rhode Island as early as the mid-17th century, they were almost immediately placed in environments where they would live, work, and worship near Indigenous people. The Colony of Rhode Island, in its early laws, consistently lumped Africans and natives together. The laws restricted the behaviors of both groups. A May 7, 1718 law directed at both enslaved Africans and natives stated:

> *"An Act the speedier Trial of such Negro and Indian Slaves, who shall be found Purloining and Stealing, &c. BE it enacted by the General Assembly of this Colony, and by the authority of the same it is Enacted, That all Negro and Indian Slaves that shall be found Purloining, Stealing or Thieving, shall be Tried and Adjudged for the same, in the Town where such Offence shall be committed; And the Assistants,*

Justices of the Peace, and Wardens of such Town, or any two of them, are hereby fully Empowered to Hear, Try and Adjudge the same; and upon Conviction thereof, Defined if Sentence to give, as fully and effectually, by Whipping, Banishing, &c. as the General Court of Trials, and General Delivery, within this His Majesty's Colony have been Authorized, Used or Accustomed to do."[250]

Within this backdrop of shared space and restricted lives, African and Indigenous people formed interpersonal relationships. The offspring of African and native relations were oftentimes recorded as "Mulattoes." The cohabitation or marriage between people of different racial groups has been commonly referred to as miscegenation. As noted by historian Rhett Jones, *"Miscegenation was common in the Narragansett Country, scholars agreeing that the Narragansett Indians had considerable sexual contact with both whites and Blacks. The Indians were as unprepared for the cultural consequences of miscegenation as were Blacks and whites so that for a number of years it was not clear whether persons of mixed ancestry were members of the tribe."*[251] Rhode Island officials were so concerned about race mixing they passed a 1798 law forbidding interracial marriages, *"That no person, by this act, authorized to join persons in marriage, shall join in marriage any white person with any Negro, Indian or mulatto…."*[252]

The most challenging consequences of African and native interactions culminated in the late 19th century, when Rhode Island authorities determined by legislation who was native and entitled to membership within the Narragansett tribe. The concept of "Indian blood" would play a central role in determining Narragansett identity. Even worse: it would be used to diminish the tribe's political and sovereignty status in the very land they had inhabited for thousands of years.

1880 Act to Abolish Narragansett Tribe & Reservation Negroes

The 1880 law to abolish the authority of the Narragansett Tribe was preceded by a series of state hearings. Many white so-called authorities justified their position on tribal abolishment by claiming tribal members possessed "Negro blood." They based their claims on a pseudo-science popularly referred to as the "One-Drop Rule," a highly subjective and discriminatory legal principle of racial classification that asserts that any person with even one Black ancestor is considered Black or colored.[253] This highly racialized tactic effectively denied Narragansett tribal members of their legal rights to their ancestral land and identity. A newspaper account of the hearings reveals the racist beliefs that would result in tribal abolishment:

"Several meetings of the General Assembly committee have been held for the purpose of hearing testimony which might govern a decision upon the feasibility of abolishing the tribal relations of the so-called Narragansett Indians to the State by the purchase of the lands and placing them on a par with other citizens. From the hearings thus far held, it is shown that very little Indian blood is to be found upon the reservation, it being mostly negro. It is doubtful if a full-blooded Narragansett Indian is to be found among the tribe. The reservation is only serving the purpose of a place of refuge for a thriftless class of negroes whose manner of living is a disgrace to the State. Living in almost total disregard of moral law, these reservation negroes cannot but send forth among the community a large number of depraved characters. There is no justice in the memory of the extinct Narragansett Indians in continuing the reservation."[254]

Gideon Ammons, a deacon in the Narragansett Church, testified during the 1880 hearings. He served on the

Narragansett tribal council from 1847 to 1873 and died in 1899. The Evening Bulletin called him the "Last Chief and Head of the Narragansett Tribe of Indians."[255] He was called as a witness during the 1880 hearing to abolish the Narragansett Tribe, and the questions put before him center around how natives determined who a member of the tribe and what position did those of "Negro Blood" occupy in tribal status:[256]

GIDEON AMMONS, SWORN TESTIMONY

Q. (By Mr. Peabody.) You were before the committee, were you not, at the —meeting house?

A. Yes.

Q. You spoke before them, and were asked questions?

A. Yes, sir.

Q. Mr. Adams was there, wasn't he?

A. Yes.

Q. Do you remember Mr. Adams asking you are members ever voted into your tribe by a vote of the Council?"

A. No. He asked me how members were made.

Q. Now, do you remember of making this answer to him:

A. No, sir; all the way we can make members is when anybody comes and claims to be a member of the tribe they inform the Council, and the Council is bound to attend to them at any time when they call. Then they must present living witnesses. We can't take paper.

We want a witness that can go back and trace their pedigree from the stump; and when they can trace from the stump, and bring clear evidence, then we will receive them as members of the tribe ; and if they can't do that, they pass on?"

A. Yes, sir; that was my reply to that.

Q. Then the fact whether they live on the reservation makes no difference. If they can prove their pedigree, you consider them members of the tribe?

A. Yes, sir.

Q. Also, your answers to the following: "Mr. Carmichael. - Has there ever been any members of the tribe taken in by vote?

(A) Ammons. - No, sir. They would have to prove themselves by living witnesses. If anybody can prove themselves by living witnesses, and can trace their pedigree to the tribe, we let them in; but if they cannot do it in that way, they can stay out.

Q Mr. Adams. - If born in wedlock, they can prove themselves? Mr. Ammons. - Yes, sir. Mr. Adams. — Suppose they were born out of wedlock? Mr. Ammons. The child follows the mother. The Government *made a regulation, in 1792, that if they were not married the child couldn't inherit the tribal property from the father, but the woman being in the tribe the child would follow her anyhow."*

A. What they call tribal land we call public land.

Q. If a man and woman were lawfully married, their children would be members of the tribe, if either one of them was a member of the tribe?

A. Yes, sir.

Q. So it would make no difference if one of them was a negro, if one was a member of the tribe?

A. When that regulation was made there were slaves sent to Rhode Island, and you people wanted the benefit of the children. If a nigger woman said she had a child by an Indian, she would claim the child. That was what that was put in for. The Government of Rhode Island said nothing about it after slavery had passed away.

Q. If an Indian and a negro were married lawfully, and had a child, the child would be an Indian?

A. Yes, sir.

Q. (By Mr. Carmichael.) Has that been the custom of the tribe?

A. When slavery died out of the State. When they had slaves in the State, they called a negro a slave. If you had children by a slave, it belonged to your chattels; but if he was lawfully married, this child would inherit his rights.

Q. (By Mr. Peabody.) That was after 1792?

A. Yes, sir.

Q. Before that time, if they were married, they were all Indians?

A. Yes, sir.

Q. (By Mr. Carmichael.) In a case like this, where it has been generally known that there were members of certain families who originated in that way - by an Indian father and a negro woman, has the custom of the tribe been such since that time that they have been recognized as members of the tribe, and treated as such?

A. Yes, sir.

Q. When not married how was it?

A. If they were not married, and it was a negro woman, the children follow her out.

Q. The Council have cut them off?

A. Yes. But if a woman that belonged to the tribe had children by a negro man, the children followed her in the same way as if they were not married.

After weeks of testimony, the Rhode Island General Assembly, at its January 1880 session, passed "An Act to Abolish the Tribal Authority and Tribal Relations of the Narragansett Tribe of Indians." It said:

> *Section One: A Board of three Commissioners shall be appointed upon and after passage of this act.*
>
> *Section Two: Said Commissioners are hereby authorized, empowered, and directed for and on behalf of the state, to negotiate with and purchase from the Narragansett Tribe of Indians all their common tribal lands, now contained within the Indian reservation so called, as bounded, A.D. 1709, and all their other tribal rights and claims, of whatsoever name and nature, for a sum not exceeding 5,000 dollars.*
>
> *Section Three: Said Commissioner shall have full power and authority to hear and determine all questions which may arise in reference to said lands, rights, and claims, quit-claimed to the state as provided in section 2 of this act and shall have full power and authority to ascertain and determine what persons, member of said Narragansett tribe of Indians, are entitled to receive portions of said purchase money to be paid by the state.*
>
> *Section Nine: From and after the passage of this act, the tribal authority of the Narragansett tribe of Indians shall cease, except for the purpose of carrying the provisions of this act into full effect; and shall all persons who may be members of said tribe shall cease to be members thereof, except as aforesaid, and shall thereupon and thereafter be entitled to all the rights and privileges, and be subject to all the duties and liabilities to which they would have been entitled or subject had they never been members of said tribe; provided however, that all members of said tribe who shall at that time be paupers, and all members of said tribe who shall thereafter, and before gaining settlement in any town, become paupers, shall be held and considered state paupers to all intents and purposes; and provided, also, that settlement of any member of said tribe in any town prior to the confirmation and establishment of said report (plat?) shall in no event be construed as part of the time for gaining such settlement in such town.[257]*

The state-led attempts to abolish the tribe and take its lands had a devastating effect on Rhode Island's native population. Tribal members continued to fight for their ancestral land and sovereignty rights, culminating in a Rhode Island Supreme Court decision on February 24, 1898, which supported the 1880 state act of tribal abolishment:

> *"Finally, although the United States have never recognized the Narragansetts as a tribe of Indians, the State of Rhode Island has recognized them as such, or as a community, or as a something, by whatever name called, which possessed an interest in, or title to, the so-called common tribal lands worthy of compensation when constitutionally parted with; and we think it may be so constitutionally parted with under and by virtue of said Chapter 800, amended by Chapter 897; and that interest or title, when acquired by the State, combined with the title the State already had, makes a full and valid title in the State, which it might in turn sell and dispose of in the way and manner provided for in said Chapter 800 and give to the purchasers thereof a like full and valid title to said common tribal land. We also think*

the tribal relations of the so-called Narragansett tribe could be, and were, constitutionally terminated by said Chapter 800. The conclusions to which we have arrived from the foregoing considerations lead us to the opinion that all the questions put to us by your honorable body must be answered in the affirmative, and we hereby answer them accordingly." [258]

PART 3: THE GREAT WAR & THE NEW CIVIL RIGHTS ERA (1900-1940)

Combating Jim Crow Traditions in Rhode Island & Formation of Black Associations

African heritage Rhode Island men and women embraced a new century by forming new civic groups organized around collective civic and political action. George T. Downing, one of Rhode Island's and America's leading civil rights voices, led the movement. In 1902, he and other Providence and Newport leaders published a pamphlet called "An Expression from The Oppressed." The statement called public attention to the ongoing disfranchisement and discrimination across America and Rhode Island:

> *Our present purpose is to agitate: to beget actions that will bear evidence that we are regarded as worthy American citizens; equals before the law, not to be tampered with. We bear in mind that what has been sent to us in letters of others that have been unjustly treated in Rhode Island. We sympathized with them at the time. We will not be content until a citizen, let the shade of his complexion be what it may, is treated fully all over the land as he shall merit. We ask, when does the right obtain to look upon the complexion of citizens of a common country and make individual distinctions among them? We are colored, but we feel ourselves the peers of our fellow countrymen. We refer to the fact that Negro blood was the first to flow for American Independence, and that it has been flowing ever since, freely in a very marked manner in defense of the Nation in all its battles. Why treat us as you do?*[259]

Benevolent associations became an essential means of collective expression for the African heritage community and began to flourish during the early 20th century, particularly in Providence. These groups, mainly an extension of church organizations, became the social lifeblood for Black community service. They organized and acted against oppressive Jim Crow laws meant to marginalize Blacks by denying them jobs, the right to vote, and other opportunities. The new associations provided two critical benefits for the Providence African heritage community. First, they brought together large groups of people with shared interests. Second, they provided a forum to advance purpose and power. While some associations organized around fellowship, worship, and social interests, others organized around political interests, civil rights, and social advancement. An early attempt at forming a civil rights organization in Providence was led by George T. Downing, Reverend Mahlon Van Horne, and Governor Herbert H. Ladd in 1889. At a December 14 meeting of Colored Citizens at Union Hall, they proposed an "Afro-American League," but broader interest soon waned.[260]

The 1898 Afro-American Council, a descendant of the antebellum-era American Society of Free Persons of Colour, was perhaps the first nationwide African heritage civil rights organization.[261] Its purpose was to provide a national forum for African-heritage people to respond to growing racial discrimination, Jim Crow segregation laws, and white violence against people of color, including widespread lynchings.[262] Providence would establish an Afro-American Council chapter for a short period, but local interest favored combined social and political interest organizations. The Providence-based Irreproachable Beneficial Association brought together Black cooks, waiters, and porters. Incorporated on October 24, 1904, the all-male group was sometimes referred to as the "Black Hope Club."[263] While most of the Irreproachable Association activities were social, the meetings often included talk of commerce and politics.

Marathon Football Club, c. 1915, Rhode Island Black Heritage Society Collection

The Marathon Club was organized in Providence in 1905.[264] The Club was part of a broader strategy within the African heritage community to improve Rhode Island's young men socially, culturally, and physically through early baseball, track, and football teams comprised of African heritage and Indigenous young men from Providence and Newport.[265] The Marathon Club's work was led by Roberta J. Dunbar and Joseph G. LeCount, Esq. These young Providence activists would go on to become the founders of the Providence Branch of the National Association for the Advancement of Colored People (NAACP).

An important equal rights organization formed in the early 20th century in Providence was the Rhode Island Union of Colored Women's Clubs. Providence-born Mary Elizabeth Jackson became a founding officer of both the NAACP and the Colored Women's Clubs. She was joined by other activists, including Bertha Higgins, Roberta J. Dunbar, Susan Williams, Jacynthia Perry, and W. Worthen.[266]

Unquestionably, the most important and influential African heritage association organized in the early 20th century was the National Association for the Advancement of Colored People, led by W. E. B. Du Bois and chartered in 1909 to advance justice for African heritage people across America. Rhode Island African heritage citizens formed one of the NAACP's earliest local chapters. On November 5, 1913, 600 African heritage people crowded into Beneficent Congregational Church, known as the "Round Top Church" in downtown Providence, to hear Dr. Joel Spingarn, president of the NAACP New York Branch. Dr. Spingarn was there to gauge Rhode Island interest in a state chapter of the NAACP.[267] Founding members included Dr. Julius J. Robinson, president; Reverend C.C. Alleyne of Providence's People's African Methodist Episcopal Church; Roberta J. Dunbar, secretary; Reverend Zachariah Harrison of Pond Street Baptist Church, treasurer; and executive committee members John C. Minkins, William P.H. Freeman, William A. Heathman, Esq., Julius Mitchel, Esq., and James E. Dixon.[268] Early meetings of the Providence branch were held at the Opera House, Strand Theatre, Trinity Auditorium, and the First Baptist Church.

In 1915, the Providence NAACP protested the showing of "The Birth of a Nation." The silent film, directed by D. W. Griffith, is recognized today as one of the most controversial films ever made. It depicts the Ku Klux Klan as heroic figures and African heritage people as marauding sexual predators menacing white women in the years immediately following the Civil War. White audiences attended sold-out shows across America, while the national NAACP led an effort to ban the movie.[269]

Following the national branch's lead, the Providence NAACP mobilized a campaign to stop the movie from showing in Providence.

Simultaneously, Col. Felix R. Wendelschafer, manager of the Providence Opera House, prepared to show the film for great profit, boldly guaranteeing the film's owner $5,000 in ticket sales.[270] The Providence Branch took immediate action. At a lively meeting led by attorney William A. Heathman at the Bethel AME Church, NAACP members called for a ban on the film. Despite the best efforts of the NAACP, the film appeared in Providence. The best the community of color could achieve was removing several of the most racist scenes, with the decision causing a deep divide between community leaders. [271] According to Col. Wendelschafer, the movie ran for two weeks, drawing capacity audiences at every performance.[272] With the release and popularity of "Birth of a Nation," the Ku Klux Klan experienced a significant resurgence in America in the years following the First World War, most notably across Rhode Island.

The Providence NAACP also fought for anti-lynching legislation at the state and national levels. From the end of the Civil War through the mid-20th century, newly freed African heritage people bore the brunt of white violence, many times in the form of mob executions by hanging or lynchings. According to the Tuskegee Institute, lynchings in American occurred most frequently in the period between 1890 and 1920. In all, 4,743 people were lynched between 1882 and 1968. Of that number, 72 percent were African-heritage men and women.[273] On March 3, 1904, nationally renowned Black journalist and activist Ida B. Wells spoke to a standing-room-only crowd at the Congdon Street Baptist Church. She urged the attendees to stand together against "mobs of white savages."

> Miss Wells-Barnett opened her address by describing the recent events in the South in the direction of meting out punishment to the Negroes there for the most atrocious of crimes, characterizing white people who were concerned with lynchings as "mobs of white savages, human devils, etc." In conclusion, Miss Wells-Barnett said that the Negro could never hope to better his condition until he woke up to the fact he must help himself; that God would not bring about the betterment of the race when he had given the colored man the strength to help himself. The Negroes must get together![274]

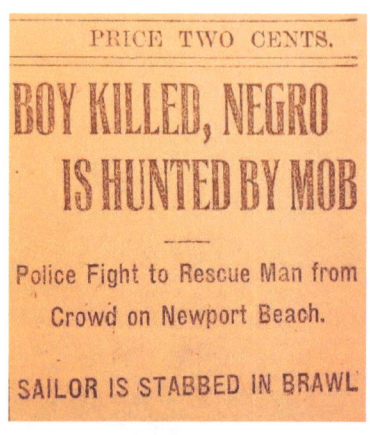

Providence Journal, July 5, 1913, Stokes Family Collection

While Rhode Island was one of five states that did not experience lynchings during that dark era, it came very close during a Fourth of July celebration in 1913. In Newport, a mob of about 5,000 men, women, and children chased Charles Smith, a 20-year-old African heritage man, across Easton's Beach crying, "lynch him." According to one report, "women became infuriated and screeched themselves hoarse."[275] The mob formed after Smith reportedly stabbed a sailor during a fight. Several white sailors chased Smith down the beach, prompting him to turn and fire a single shot from his revolver. Tragically, the bullet struck and killed William Egan, Jr., a 13-year-old Newport boy. Word rapidly spread through the beach about a Black man killing a white boy, and shoreline revelers, comprised of men, women, and children, transformed into a raging mob.

Fortunately, several police officers on the scene quickly took Smith to the beach office and called for a patrol wagon to escort him to the police station on Market Square. The incident made news across Rhode Island, and racial tensions between Black and white citizens were at an all-time high that year. Newport and Providence African heritage leaders came together to retain Julius L. Mitchell, soon to be a founder of the Providence NAACP and one of Rhode Island's early Black and civil rights attorneys. Mitchell successfully moved the trial from Newport County to Providence County to ensure a fair hearing. While the first trial ended in a hung jury in December 1913, Smith was convicted of manslaughter at a second trial and sentenced to life in prison.[276]

The near lynching and subsequent trial galvanized the African heritage community. Black leaders organized a local branch of the NAACP to ensure that a lynching would never occur in Rhode Island. On April 15th, 1920, a pre-membership drive meeting was held by the NAACP at the Winter Street AME Church in Providence. Dr. W. E. B Du Bois, the nation's leading Black equal rights leader and a founder of the NAACP,[277] was the featured speaker, and the topic was advancing state and federal anti-lynching legislation.[278] As reported in the Providence Evening Bulletin, *"Dr. W.E. B. Du Bois, the main speaker of the evening, called on the colored people to tell the truth to the people of the other race and said that the history of lynching had been made into a story recently and sent to every paper in Europe including Germany and the Russian Soviet."*[279] The Providence NAACP, led by president John F. Lopez and attorneys William A. Heathman and Julius L. Mitchell, was incensed by Rhode Island House Judiciary Chairman Fletcher W. Lawton, who stood firmly against a state anti-lynching law. In 1930, the NAACP branches in both Providence and Newport included a call for federal anti-lynching legislation within the Rhode Island Republican Party platform and Clark Burdick's reelection to Congress. It said, in part:

Providence Branch NAACP Membership Drive 1920, Rhode Island Black Heritage Society Collections

> We urge Congress to consider the most effect means to end lynching in this country, which continues to be a terrible blot on our American civilization. Our Negro citizens have the inalienable right to live peacefully and to receive the equal protection of our laws, and to participate in government and the choice of national, state, and municipal officials. It is well recognized that every state under Republican administration grants these rights, just as it is well known that many states under Democratic administration has denied them. Rhode Island is the traditional friend of the Negro.[280]

The anti-lynching federal law was denied. Undaunted, the NAACP would grow stronger and bolder in the 20th century, advancing employment and equal housing rights throughout the city and state.

The Fight Overseas & At Home

World War I transformed America. It propelled the young nation into a worldwide conflict and required an unprecedented mobilization of troops and supplies. By 1918, the federal government was asking everyone to sacrifice for the war effort. During the war, 350,000 African-heritage men and women served in practically every military service branch. As the country prepared for war, many factories put aside manufacturing cars, appliances, and home goods to make planes, tanks, and weapons for the troops. Here in Rhode Island, companies like the Gorham Manufacturing Company turned from making silver jewelry and flatware to making hand grenades. The need for labor increased as the war went on, and Rhode Island women, in particular, found more opportunities to enter the labor force. Nearly every day, Rhode Island papers carried advertisements for *"Girls Wanted,"* promising good pay, bonuses, attractive surroundings, and light work. What the ads did not state was "colored women" need not apply.

The New York Age, the nation's leading African heritage newspaper of the day, reported on November 9, 1918, that the Gorham Company's Providence plants refused to hire women of color.[281] The company's management stated they did not employ colored women because white women refused to work with them. Outraged, the New York Age declared, *"This vicious form of discrimination is being practiced in Rhode Island – not Mississippi."* Several organizations looking into the matter filed a complaint with then-Governor Robert Beeckman. The Providence NAACP eventually convinced Gorham and other companies—all in need of workers— to hire women of color. Still, it took a Providence woman of color to advance the cause of equal employment for women in Rhode Island and across America.

Born in 1867 in Providence to Henry and Amelia Jackson, Mary Elizabeth Jackson was a member of the Pond Street Baptist Church, a charter member of the Providence NAACP, and an officer with the New England Federation Of Colored Women's Clubs.[282] Jackson worked tirelessly to halt discriminatory practices and improve working conditions for women of color. A statistician at the Rhode Island Labor Department during WWI, she was appointed as a Special Worker for Colored Girls on the YWCA War Work Council, where she analyzed employment trends and recommended programs to encourage the fair employment of women of color. As an early advocate of women's rights, she wrote an article in the NAACP's The Crisis magazine in November 1918 entitled "The Colored Woman in Industry." She detailed the working conditions of women in factories and wrote about a future where women of African heritage worked alongside other women. This forward-thinking woman discussed the prejudice and poor working conditions that

Mary Elizabeth Jackson c. 1917, Crisis Magazine

women faced, and she wrote about the wage inequalities between Blacks and whites and men and women. "Thousands and thousands of eager boys have gone to France; we all know about them. Few of us realize that at the same time, an army of women is entering mills, factories, and all other branches of industry."[283] Jackson wrote a second article that year in the Young Women Christian Association Magazine.

> *For more than two centuries, the colored woman gave to this country an unrecognized contribution of love, loyalty, and unrequited labor. Both the skilled and unskilled woman labor of the South was for years the colored woman's. Neither in gold nor in gratitude has she been repaid for those years of faithful toil. Is this*

not the day for the Nation to pay to the daughters of today its debt to the mothers of yesterday by throwing wide the door of economic opportunity that they may become skilled trained competitors in the land to which their mothers gave their all?[284]

Rise of the Ku Klux Klan in Rhode Island

The Great War ended. In a Crisis magazine piece called "Returning Soldiers," W.E.B. Du Bois described the scene:

We are returning from war! The Crisis and tens of thousands of back men were drafted into a great struggle. For bleeding France and what she means and has meant and will mean to us and humanity, and against the threat of German race arrogance, we fought gladly and to the last drop of blood; for America and her highest ideals, we fought in far off hope; for the dominant southern oligarchy entrenched in Washington, we fought in bitter resignation. For the America that represents and gloats in lynching, disfranchisement, caste, brutality, and devilish insult for this, in hateful upturning and mixing of things, we were forced by vindictive fate to fight. But today, we return! We return from the slavery of uniform, which the worlds' madness demanded us to don, to the freedom of civil garb. We return. We return from fighting. We return fighting. Make way for Democracy! We saved it in France, and by the Great Jehovah, we will save it in the United States of America or know the reason why.[285]

African heritage troops returned to their hometowns, cities, and states with high expectations of equality, employment, and respect. Instead, they faced steadily growing racial tensions that culminated in race riots across three dozen cities during the summer of 1919, dubbed "Red Summer" by civil rights activist and author James Weldon Johnson.[286] The Providence NAACP organized a "Silent Parade" of over one thousand people who walked down Providence's streets to protest the race riots sweeping across postwar America.[287] Tragically, the lynching of African heritage people soared like no other time since the Jim Crow days. Some African heritage veterans were lynched while in uniform. The Ku Klux Klan claimed more than four million members.

A group of ex-Confederate soldiers started the Klan in 1865 in Pulaski, Tennessee. At first, it was only a social club. But in 1867, when freed Black men gained the right to vote, the group became more political and more violent as they tried to discourage African-heritage men from voting. The following year, the Klan selected former Confederate Army General Nathan Bedford Forrest as their leader.[288]

Klan activity in Rhode Island occurred during the world war years, peaking in the mid-1920s. Klan-supported events included a June 21, 1924 rally with an estimated 8,000 Klan members assembling at Old Home Day Grounds in Foster. After the rally, they served a clam chowder dinner and initiated several hundred new Klansmen under a blazing cross.[289] In the

K.K.K Rally at Oaklawn Cemetery, Broad St. Providence
Rhode Island Historical Society

fall of 1924, more than 3,000 Klansmen in hooded robes met near Chepachet Road in Smithfield. Some 200 new members were inducted. Five hundred automobiles at the nighttime event illuminated the field.[290] To understand how openly the Klan operated in early 20th century Rhode Island, consider the following: Klan rallies and membership drives occurred across the state, including at Washington Square in Newport,[291] the Oaklawn Cemetery on Broad Street in Providence, an oyster supper in Coventry, and a dinner dance held at Rhodes-on-the-Pawtuxet on January 30, 1925. The Pawtuxet affair was sponsored by the Providence County Klanton and its women's auxiliary for an estimated crowd of one thousand celebrants.[292]

Given the Klan's intimidation tactics against African heritage people and the state's rapidly growing Catholic and immigrant population, the fear of violence was palpable. These concerns became a painful reality when a series of fires were set at the Watchman Industrial School in North Scituate, a vocational school for African heritage children. As activity peaked in the area, so too did a series of damaging fires at the school.[293] Sending a clear message that the Klan was officially part of the state's political landscape, Secretary of State Ernest Sprague granted a charter to the Ku Klux Klan of Rhode Island in the fall of 1925, declaring:[294]

> The purpose of the organization, as contained in the charter, are as follows:
>
> A. Fostering and promoting fraternity and good-will toward its members.
>
> B. Encouraging participation by its members in the community and civic activity.
>
> C. Encouraging a fearless and faithful administration of justice through due process of the law.
>
> D. Teaching respect for and obedience to the Constitution of the United States and the Constitution and Laws of the State of Rhode Island.
>
> E. Educating its members in the duties of American citizenship and inspiring both by precept and example, an exalted patriotism.
>
> F. Devoting, under the direction of its chief officer, to charitable, benevolent, and educational purposes all surplus funds which may be accumulated from the collection of dues of its members.
>
> The headquarters of the organization under its charter will be in Providence.

The Emergence of Cape Verdeans in Providence

One important group of African heritage immigrants to arrive in early the early 20th century was the Cape Verdean community. The Cape Verdean people have a deep and rich history in Rhode Island. The Cape Verde archipelago consists of twenty-one islands that lie several hundred miles off West Africa's coast. By the 15th century, explorers from Portugal used the islands as a staging area for their West Africa slave-trading interests. In 1466, a Royal Charter established by the King of Portugal gave Cape Verde's merchants the right to trade in slaves.[295] The introduction of enslaved Africans and the resulting interrelationships with the Portuguese mariners and settlers created the mixed heritage Cape Verdean people of the present day. Also present in Cape Verdean ancestry are those who arrived as "New Christians"— Sephardic Portuguese Jews who had converted to Christianity or concealed their Hebrew faith during the Spanish and Portuguese Inquisition of the 15th century.296 Cape Verdeans are also distinct among early American populations of African heritage or mixed origins because they came to America as free laborers rather than slaves.297 The United States took an interest in the area in 1843 when it formed an African Squadron, led by Rhode Island Commodore Matthew Perry, to curb West African slave-trading activity that included several Cape Verdean ports.298

The earliest Cape Verdeans arrived in America in 1860, followed by larger migrations between 1900 and 1921. Many entered America through New Bedford, Massachusetts.299 Arriving from a seafaring island nation, many Cape Verdeans, particularly the Brava seamen, moved from New Bedford to Providence and East Providence along the Seekonk River. They worked as mariners, longshoremen, fishermen, laborers, and dockhands. Beginning as early as the late 19th century, Cape Verdean immigrants created a tightly knit, family-oriented community within Providence's Fox Point and College Hill neighborhoods. They established a place of worship at 51 Sheldon Street—the oldest Cape Verdean Church in America.300

Lou Costa Collection on Fox Point, Providence Public Library, Special Collections

A review of census records, World War I registration cards, and city directories during the early 20th century reveals Cape Verdean people and families living throughout the Fox Point neighborhood:

Anthony Lima Residence Year: 1930/ Immigration 1911 Street Address: 192 Transit St. (1930) Street Address: 153 Transit St. (1940)	**Valentine Tavares** Residence Year: 1935 Street Address: 244 India St.	**Arania Fonces** Residence Year: 1920 Street Address: 42 Wickenden St.
Louis Gomes (Birth: French Africa) Residence Year: 1930 Street Address: 216 Wickenden St.	**Grayton Silvia** Residence Year: 1920 Street Address: 349 South Main St.	**Peter Forte** Residence Year: 1930 Street Address: 106 India St.
Gertrude Correia (Widow 36) Residence Year: 1930 Street Address: 569 South Main St.	**Freeman Almeida** Residence Year: 1936 Street Address: 74 Trenton St.	**John F. Lopez** Resident Year: 1935 Street Address: 445 Wickenden St.

One Cape Verdean inhabitant in the Fox Point neighborhood became one of Rhode Island's greatest civil rights leaders, actively engaged in nearly every major equal rights organization and event of his day. John F. Lopez Jr. was born in 1888 in New Bedford, Massachusetts, to immigrant parents. He moved to Fox Point, where he ran a successful funeral business at 445 Wickenden Street. Lopez was also an early member of the Providence Branch NAACP, serving as president and chief spokesperson during the World War II era.301 His work on advancing fair employment laws within the state of Rhode Island reached heroic levels and set the stage for other Cape Verdean social justice and political leaders, most notably George Lima, Isadore Ramos, Peter Coelho, Clifford Monteiro, John DaLuz, George Castro, Maria Lopes, and Jim Vincent.302

The Fox Point inhabitants faced significant challenges during the 20th century, including the devastating effects of the 1938 and 1954 hurricanes, the construction of the I-195 highway, urban redevelopment, and residential gentrification.[303] Many of these occurrences created both intended and unintended far-reaching consequences that led to the disruption and displacement of working families. The new I-195 highway cut directly through the heart of Fox Point and the historic Cape Verdean neighborhood, destroying houses and businesses and dislocating many people. The highway also separated the Fox Point people—many of them waterfront workers—from the city's historic waterfront.

Mary Elizabeth Sharpe, the wife of Henry Dexter Sharpe, the president and treasurer of the Brown and Sharpe Manufacturing Company, delivered another blow to the Fox Point community. In 1962, she launched a campaign to transform the working waterfront along India Point into a recreational park to be named India Point Park:

> *From the late 18th century to the early 20th century, India Point was part of Providence's working waterfront. The area was a primary setting for the city's maritime and economic history. Shipbuilding, the East India trade, passenger, and freight steamers, and railroads all flourished here during the period. India Point had declined to become a center for scrap metal shipping when in 1962, a Providence resident, Mary Elizabeth Sharpe, began urging the city to establish a waterfront park on the site. By 1964, Mrs. Sharpe's idea had taken hold enough to have the idea for a park at India Point included in a 1964 Master Plan. By 1966, I-195 was constructed, cutting off India Point from the Fox Point neighborhood. A series of events, including a large financial donation by Mrs. Sharpe, the relocation of the scrap yards to the west banks of the Providence River, and the assistance of the US Department of Housing and Urban Development enabled the construction of India Point Park to begin in 1971.[304]*

The actions of Mrs. Sharpe and government officials were initially seen as an attempt to replace urban blight with a city park. As in other urban renewal projects, little thought was given to the project's impact on people of color and their communities. The permanent loss of the working waterfront had significant socioeconomic consequences for the Cape Verdean families of Fox Point, who were historically dependent upon the many employment opportunities tied to the harbor.

Political Transitions: From Republican to Democrat

Nearly all African-heritage voters sided with Abraham Lincoln's Republican Party after the Civil War.[305] After many years of allegiance, many Black Republican loyalists worried their votes were being taken for granted. These concerns were sparked by comments like those of New York Congressman Lemuel E. Quigg, the chairman of the Republican State Conventions. When asked about Black patronage within the party, he answered smugly, *"I know the Negroes better than they know themselves. You couldn't drive them out of the Republican Party with a sledgehammer."*[306]

In 1922, the Colored Independent Political Association at the AME. Zion Church in Providence pushed back against the Republican Party, stating, *"We reaffirm the right of the colored citizens of Rhode Island to equal opportunity and responsibility before the law."* Its founding member, Zion Church Reverend R.A. Carrell, directly assailed the state's Republican Party as *"a party that uses the Negro for its selfish ends in Rhode Island, and for the wrongs which it has visited on the member of his race in Rhode Island."*[307] Another prominent member of the new organization was Dr. William H. Higgins, who *"scored the Republicans for what he termed the conciliation of racial and national groups and awarding of political places to members of these groups."*[308]

Dr. Higgins and his wife, Bertha, were political powerhouses within the Providence African heritage community in the early 20th century. Dr. Higgins was born in Marion, North Carolina, in 1872.[309] He graduated from Livingston College in 1889 and graduated with high honors and a medical degree from Shaw University in Raleigh, North Carolina, the first historically Black institution of higher education in the South and the first to offer a four-year medical program.[310] Higgins moved to Providence in 1903 and opened a medical practice in the west end of the city at the corner of 43 Wendall Street and 144 Dexter Street.

In 1911, Dr. Higgins was elected to the Republican City Committee representing the Seventh Ward of Providence, the first time that a person of color was so honored by the Republican Party. Later, in 1928, Black voters in the district refused to take part in the Republican caucus because the Seventh Ward Republican Committee refused to forward the name of Dr. Higgins and a member of the same committee to run for the vacant city council office.[311]

His wife, Bertha G. Higgins, also an influential political activist, founded the Julia Ward Howe Republican Women's Club of Providence and devoted her life to advancing African-heritage women's equality and political rights.

By the early 1930s, Bertha joined her husband as an outspoken critic of the lack of support for African heritage people by the Republican Party. Soon after, Bertha Higgins and John F. Lopez helped form the Providence Colored Democratic Club. The Colored Democratic Club played an important role in electing Democrats to major state offices. At a mass meeting of African heritage voters at the Eagles Auditorium on Westminster Street on November 5, 1934, they hosted Governor Theodore Francis Green as the featured speaker.[312] Green, in turn, secured appointments of African heritage people to public positions, including a State House appointment for Lopez.

Governor Green and the state Democratic leadership were tested in 1934 when the newly built Narragansett Park and Racetrack placed "For Colored and For White" signs at the horse stables and restaurant. The Providence Colored Democratic Club and the Providence Branch NAACP convinced Governor Green to promptly remove the signs.[313] These local actions and the popular national New Deal investments by Democratic President Franklin Delano Roosevelt successfully transformed Black Republicans into Blue Democrats across America and in Rhode Island.

A Distinct People: Indian Reorganization Act of 1934

The State of Rhode Island's legislative actions in 1880 to abolish Narragansett tribal sovereignty and sell off tribal land was part of a national policy of detribalization that swept across America:

> *During the nineteenth-century military conquest, fraudulent or unobserved treaties and the increasing pressure of advancing white settlement disposed of the Indian tribes of virtually the entire continental United States. White encroachments on their lands, military subjugation, and even intermarriage,*

had not, however, disrupted the political organization of many Indian tribes.[314]

Rhode Island's deconstruction of the Narragansett tribe would remain in place for over fifty years until a new generation of Narragansett leaders seized an opportunity for recognition through a progressive-minded governor—Theodore Francis Green. Green and his Democratic party had come into power in Rhode Island by building a coalition of labor unions, working-class immigrants, and a rising ethnic middle class. His support of the political aspirations of Rhode Island's African heritage community lured Blacks away from the GOP. During his time as Governor (1933–1937), Green guided Rhode Island through the Great Depression and also reestablished a bond with the Narragansett tribe. As part of the state's Tricentennial Celebration, he established "Rhode Island Indian Day."[315]

Rhode Island Indian Day Celebration, Narragansett Indian Church, Charlestown, R.I., Rhode Island Collection, Providence Public Library

In 1936, the Rhode Island General Assembly enacted General Law 25-2-4 under "Days of Special Observance," proclaiming, *"The last Saturday before the second Sunday in August shall annually be set apart as a day to be known as the 'Rhode Island Indian Day of the Narragansett tribe of Indians.' The day is to be observed by the people of this state with appropriate exercises in public places and otherwise commemorative of the Narragansett tribe of Indians."* Princess Red Wing, a Narragansett elder and historian, seized this public recognition to advance tribal autonomy in the Narragansett Dawn, a tribal newspaper she co-founded:

The weary struggling years of history of Rhode Island have been lived and relived in this Tercentenary Year of the state's foundation, in which the Narragansetts have been featured and re-featured. In these great celebrations by white Rhode Island, Narragansetts have been called upon to do their part from the days of Canonicus to Queen Esther. Rhode Island can show no great pageant of her historic years of the past without her Indians. In the many programs of the year, only a pleasant, bright, and cheerful side of the Narragansetts have been portrayed. Always the Indian is giving up to the paleface. In the long run, "giving" brings a reward. We have given what we had to give in the past. In the present, we gave of our members for entertainment and enlightenment into historic facts. Our reward is, Rhode Island knows now, THE NARRAGANSETT TRIBE STILL EXISTS![316]

The fearless leadership of Princess Redwing and others greatly advanced Narragansett and Indigenous recognition. But it took a federal act to bring a new level of native independence and sovereignty across America. The Indian Reorganization Act, also called the Wheeler-Howard Act, was signed into law by New Deal President Franklin D. Roosevelt on June 18th, 1934. The law strengthened, encouraged, and preserved the

Indigenous tribes and their historic native cultures. Rhode Island state and local governments would rely on one section of the law to limit the Narragansett tribe's sovereignty. Sec. 19 of the law states:

> *The term "Indian" as used in this Act shall include all persons of Indian descent who are members of any recognized Indian tribe now under Federal jurisdiction and all persons who are descendants of such members who were, on June 1st, 1934, residing within the present boundaries of any reservation.*[317]

The Indian Reorganization Act of 1934 reestablished native tribes across the country as distinct people with significant self-determination and sovereignty powers. Still, for Narragansett tribal members, who were not recognized by the state at the time, the federal law had little real benefits. Only those tribes that signed treaties were federally recognized and given access to resources.[318] The state's 1880 law of abolishment would continue to be used against Narragansett sovereignty by a succession of Rhode Island governors and congressional leaders well into the late 20th century.

1934 Federal Housing Administration Act & Redlining

A major law enacted as part of the federal New Deal was the National Housing Act of 1934, intended to make housing and home mortgages more affordable. During the Great Depression, many banks failed, causing a drastic decrease in home loans and ownership. The federal act established the Federal Housing Administration (FHA), which offered mortgage insurance to FHA-approved banking institutions. The insurance protected lenders against losses from defaults on mortgages by borrowers. In the case of a loan default, the FHA paid the lender a specified claim amount. While the innovative New Deal program opened the doors to homeownership to scores of Americans, not everyone got a loan—especially people of color. As detailed by Richard Rothstein, a Distinguished Fellow of the Economic Policy Institute:

> *To solve the inability of middle-class renters to purchase single-family homes for the first time, Congress and President Roosevelt created the Federal Housing Administration in 1934. The FHA insured banks mortgages that covered 80 percent of purchase prices had terms of twenty years, and were fully amortized. To be eligible for such insurance, the FHA insisted on doing its own appraisal of the property to make certain that the loan had a low risk of default. Because the FHA's appraisal standards included a whites-only requirement, racial segregation now became an official requirement of the federal mortgage insurance program.*[319]

FHA policy was anchored on the premise that neighborhoods occupied by the same racial groups would be the most stable over time and produce the highest returns, or property values, for residents.[320] The federal underwriters' manual mandated racial and class segregation in housing:

> *The Valuator should investigate areas surrounding the location to determine whether or not incompatible racial and social groups are present to the end that an intelligent prediction may be made regarding the possibility or probability of the location being invaded by such groups. If a neighborhood is to retain stability, it is necessary that properties shall continue to be occupied by the same social and racial classes. A change in social or racial occupancy generally leads to instability and a reduction in values. The protection offered against adverse changes should be found adequate before a high rating is given to this feature.*[321]

This highly discriminatory practice that restricts or denies access to loans, mortgages, and other financial

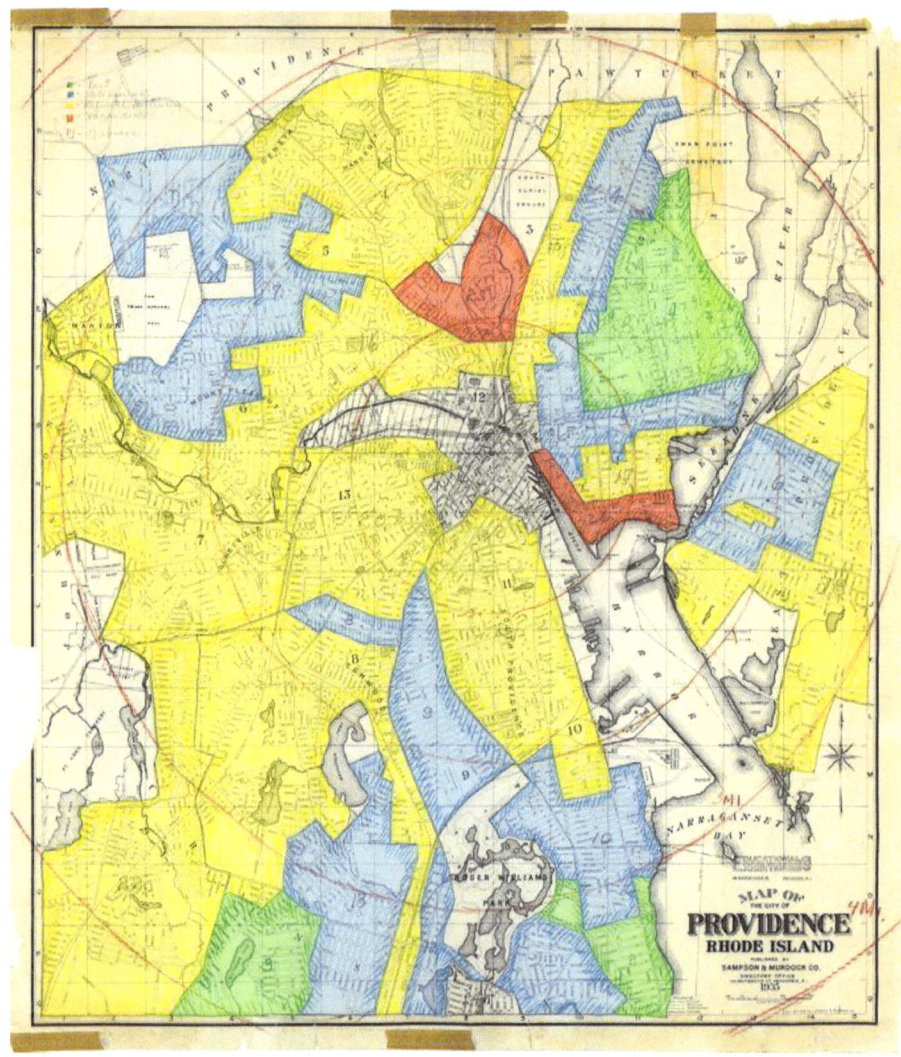

Homeowners Loan Corporation Map, City of Providence, 1935, Providence City Archive

resources based on race, class, and location is popularly known as *"redlining."* As part of the New Deal, the Homeowners Loan Corporation (HOLC) was established to refinance home mortgages in danger of foreclosure, as well as to expand home-buying opportunities. HOLC investments were predicated upon neighborhood risk assessments. Homes within neighborhoods considered to be high risks for loans were often "redlined" by real estate brokers, mortgage underwriters, and lending institutions, denying home buyers access to capital investment within those communities.[322] In 1935, HOLC developed an investment map for the City of Providence that, not surprisingly, mainly identified neighborhoods of color as either *"Hazardous or Declining,"* including Fox Point, South Providence, West Elmwood, Lippitt Hill, and large sections of College Hill.[323]

The FHA mortgage insurance and related programs continued its official policy of racial exclusion for decades. This policy was primarily directed towards African heritage home buyers and lower-income neighborhoods. Twenty-five years later, at a United States Senate Hearing on amending national housing laws, it was disclosed, *"FHA has continued to insure loans with the full knowledge that builders and developers were excluding racial and religious minorities. Even as far as production of segregated homes for minority families is concerned, the FHA record is a sorry one."[324]*

During the Great Depression, the demand for decent and affordable housing in Providence reached epidemic proportions. In 1935 alone, more than 40,000 citizens were dependent upon local relief efforts. Many of the poorest men, women, and children lived in neighborhoods identified as having high instances of substandard housing, including Fox Point, Federal Hill, Smith Hill, Olneyville, Wanskuck, and South Providence.[325] The demand for safe and affordable housing and employment security became major national and local public policy matters in the mid-20th century. Public housing had its start in Providence in 1935 when the General Assembly passed the Housing Authorities Act. Its "Declaration of Necessity" section said, in part:

> (1) Unsanitary or unsafe dwelling accommodations exist in various cities of the state, and that these unsafe or unsanitary conditions arise from overcrowding and concentration of population, the obsolete and poor condition of the buildings, improper planning, excessive land coverage, lack of proper light, air, and space, unsanitary design and arrangement, lack of proper sanitary facilities, and the existence of conditions which endanger life or property by fire and other causes; that in all these cities many persons of low income are forced to reside in unsanitary or unsafe dwelling accommodations;

> (2) In various cities, there is a lack of safe or sanitary dwelling accommodations available to all the inhabitants, and that consequently many persons of low income are forced to occupy overcrowded and congested dwelling accommodations.

> (3) These conditions cause an increase in and spread of disease and crime and constitute a menace to the health, safety, morals, and welfare of the citizens of the state, and impair economic values; that these conditions cannot be remedied by the ordinary operations of private enterprises.

> (4) The clearance, re-planning, and reconstruction of the areas in which unsanitary or unsafe housing conditions exist and the providing of safe and sanitary dwelling accommodations for persons of low income are public uses and purposes for which public money may be spent and private property acquired.

> (5) It is in the public interest that work on these projects be instituted as soon as possible in order to relieve unemployment, which now constitutes an emergency, and

> (6) The necessity in the public interest for the provision enacted by these chapters is declared a matter of legislative determination.[326]

This state measure would lead to the establishment in 1939 of the Providence Housing Authority. As local, state, and federal governments responded with bold and new social programs, Providence's civil rights groups tackled the ghosts of Jim Crow and the "separate and unequal" treatment of people of color and their neighborhoods.

PART 4: FAIR EMPLOYMENT DURING WWII ERA (1940-1955)

Fight for Fair Employment

World War II transformed America and Rhode Island. As in the previous war, Rhode Island mobilized men, women, and resources to prepare for the largest war in human history. Many of Rhode Island's jewelry factories made medals and other military materials; Brown and Sharpe in Providence turned out ammunition parts and largely employed women.[327]

As African-heritage men served overseas and at home throughout the war years, women contributed to the war effort in different but important ways, individually and through service organizations, including the YWCA and American Red Cross. African-heritage women sacrificed as well, but their efforts were hard-fought and continuously met with resistance as second-class citizens simply because of their race and gender. As noted by historian Karen Tucker Anderson, *"few have considered the impact of the wartime expansion on black women, who constituted 600,000 of the 1 million blacks who entered paid employment during the war years."*[328]

In 1939, as Rhode Island braced for possible conflict, James N. Williams helped organize the Providence Urban League. Williams was born in Des Moines, Iowa, in 1909. He earned a bachelor's degree from Des Moines University and a master's from the New Jersey State Teachers College. He arrived in Rhode Island as the director of the Rhode Island Conference of Social Workers, and by 1939, he became the director of the newly established Providence Urban League.[329]

African-heritage men and women had to repeatedly fight both to serve their country overseas and support the war effort at home. The newspaper headlines from the era show some of the challenges they faced and how they met them:

"More Employment Urged For Negroes," Providence Chronicle, September 1942
A report shows that Negroes were employed in mostly unskilled defense positions.

"More Skilled Jobs Go To Negroes," Providence Chronicle, October 1942
Chief of Negro Manpower Service says the number of blacks in war jobs has increased.

"Woman Power For War Plants," Providence Chronicle, November 1942
American Women of many racial groups man machines for our war production needs.

"Cranston Dance Called Off," Providence Journal, October 1943 *A performance by the Count Basie Negro Orchestra, scheduled for Rhodes-on-the-Pawtuxet, is called off because Negro men and white women might dance together.*

"Order Violations Claimed Negro Shipyard Worker's Attorney," Providence Journal, June 1944
A story about a union dues setup at Kaiser-Walsh Shipyard.

"Negroes Will Open USO This Evening," Providence Journal, October 1944
A segregated Negro USO is completed in Newport.[330]

The headlines reveal acceptable gains for African heritage war workers. While many worked at unskilled jobs, capable men and women of color found better job opportunities as the war progressed. Major General Philip

B. Fleming, the administrator of the Federal Works Agency, addressed the fourth annual Urban League of Providence dinner at the Beneficent Congregational Church, declaring:

> *"As a beneficiary of the wartime situation and manpower shortage, the Black worker was taking a long step forward along the way to economic emancipation. The problem would be to maintain and extend the gains already won. Most Negros are making good. He has to be just as good as the white man with whom he competes. If not, just a little bit better. And I think there is a very real responsibility upon such organizations as the Urban League to see that the Negroes it recommends for employment in industry are thoroughly competent to do the work required. Nothing is to be gained, either for the individual or for his race, when the Negro is placed in a job he is not qualified by education and training to fill."[331]*

Civil rights leader W. E. B. Du Bois recognized the paternalistic and patronizing beliefs of white leaders such as General Fleming towards the African heritage worker. Writing about the stereotypes plaguing Black workers, he asserted in a 1923 article:

> *"American industry is slowly beginning to awake to the fact that there is in this country a great reservoir of labor which has been only partially tapped. The South has nine million black folk, of whom five million are productive workers. As a mass, they are ignorant and unskilled, but they are ambitious, willing to learn, and, for the most part, at present, wretchedly underpaid. Lynching, lawlessness, lack of schools, and disfranchisement have slowly but surely made them ripe for change. The public, therefore, in the end, must say: There is but one way out. The South must reform its attitude toward the Negro. The North must reform its attitude toward common labor. The unions must give up monopoly and aristocracy as methods of social uplift. The Negro must develop democracy within as well as without the race."[332]*

As Rhode Islanders retooled their factories for war work, the Providence NAACP and Urban League prepared to fight for military and private sector jobs. Their advocacy campaign would require documented evidence that both demonstrated the challenges faced by non-white applicants and, particularly, women who faced employment discrimination by race and sex.

1943 Report on the Employment Problems of the Negro

Many of the Urban League organizers in Rhode Island were veteran members of the Providence Branch NAACP. They saw the Urban League as a dedicated means to secure fair employment rights. Led by the NAACP legal counsel Joseph LeCount and Urban League's James Williams, the State of Rhode Island in 1942 established a Governor's Commission to look into Black employment. The Commission published a landmark report in 1943 entitled *"Report of the Commission on the Employment Problems of the Negro."*[333] Prominent Commission members included Bertha Higgins, Ella Solomon, Ramona Barros, and Mrs. S. Foster Hunt, serving as Providence Urban League chairperson.[334]

The report looked at the hard, "unpleasant" facts about Black employment:

> *"The fact that there are some 12,000 of our fellow citizens in Rhode Island who are denied equal opportunity with their fellow citizens is a hard and unpleasant fact. The rank discrimination against*

the Negro race in every city and State in the Union, the denial of the Negro of even the right of suffrage in certain sections of this Democracy, are hard, unpleasant facts. More than that, they are dangerous, explosive facts which, if not altered, may well determine the future course of history."[335]

The Commission conducted hundreds of interviews with men and women of African heritage across the state, but mostly in Providence. Officials interviewed Blacks about routine discrimination across many skilled, semi-skilled, and professional industries. The examples were numerous:

- *Received word to report to a company where there was a vacancy for a shipping clerk. Employer enthusiastic over the phone, but when I reported for job, was not hired as company did not hire Negroes. (Clerk)*

- *Applied W. A. Co., Conn., G. R. Co. and other large concerns to get a job as chemist. All of these places, upon learning he was a Negro, made excuses for not hiring him. Took an out-of-State examination, placed seventh on list; although offered job, when appeared was sent home to await final notice, which was never received. (Machinist)*

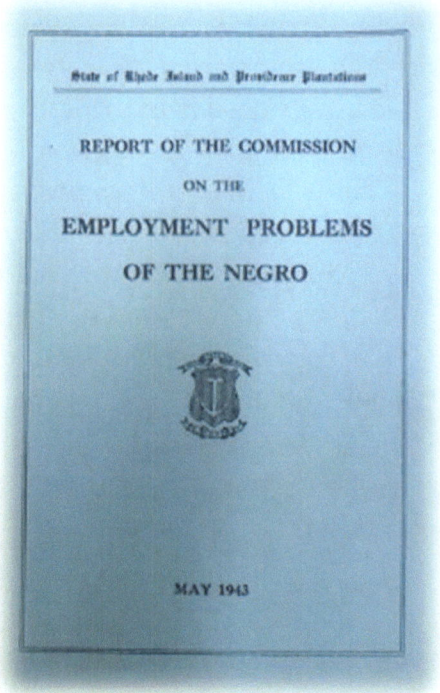

Report Of the Commission on the Employment Problems of the Negro, Rhode Island State Archives

- *Difficulty is color. Even smart people don't have a chance. Kids get disinterested and drop out of school. (Domestic)*

- *One friend tried to get a clerk's job in a local store. Told they were sorry that they never employ colored people. If they did, most of present clerks would cause friction. Some stores and firms come right out and say, "No Negroes!" (Clerk)*

- *Providence is the worst place on the map for race difficulties. The prejudice here against Negroes is worse than it is in Mississippi. The war industries have helped a lot, but there will be a post-war setback. (Minister)*

- *There's discrimination; you know, color. When we go for a job, the guy just looks at us and says, "Sorry, someone else is coming in." (Longshoreman)*

- *Extreme discrimination in many lines, especially in any kind of skilled labor. Says it's worse in Rhode Island than in any other New England State. (Teacher)*

- *There's Y. store, just around the corner. A group of Negroes got together recently and went to the store and asked the manager if he would employ a Negro boy, either as a clerk or delivery boy. Ninety per cent (90%) of the store's business comes from Negroes. The manager got in touch with the district manager of the company, who said he'd close the store before he'd hire any Negroes. Rhode Island is the meanest little State in the Union. (Clerk)*

- *My husband has not had much difficulty. He passes as an Italian. (Teacher)*[336]

After documenting numerous instances of employment discrimination directed at African heritage people, the Commission concluded that: *"the Negroes of this State are being refused equal economic opportunity with the general population, in pursuing employment for which they are qualified."[337]* The Commission also recommended *"legislation be enacted to prohibit discrimination in the employment of persons of any race, color or sex or nationality, in any public utility or public works operating within the State or subdivision thereof."[338]*

In response, Governor John O. Pastore called for a Rhode Island Fair Employment law in his February 3, 1948, state budget address, stating, *"Prejudice, bigotry, and racial discrimination have no place in American life. These evils cannot be stamped out by legislation alone. They can be eliminated and only by education, but the legislation is a stride forward toward the desired goal."[339]*

The actions of Providence Urban League and NAACP leaders, coupled with efforts by local and state elected officials, spurred the adoption of the Rhode Island Fair Employment Practices Act.[340] The July 1, 1949 law provided for a commission of five to be nominated by the governor with the Senate's advice and consent. The Commission was given explicit authority *"to receive, investigate, and pass upon charges of unlawful employment practices."[341]* The powerful civil rights law also established the Rhode Island Commission Against Discrimination. The practice or policy of discrimination against individuals *"is a matter of state concern,"* the commission said, adding that *"discrimination foments public strife and unrest, threatens the rights and privileges of the inhabitants of the state, and undermines the foundations of a free democratic state."[342]*

The new Rhode Island law stood out from other early state fair employment practice laws in several important regards:

> *It allows a period of one year within which complaints may be filed, whereas, under earlier legislation, only ninety days or six months was allowed. Another distinguishing provision permits the filing of complaints by "any organization chartered for the purpose of combating discrimination or racism or of promoting full, free or equal employment opportunities," thereby making it possible for civic-minded organizations to seek redress on behalf of persons who, because of fear of reprisal or lack of funds, might be unwilling to appear as complainants. Similar authority is given to State officials in other States, but experience shows that they are, sometimes reluctant to start proceedings.[343]*

Three years later, the Rhode Island Commission Against Discrimination declared in its 1952 Annual Report, *"The complete elimination of discrimination and segregation is our goal, and such is only attainable by the changing of deeply ingrained customs and traditions of the past through the substitution of patterns which will reflect the true ideals of America."[344]* These lofty words, born out of a decades-long struggle to prohibit discrimination in employment towards African heritage Rhode Island citizens, gave people of color hope. But the complete elimination of discrimination in employment would require a more comprehensive approach to dismantling employment barriers ensuring equal access to workforce training and education—critical issues well understood by the Urban League and NAACP as future goals.

Walsh-Kaiser Shipyard & Nursing School Integration

The WWII years ushered in two significant achievements in fair employment opportunities for Rhode Island's African heritage community. In 1944, Rhode Island civil rights attorney Joseph LeCount, NAACP Providence

President John F. Lopez, and Providence Urban League leader James Williams, joined Thurgood Marshall and the national NAACP in successfully bringing suit against the Local 308 of the International Brotherhood of Boilermakers, Iron Shipbuilders, Blacksmiths, Forgers, and Helpers. The suit helped over 500 African heritage men join the huge workforce at the Walsh-Kaiser shipyard in Cranston and Providence as equal union members.[345]

As reported in the leading African heritage newspaper of the day, *"Walsh-Kaiser Shipyard Company in Providence, R.I. has hired more than 250 Negro workers as welders, riggers, warehouse-men, maintenance mechanics, chippers, drillers, riveters, steamfitters, carpenters, and shiplifters"*.[346] But later that year, as African heritage workers continued to land jobs and work at the shipyard, their status as union workers changed. As Patrick Crowley notes in an article on the event:

> *On August 3, 1943, an African American man named George Schmoke walked into the National Urban League offices on Broadway in New York City with a story to tell. Mr. Schmoke worked as a laborer at the Walsh-Kaiser shipyard in Providence, Rhode Island, making Navy ships for the allied war effort. He was one of the lead men in his department and tasked with trying to get help for his fellow African American shipyard workers. Mr. Schmoke told Julius Thomas, head of the Urban League's Industrial Relations Department, the workers were represented by Local 308 of the International Brotherhood of Boilermakers, Iron Shipbuilders, Blacksmiths, Forgers and Helpers (IBB), but because they were people of color, they were not granted full membership in the local union. Instead, the IBB was forcing the African American boilermakers into an auxiliary union without the same full union rights as their white counterparts.*[347]

In June 1944, the Urban League suit took on national momentum. The New York Age newspaper reported on new twists in the legal challenge under the headline, *"Suit Against Jim Crow Boilermaker Union in Rhode Island Continues. New Cases Heard."*[348] This landmark case had national repercussions and eventually ensured African-heritage men and women the right to work and equal wages and benefits in labor unions. As Providence was at the center of World War II shipyard construction, the city was also at the center of combating persistent Jim Crow employment policies that were eventually defeated through the efforts of the NAACP and Urban League.

That same year, Mrs. S. Foster Hunt, the chairperson at the Providence Urban League, secured an agreement with the Nursing School Council at Rhode Island Hospital to accept "colored applicants" for the first time, opening up employment opportunities for scores of African heritage women in Rhode Island. The Urban League's steady advocacy was highlighted in an April 1944 letter to the Rhode Island Hospital Trustees:

> *The Providence Urban League, as part of its effort to secure equal opportunities for Negroes, has for some time tried to get qualified colored girls accepted as student nurses in Providence training schools. As you may know, the State Committee on Nursing Education recommended last spring to every training school in the State that this non-discriminatory policy be adopted, as it has been in five great hospitals in Boston, including the Massachusetts General.*[349]

In a November 21, 1944 letter to Hunt from Dr. Alex M. Burgess, the trustee noted the hiring breakthrough:[350] *"At a meeting of the Nursing School Council held April 25, 1944, at the Rhode Island Hospital, the following motion was adopted. 'That colored applicants may be accepted upon proof of their intelligence, scholarship, adaptability, home background, personality, and character. That they be admitted only on the same basis as to all other students.'"* Dr. Burgess sent another letter to the Board of Trustees at Rhode Island Hospital, declaring:

> *Discrimination against any racial group is certainly not compatible with Rhode Island tradition, but, unfortunately, colored people have not been given an equal chance here in our State. I am aware that no action was taken by the board because classes were already filled. It is, in my judgment, however, not important whether or not colored nurses are admitted at once, and I assume that until superior applicants present themselves, none would be. The important thing, I believe, is for it to be known that the Rhode Island Hospital, with its many years of service to all on an equal basis, does not draw the "color line."* [351]

The Providence Urban League's work received national attention. The 1945 issue of *Opportunity: A Journal of Negro Life* reported that *"Mrs. S. Foster Hunt, President of the Providence Urban League, headed a committee which, after a series of conferences, discovered that two Providence hospitals would accept Negros and that had already accepted one."*[352]

Another important victory in the fight for fair employment occurred when the Urban League and the NAACP convinced law enforcement officials to hire African heritage police officers in Providence. After much discussion and protest, the first Black policeman, Al Lima, was hired in 1946. Two years later, Horace Craig, Manuel Rodrigues, and Vernon Dunlop, all WWII veterans, became Providence police officers.[353]

At the conclusion of WWII, soldiers returned to America hoping to snag good jobs and good homes at the start of a new era of prosperity. The federal American Housing Act of 1949 greatly expanded the role of the government in mortgage issuance and public housing construction. It also provided federal funding for slum clearance programs associated with urban renewal projects in American cities.[354] This law propelled the issue of Fair Housing and Urban Redevelopment into the center stage of public equal rights advocacy efforts nationally and dramatically within Rhode Island. Seen as a remedy for urban blight, urban renewal became a controversial solution in some cities, including Providence.

Urban Living: The Indigenous Neighborhoods of Providence

Denied their rightful place and livelihoods in their ancestral lands, many of Rhode Island's Indigenous people returned to their historic settlement areas within the City of Providence. Archaeologists working in the historic cove area and north shoreline (the present-day Waterplace Park and train station) have recently recovered native tools and artifacts that predate European settlement.[355] Often living and working in a shared existence with African heritage people, the later Indigenous inhabitants of Providence resided within the historic neighborhoods of Fox Point, Lippitt Hill, College Hill, and South Providence.[356] Their occupations varied, but they worked at jobs similar to those held by African heritage and working poor whites, as laborers or jobbers, peddlers, teamsters, and mariners.

The State of Rhode Island's efforts to abolish the authority and identity of the Narragansett people in 1880 included a list of tribal members who received settlement money for their land. The City of Providence listed the following residents as tribal members:

> Alexander R. Ammons, William H. Bent, Ida Bent, Sarah C. Cone, Mary R. Cone, Francis Cone, Charles H. Cone, Henrietta F. Cone, Fred Cone, Mary Jane Cone, Benjamin R. Champlin, Ellen M. Champlin, Jane R. Champlin, Walter H. Champlin, Mary A. Carpenter, Martha Creighton, Benjamin G. Gardner, Hannah M. Hazard, Harry N. Hazard, Grace E. Hazard, Sarah Hazard, Howard Hazard, Minnie B. Hazard, Lydia Harris, Eliza L. Hilton, Clarence Hilton, Amy Jackson, Edward Noka, Frank E. Nichols, Georgina Nichols, Mabel Nichols, Charles Nichols, Grace Nichols, Hannah Nichols, Olive Nichols, George Nichols, Priscilla Nichols, Mary E. Sullivan, F.D. Thomas, Annie Thomas, B.F. Thomas, Lizzie Thomas, Carrie Thomas, Willie Thomas, Lorenzo Thomas[357]

A review of census records and city directories during the late 19th and early 20th centuries uncovers family names directly associated with Narragansett tribal members, including Charles H. Cone and family on Grove Street near Federal Hill; Christopher Rhodes Champlin, on Freemont Street in Fox Point; John and Sarah Hazard in the 7th Ward; Hannah Nichols, also in the 7th Ward; and Fredrick D. Thomas, a teamster in the 1st Ward. They faced similar challenges, particularly living away from their original homes of North Kingstown, South Kingstown, Charlestown, and Narragansett, where white officials decided what their race and ancestry should be. Between 1850 and 1880, the codes for enumerators for United States Census did not include a category for native people, only white (W), black (B), and mulatto (M).[358] This official action denied Indigenous people a native identity at the time.

These Narragansett tribal members, who would be officially identified in the 1880 land sales,[359] are intermittently listed in public records while residing in Providence as Negro, Mulatto, Colored, White, Black, and in rare cases, Indian. This purposeful misidentification of their native heritage can be seen in the case of Nancy Noka Chevees. At the 1880 hearing on Narragansett Tribal Affairs, Chevees, born in South Kingstown, was listed as the daughter of Sam Noka. She was 65 years old at the time of the hearing. According to records, she lived on Benevolent Street in Providence and had not lived in Charlestown or South Kingstown for thirty years. She was also listed as the wife of George Chevees, an African.[360] She and her husband George lived in Warwick in 1870 and were both listed as Black. A decade later, the couple still lived in Warwick. George was identified as Black, and Nancy as Mulatto. By the 1885 census (and after Narragansett tribal abolishment), she was a widow and was identified as an Indian.[361]

The consistent government confusion and misidentification of Indigenous people in Rhode Island history greatly restricted Narragansett and other native people from pursuing their basic civil rights. As scholar Hilary N. Weaver notes the practice was even more insidious:

> *In the end, although it is clearly inappropriate to make assumptions about an individual's cultural identity based on appearance, or blood quantum, most attempts to measure identity are of questionable adequacy and accuracy. Federal policies that treated Native people of mixed heritage differently than those without mixed heritage effectively attacked unity within Native communities, thereby turning Indigenous people against each other.*[362]

PART 5: FAIR HOUSING & URBAN REDEVELOPMENT (1950-1975)

1949 Fair Housing Act & Jim Crow Tradition

There is an old folk saying that deftly captures the subtle differences in racial discrimination in the North and the South, particularly in the areas of housing and shared living environments faced by African heritage people during the post-World War II years. And it goes like this:

> *In the South white people don't mind how close a Negro gets to them as long as he doesn't rise too high (economically or socially), while in the North, white people don't mind how high a Negro rises as long as he doesn't get too close.*[363]

The vastly unequal conditions between black and white in America dates back to the Jim Crow laws established in the American South immediately following the Civil War that justified and formalized racial segregation.[364]

James N. Rhea was an African heritage reporter with the Providence Journal. In the early 1950s, at the dawn of the modern civil rights movement, the Journal partnered with the American Civil Liberties Union to survey Negroes grappling with discrimination. Rhea provided a provocative and insightful view of Providence at the time. He obtained first-person accounts (including his own) of African-heritage people who faced the Jim Crow traditions of the constant discrimination in employment, housing, and access to basic services as he traveled through Lippitt Hill, Fox Point, College Hill, and South Providence. His report uncovered the following:

EMPLOYMENT

Providence Negroes, who number approximately 7200, are still marginal workers. The overwhelming majority of them are in unskilled and semiskilled job categories. Consequently, they are, as a group, at the bottom of the city's economic ladder. According to job placement specialists, social workers, and local Negro leaders, this condition is largely traceable to the fact that race is a significant factor in employment.

HOUSING

The recent experiences of two of my acquaintances show how the pattern of discrimination keeps Negroes in "Negro sections." The Negro head of a small family was seeking to buy a house. The best one available at a price he could afford was in a white neighborhood. The only thing that came between him and the purchase was his race. Occasionally white residents have signed petitions to keep Negroes from moving into a neighborhood.

NEIGHBORHOODS

At the time of the 1940 census, there were three distinct Negro communities, one large area with a scattering of Negro households and several blocks throughout the city with from 10 to 50 percent Negro population. The largest of the Negro communities was on both sides of Benefit Street, north of Meeting Street; along North Main Street to Doyle Avenue, and between Doyle Avenue and Olney Street from North Main Street to Hope Street.

PUBLIC AMENITIES

One prominent Providence restaurant has developed the art of discouraging Negroes to a fine degree. I entered that place several times and, on all but one occasion, was shown to a seat in the extreme rear. And each time I ate, a tall, scowling official would stand or sit near me, watching every bite I took, never changing his expression. Once, when no one bothered to show me to a seat, I took one upfront. The scowling official looked at me with an expression of alarm as if to say, "You know better than that!" I stared back at him between bites and did not enjoy my food. This same restaurant has a policy of over-charging Negroes, and over-seasoning food served to them.[365]

At the start of 1950, President Turman's recently enacted Federal American Housing Act of 1949, dubbed a "Fair Deal," greatly expanded the previous FHA policies tied to mortgage insurance and public housing construction. The new law took on the task of municipal slum clearance through the expansion of local redevelopment authorities. One important part of the law allowed local public housing agencies to continue to finance and build separate public housing projects for Blacks and whites or separate them within projects.[366] This federal policy was carried out with active compliance in Rhode Island, particularly by the City of Providence's public housing authority.

Immediately after WWII, Providence, like most urban cities, experienced a significant influx of returning young veterans. Mayor Dennis J. Roberts initiated a plan to expand the city's WWII-era housing projects, named Roger Williams and Chad Brown. The plan called for clearing blighted areas to make way for new public housing units.[367] Encouraged by a federal policy that encouraged "separate and equal" housing, the City of Providence hoped to build a project that would meet African heritage citizens' needs but also stand apart from the white public housing population.

As far back as 1939, Black and white leaders decided to construct a public housing project in one of the city's Black neighborhoods. The area between Codding, A, and Dodge Streets was the agreed-upon location.[368] While Jim Crow laws dominated the American South during the middle 20th century, they surfaced in northern cities like Providence, too. The need for safe, clean, and affordable public housing for the needy families of color in Providence trumped the need for integration. Both Black and white leadership supported a "Negro Only" public housing project to be named Codding Court. As reported in the 1943 edition of *Opportunity: A Journal for Negro Life*:

> *"Volunteer workers organized by the Providence Urban League have started leveling land and filling holes on a site where the Codding Court low-cost housing project was to have risen. These workers have started making a playground. The rough grading and leveling are being provided by the Providence Housing Authority through a private contractor. But the stones and rubble are being cleared away by a large group of volunteers from the Urban League, Brown University, and Pembroke College, as well as boys and girls in the neighborhood."*[369]

Officials broke ground on the Codding Court public housing project on April 27, 1950, with a large ceremony led by Mayor Roberts and representatives from the African heritage community.[370] The Providence City Council passed a resolution in 1951—the same year that Codding Court was completed—opposing racial discrimination in public housing. But the resolution was only an expression of opinion and not a law.

The project created 119 affordable housing units for a city-wide African heritage population representing over four thousand citizens. The Codding Court project also did not solve the standing Jim Crow housing policies of Providence, where racial discrimination and segregation plagued Black-qualified applicants who had very limited access to other publicly funded housing projects across the city. Both the Providence NAACP and the Urban League, led by John Lopez and Andrew Bell, demanded the Providence Housing Authority adopt an anti-discrimination policy, leading Mayor Roberts to issue a January 6, 1950 statement informing the Providence Housing Authority that is was administration policy and his personal desire *"that no restriction or discrimination shall be imposed on the use of any public facility, including public housing because of race, creed, color or national origin."*[371] The Providence Public Housing Authority stubbornly refused to adopt an anti-discrimination and integration policy, instead maintaining its policy of building racially separate housing projects or placing African heritage families in isolated sections within other existing housing projects.[372]

Over the next decade, the Providence Public Housing Authority steadfastly rejected the adoption of an anti- discrimination policy. Joining the many calls for equality and fairness, the *Providence Journal* published a series of editorials through the summer of 1956 with telling headlines:

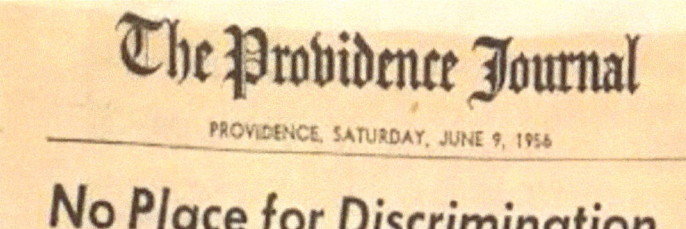

NO PLACE FOR DISCRIMINATION (JUNE 9, 1956)

LET'S HAVE NO COLOR LINE IN PUBLIC HOUSING (JUNE 22, 1956)

A SHAMEFUL SUPPRESSION OF A STATE RULING (JULY 21, 1956)

The Providence Journal's most forceful statement, in a June 22, 1956 editorial, boldly stated, *"The Providence Housing Authority is deceiving nobody but itself with this studied effort to duck a critical social problem. It is looking like what may well be its last chance to do voluntarily what the city has the right to expect it ought to do. Unless the agency wakes up, the Rhode Island courts will have to write the policy that law, a good conscience, and democracy demands."*[373] The Urban League and the American Civil Liberties Union[374] announced that they would organize a class action suit against the Providence Housing Authority.[375] The public demanded equality and justice, too. In September 1956, Roberts, now governor, announced a new policy directive. *"All public housing projects in this state are operating on a policy of open tenant selection on a non-segregated basis,"* he said. *The agreement, he added, came about through an agreement with the Providence Housing Authority and the Rhode Island Commission Against Discrimination.* [376]

After years of protest, public housing in Rhode Island was finally available to all qualified citizens. Ironically, it took nearly twenty-five years after the very creation of public housing for authorities to embrace the idea of housing fairness. Unfortunately, the forgone benefit to so many African heritage men, women, and children during that time—people denied the basic rights to safe and affordable housing—has never been measured. Many questions were never answered, such as, How many lived in poverty and squalor because of city, state, and federal government-sanctioned racist practices? How many simply left the city? The traumatic impact of racism and discrimination on Providence's citizens of African heritage continued well into the 20th century through redlining, private home sales, and urban renewal.

Separate & Unequal Private Housing

An eclectic group of public and private organizations took on the next housing issue: racism in the private housing market. In 1958, businessman Irving Jay Fain led a group called *"Citizens United for Fair Housing."* Born in Providence in 1906, Fain was the son of Russian immigrants. He grew up near the Lippitt Hill neighborhood, attended Classical High School, and graduated from Harvard College in 1927. A lieutenant in the United States Army during World War II, he encountered discrimination against African heritage soldiers. After the war, he returned to Providence to work in his family's textile businesses, including Apex Tire and Rubber. Every Sunday, he taught at Temple Beth El.[377] Providence Urban League Chairman and civil rights champion Andrew J. Bell described Fain this way:

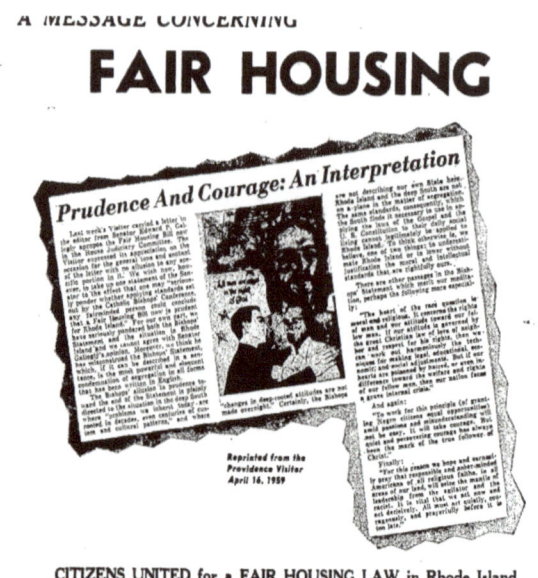

Providence Journal Newspaper, April 21, 1959

Once in a while, a person appears on the scene and conducts his life in an attempt to resolve the problems of the downtrodden. This person usually ends up being the community's most unforgettable character. In the opinion of many, Irving Jay Fain was such a person.[378]

Fain's fair housing group included business, religious, and civil rights organizations from across the state, among them Democratic and Republican leaders, the Catholic Diocese of Rhode Island, Temple Beth-El, the Rhode Island State Council of Churches, the AFL-CIO, and major Rhode Island businesses. Prominent Rhode Island leaders who led their names and support of the cause included John Lopez with the NAACP, Andrew Bell of the Urban League, George Lima of the Catholic Interracial Council, civil rights attorney Alton Wiley, Rhode Island Governor Christopher Del Sesto, former governor Dennis Roberts, U.S. Senator John Pastore, U.S. Senator Claiborne Pell, Providence Mayor Walter Reynolds, Gilbane Building Company president William Gilbane, Thomas Policastro of the AFL-CIO, and T. Dawson Brown of Industrial National Bank.[379]

This unprecedented collaboration had a singular focus: to pass a state law prohibiting housing discrimination within privately held properties in Rhode Island. The Providence Journal, in a January 18, 1959 editorial, presented a clear and powerful statement of support of what would be called the "Fair Housing" law:

> *The Citizen's committee has laid before the General Assembly a bill that would seek to guarantee all citizens of Rhode Island, regardless of race, color, religion, or national ancestry, an equal opportunity*

to rent, lease, or buy a home. This is, in one sense, a revolutionary proposal because, for the first time, it would deny the right of an individual to refuse to dispose of private property purely for reasons of racial discrimination. No other state in the union has such a law in force. Nobody with two eyes in his head could seriously deny that racial discrimination in housing does not exist in this state. If the bill becomes law, and we think that in the end, Rhode Island will be the better for it.[380]

In 1959, Irving Fain, in an op-ed response to the *Journal* editorial, stressed the importance of fair housing for private properties, stating, *"Your support will be echoed by all Rhode Islanders who recognize that discrimination in housing is immoral and contrary to the spirit of American democracy. Anti-discrimination legislation serves to protect the right of the individual and to improve the health of the community. It matters not what may be the incidental financial transactions of the transgressor. To restrict such moral legislation by such irrelevant considerations implies indifference to, and almost denial of, the basic moral principles on which the legislation is founded."*[381]

That year, Citizens United for Fair Housing submitted state legislation *to "prohibit racial and other group discrimination in the sale or rental of private houses in the state."* The opposition was well-financed and vocal. In 1959, Providence attorney Robert Dresser led over 500 opponents of the Fair Housing legislation in a protest at the State House, stating, *"a fair housing law would infringe on private property rights, legislate social progress, lower property values and increase racial tension in the state."*[382] Dresser was joined by prominent attorney Edwin T. Scallon, secretary of the new Committee For Individual Liberty. Scallon would lend his name and beliefs to a series of advertisements that would make the case against fair housing, declaring:

Association in private housing should be by the free choice of all concerned. Association in private housing by force of law violates the individual rights of all people.

Segregation is not the issue. True integration is the result of natural development, not compulsion. The experience of our State proves this fact.

Why Invest in property you can't control?

Legislation emphasizes group differences and creates discord and tension (which Communists want); it is bad legislation.

Because it will destroy individual liberty.[383]

Not surprisingly, the Providence Board of Realtors opposed a fair housing law. In a March 6, 1962 letter, they stated that they were *"unalterably opposed to the enactment of any so-called Fair Housing Legislation which will compel the citizens of the state of Rhode Island to sell or rent their property to a person or persons, not of their own free choice."* The Realtors pointed to improving race relations in the state, adding, *"Much progress has been made over the years. This progress has been marked by a clearer and more sympathetic understanding of the minority groups concerning*

Newport Daily News, February 21, 1950

housing. We are convinced that the only equitable and effective vehicle toward eventual integration in housing is a continuance of this progress through a closer working relationship with the minority on the part of the majority."[384] The political momentum in support of a fair housing law began to shift as additional, prominent officials offered their support. They included newly elected Providence Mayor Joseph A. Doorley, who pronounced, *"I have been continually on record for a state fair housing law."*[385] In a newspaper interview, however, Doorley disagreed with National Urban League Executive Director Whitney M. Young, who stated that *"Providence has all the ingredients for a race riot."*[386] Those chickens would come home to roost for Mayor Doorley a few years later.

After eight years of long public and political battles, the governor in 1965 signed the "Rhode Island Fair Housing Practices Act."[387]

> *It is hereby declared to be the policy of the state to assure to all individuals, regardless of race, color, religion, sex, sexual orientation, gender identity or expression, marital status, military status, as a veteran with an honorable discharge or an honorable or general administrative discharge, service member in the armed forces, country of ancestral origin, or disability, age, familial status, housing status, or those tenants or applicants or members of a household who are, or have been, or are threatened with being the victims of domestic abuse, or those tenants or applicants who have obtained, or sought, or are seeking relief from any court in the form of a restraining order for protection from domestic abuse, equal opportunity to live in decent, safe, sanitary, and healthful accommodations anywhere within the state so that the peace, health, safety, and general welfare of all the inhabitants of the state may be protected and ensured."*[388]

The turbulent 1960s ushered in significant achievements both nationally and locally in the areas of fair employment and housing. Meanwhile, the Rhode Island civil rights battlefront shifted to the impact of new highways and urban redevelopment on largely African heritage neighborhoods.

Interstate RI 95 & RI 195 & Neighborhood Destabilization

The 1956 Federal Aid Highway Act established a far-reaching interstate highway system across the United States. President Eisenhower championed the law as a means to modernize the country's highway system. The law authorized the construction of over 40,000 miles of interstate highways. The government also provided $26 billion for highway construction, largely funded through a gasoline tax.[389] The super highways that crisscrossed Rhode Island—Interstates 95 and 195—broke up two historic Providence neighborhoods occupied largely by people of color: South Providence and Fox Point. Interstate advocates praised the new projects as a way to rebuild the capitol and clear away blighted housing and neighborhoods. But many of the working poor impacted by the highways lost their homes, small businesses, and places of employment.[390]

Interstate 95 Construction, c. 1959, Providence Public Library Special Collections

A MATTER OF TRUTH

The South Providence neighborhood expanded during the early 19th century, thanks in part to the extension of the railroad from the waterfront and Allen's Avenue.[391] Working-class Irish and Jewish families moved into the area, too.[392] By the mid-20th century, many of the early ethnic and religious groups had moved to other parts of the city, replaced by a new generation of workers, the poor, and largely Black residents. The area was changing.

By 1950, South Providence was densely built up. The primary physical changes that occurred in the area during the succeeding three decades were related to the painful and difficult adaptation of the neighborhood to the automobile, the increasing commercialization and industrialization of the fringe areas along Eddy and Broad Streets, the expansion of Rhode Island Hospital, the construction of I-95, the ethnic transformation of the area and the effects of urban renewal.[393]

"The scar left by the construction of Interstate 95 through South Providence was even more thorough and permanent than a mere storm," note historians Patrick T. Conley and Paul Campbell. *"Point Street School, Tyler School, and Hayward Park, as well as a commercial district along Pine Street and Beacon Avenue, were eradicated, and the southern half of Byfield Street also vanished."*[394]

In the three images of the Upper South Providence neighborhood,[395,] it is clear how I-95 blocked access by residents to the nearby working waterfront and the jobs it offered. State historic planners noted the impact:

> *No less dramatic in its effect on the physical fabric of South Providence was the construction of Interstate 95 in the 1950s. In addition to necessitating the demolition of dozens of buildings, the highway physically separated South Providence from the rest of the city, destroying its historic relationship with the downtown and the waterfront. The barrier effect on Route 95 accelerated the deterioration of the neighborhood. The containment of the developing blight in a limited area where it would not be able to spread to other parts of the city made the urgency of dealing with the problems of South Providence less pressing to the greater community. Compounding all this, South Providence became a refuge for poor minorities displaced from other areas of the city for redevelopment projects such as those at Mashapaug Pond, West River, and Lippitt Hill.*[396]

The photographic images (p. 94) also highlight the significant expansion of the Rhode Island Hospital complex over the years. The ongoing hospitals and university expansions have accelerated neighborhood disruption and transformation, impacting low-income and working-class neighborhoods such as South Providence.[397]

Completed by 1960, Interstate 195 provided a major link between Providence and Cape Cod. It ran through the heart of the Fox Point neighborhood, displacing businesses, tenants, and homeowners. In the 1700s, the area, along with India Point, served as an early seaport. In the early 1900s, Portuguese and Cape Verdean sailors migrated to the waterfront, where they toiled on docks and in factories, built ships, and worked as fishermen along the harbor and the Seekonk River. The Cape Verdeans, in particular, created a tightly-knit, family-oriented enclave at Fox Point. However, the construction of Interstate 195 displaced the community's working-class families, many of them Cape Verdeans. According to historian Claire Andrade-Watkins:

> *Over 200 people were displaced by I-195, and Fox Point was severed in two, disconnecting the once-communal neighborhood. I-195 wreaked even further havoc on the community by slowing down the business at the port. Although it had already been in decline due to containerization and industrialization in the 1960s, I-195 exacerbated the downturn.*[398]

Upper South Providence – 1952

Upper South Providence – 1972

Upper South Providence – 2020

Unlike South Providence, that maintained a working waterfront despite the interstate 95 disruptions, the Fox Point neighborhood, where many of the residents were directly dependent upon the jobs and businesses within the India Point Harbor, could only watch as the historic working waterfront and major intermodal transportation hub would soon evaporate with the demolition and relocation of businesses, many ironically moving over to the Allen's Avenue waterfront corridor in South Providence. The highway *"cleared a wide swath through the southern part of Fox Point."* [399] A 1930 graphic offers a look at the old working waterfront—and some of the businesses and structures that were demolished to make way for the interstate highway.

Urban Redevelopment & Neighborhood Deconstruction –

Fox Point, Lippitt Hill, College Hill, South Providence & West Elmwood

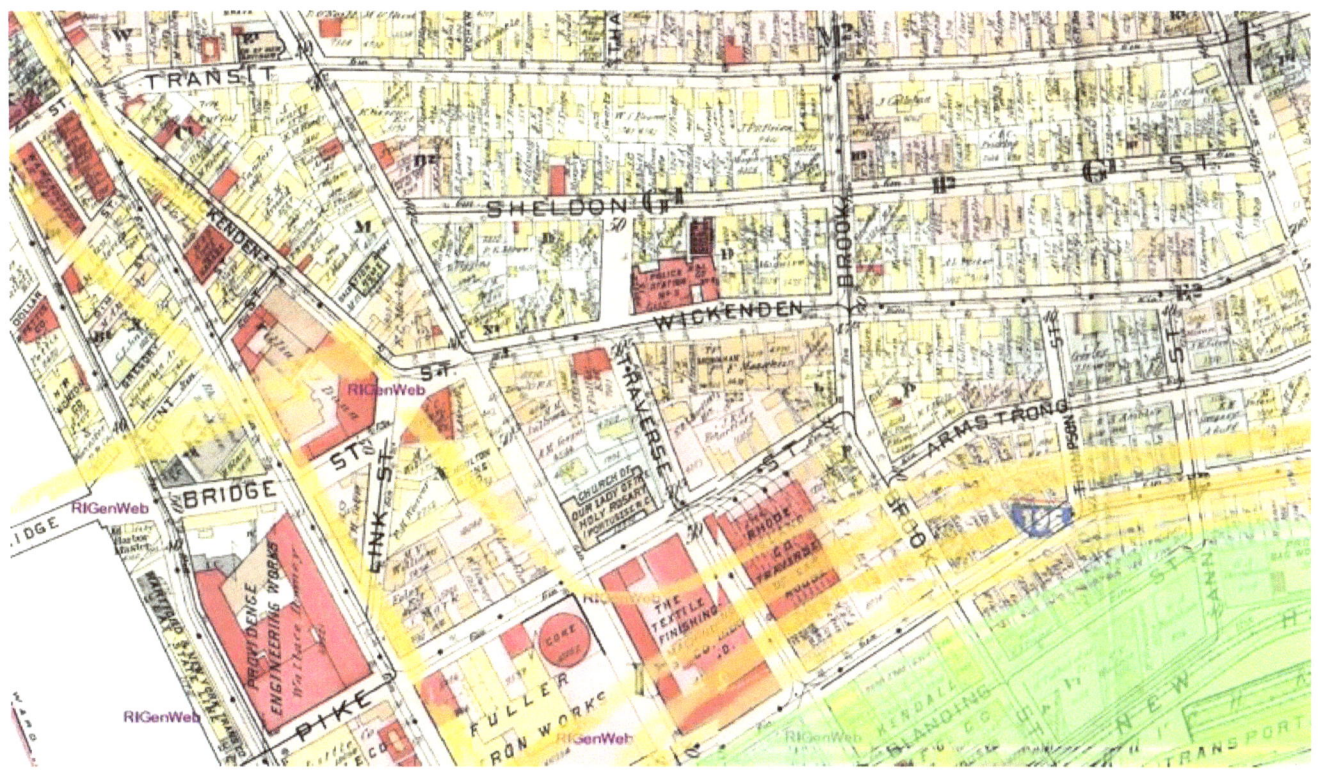

Urban Redevelopment & Neighborhood Deconstruction – Fox Point, Lippitt Hill, College Hill, South Providence & West ElmwoodImage12649.PNG

"A boy last week, he was sixteen, in San Francisco, told me on television — thank God we got him to talk — maybe somebody thought to listen. He said, "I've got no country. I've got no flag." Now, he's only 16 years old, and I couldn't say, "you do." I don't have any evidence to prove that he does. They were tearing down his house because San Francisco is engaging — as most Northern cities now are engaged — **in something called urban renewal, which means moving the Negroes out. It means Negro removal, that is what it means. The federal government is an accomplice to this fact.**"[400]

— James Baldwin

Providence underwent significant economic changes in the decades after World War II. As historians Marion Orr and Darrell West note:

> *For example, the nearby Walsh-Kaiser Shipyard, which employed more than 21,000 workers in 1944, employed fewer than 350 workers at the end of the war. Textile industries moved to cities in the southern United States or shut down completely. Across the city, manufacturing plants and mills closed or moved, including Brown and Sharpe Manufacturing, Silver Spring Bleaching and Dyeing Company, Wanskuck Company, Rhode Island Locomotive Works, and the Nicholson File Company. Thousands of jobs were lost and never replaced. From 1950 to 1975, manufacturing jobs in the state fell from 125,000 to 109,000. Many of these jobs were located in Providence.[401]*

Families left the city for the suburbs, leaving behind blighted neighborhoods and shuttered plants and factories. Federal, state, and municipal authorities looked to urban renewal strategies to turn things around. They relied on the Housing Act of 1949, which authorized $1 billion in loans to help cities acquire slums and blighted property for public or private redevelopment. The act allotted $100 million every year for five years for write-down grants to cover two-thirds of the difference between the cost of slum land and its reuse value.[402]

Cities and towns created housing authorities to identify blighted areas and substandard housing—property that could be reclaimed for the purpose of redevelopment. The Rhode Island General Assembly endorsed the idea through the 1956 Redevelopment Act, which said, in part:

> *It is further found and declared that in certain blighted and substandard areas, or portions of these areas, the physical conditions of the area and the area's relationship to the general plan for the community may be that the total public acquisition, clearance, and disposition of the entire area or an extensive portion of it may be necessary to accomplish the purposes of chapters 31 – 33 of this title; that other blighted and substandard areas, or portions of them, may be susceptible to rehabilitation and improvement to standard conditions, and the purposes of these chapters may be accomplished by the coordinated application of regulatory controls, together with redevelopment measures, short of total or extensive clearance of the entire area or portions of it.[403]*

The law gave local redevelopment agencies the power to condemn blighted neighborhoods, tear down the buildings, and resell the cleared land to private developers at a reduced price. It listed several ways in which a property might be judged "blighted," even though the guidelines could, and would, be subjectively applied:

> *Arrested "blighted area" means any area that, by reason of the existence of physical conditions, including, but not by way of limitation, the existence of unsuitable soil conditions, the existence of dumping or other unsanitary or unsafe conditions, the existence of ledge or rock, the necessity of unduly expensive excavation, fill or grading, or the necessity of undertaking unduly expensive measures for the drainage of the area or for the prevention of flooding or for making the area appropriate for sound development, or by reason of obsolete, inappropriate, or otherwise faulty platting or subdivision, deterioration of site improvements, inadequacy of utilities, diversity of ownership of plots, or tax delinquencies, or by reason of any combination of any of the foregoing conditions, is unduly costly to develop soundly through the ordinary operations of private enterprise and impairs the sound growth of the community. An arrested blighted area need not be restricted to, or consist entirely of, lands,*

buildings, or improvements that, of themselves, fall within this definition, but may consist of an area in which these conditions exist and injuriously affect the entire area.[404]

Curiously, the law did not address the concerns of the people living in "blighted" neighborhoods. Through no fault or control of their own, many of them lived in substandard housing created by absentee owners. Long-standing environmental issues contributed to the problem. As Dr. Dannie Ritchie later noted, those neighborhoods targeted for urban renewal were largely communities of color. Government-sanctioned policies consistently displaced and disenfranchised minority communities and exacerbated poverty and wealth inequality, *"in many cases under the banner of urban renewal."*[405] This groundbreaking study of housing and displacement was particularly focused on the East side of Providence and the Lippitt Hill neighborhood.

A 1956 newspaper account highlighted the issue:

One of the major problems facing the relocation of some 373 Negro families who will lose their homes when the Lippitt Hill neighborhood is condemned next month is discrimination or the fear of discrimination. A report of the Rhode Island Commission Against Discrimination released yesterday discloses this fear. The report noted that in the six preceding months, 38 Lippitt Hill Negro families attempted to purchase dwellings outside the area, with 11 successful and 27 unsuccessful. High prices, discrimination, and unsatisfactory dwelling or location were listed as reasons for failures to make purchases.[406]

In 1964, the Rhode Island Council for Community Services released a Social Plan For Community Renewal for the city of Providence. The plan urged urban redevelopers to work with neighborhood residents to overcome their "social handicaps."

There exists in many American communities among those families which are constantly exposed to the frustrations and deprivations of poverty, a particular style of life. This style of life is characterized by a sense of despair, of hopelessness, a deep-rooted belief that people's lives are at the mercy of fate. These attitudes stifle initiative and retard aspirations. They can be passed on from generation to generation as well as reinforced by those sharing the same social experiences. It is this shared way of life which recently has been termed the culture of poverty.[407]

The state's plan rested, in part, on a social theory that said poor people play a significant role in maintaining their impoverished condition. They, in fact, contribute to a cycle of poverty across generations. Critics, however, argue the *"blame the victim"* approach fails to recognize structural social barriers such as racism and sexism, barriers that can impede individual and family prosperity. Such cultural narratives, they say, can be used to advance multiple and contradictory political claims.[408]

What the Social Plan for Community Renewal for Providence and most redevelopment officials avoided are the real impacts of racial discrimination that are sustained across generations where *"inequity and injustice are not abstract things. They impact real people and real lives. In terms of poverty, annual income, wealth, health, housing, schooling, and incarceration, persistent gaps separate whites from Black, Latino, Southeast Asian, Pacific Islander, and American Indian populations."*[409]

Armed with federal and state funding, social plans, and vast redevelopment powers, the Providence Redevelopment Agency identified the Lippitt Hill, Fox Point, College Hill, and Mashapaug Pond section of West Elmwood, among others, as neighborhoods in need of redevelopment. Each of these communities contained large African heritage populations. The city's goal was to remake old and historic sections of Providence through blight removal, new roads, and utility construction. The improvements, they argued, would turn eyesore neighborhoods into attractive places to live and work. But for whose benefit?

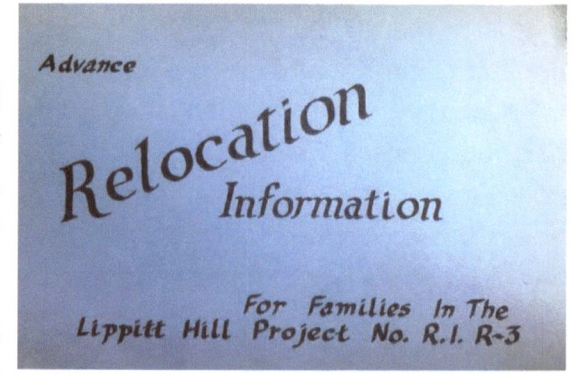

Urban League of Rhode Island Collection, Philips Memorial Library Archives, Providence College

Redevelopment agencies often relied on the use of eminent domain to turn their neighborhood dreams into realities. The practice allowed the government to take private property and convert it into public use—a practice that raised legal and ethical questions.[410]

In many cases, entire neighborhoods were deconstructed, and low- and moderate-income residents were forced to live elsewhere. That created new problems for people of color. Racist policies and attitudes restricted their neighborhood choices. The destruction of one non-white community was captured in a 1959 news story:

> *"The Providence Family and Business Relocation Service will begin this week to tackle what it acknowledges as the most difficult job in its 10-year history, finding homes for more than 400 families and individuals to be displaced by the Lippitt Hill urban renewal project. While the service has found homes for larger numbers of families and individuals in the past, the Lippitt Hill displacees will represent the largest number of non-white persons it has handled as a bloc."*[411]

Discriminatory real estate practices and high rents and home prices drove most displaced residents into other non-white neighborhoods, some of them targeted for other redevelopment plans. These actions, said Urban League of Rhode Island President Andrew Bell, *"created more of a ghetto in the already crowded areas. It was feared that there would be little chance of some of these residents returning to the Lippitt Hill area to purchase a house or rent an apartment when the development was completed. In either case, the cost would be prohibitive and beyond the budget of many families."*[412]

Residents in the Mashapaug Pond section of West Elmwood faced a similar challenge. The neighborhood's origins could be traced back to a time when the Narragansett Indians lived on the pond's shore before the arrival of Roger Williams.[413] In 1960, the City of Providence had big redevelopment plans for the area, including the construction of a 102-acre industrial park. The problem? The city had to fill in some 12 acres of the pond and move nearly 300 families.[414]

The majority of the residents forced to move were people of color. During a September 1960 hearing, residents forcefully opposed their relocation. *"Will you let me move next door to you?"* asked one Black woman.[415] The city authority won in the end, and the Huntington Industrial Park was eventually built on the Mashapaug Pond's shores.[416] The Urban League compiled a list of the families of color forced to relocate, putting a human face on **the consequences of urban redevelopment.**[417]

Legend for Map of 1961 Families of Color, derived from Urban League List

No.	First Name	Last Name	Address	Month moved out
1	Raymond	Smith	56 Niantic Ave	Feb-61
2	Edward	Long	56 Niantic Ave	Feb-61
3	Mamie	Lewis	491 Huntington Ave	Feb-61
4	Jacqueline	Fayerweather	513 Huntington Ave	Nov-61
5	Mrs. Wilson	Williams	515 Hamburg Ave 13	Sep-61
6	Leroy	Williams Sr.	515 Huntington Ave	Oct-61
7	Anne	Gaston	127 Burrington Ave	Feb-61
8	Elizabeth	Dunn	127 Burrington Street	May-61
9	Frederick	Tomlinson	125 Burrington St	Feb-61
10	Elliott	Mitchell	126 Burrington St	Apr-61
11	Clarissa	Spring	126 Burrington St rear	Jun-61
12	Ronald	Russell	126 Burrington St rear	Jul-61
13	Grover C.	Johnson	124 Burrington St	Feb-62
14	Andrew	Washington	124 Burrington St	Feb-61
15	Maggie	Geter	66 Calhoun Ave	Mar-61
16	Ruby E.	Burton	66 Calhoun Ave	Jan-61
17	Beverly	Washington	16 Clinton Ave	Aug-61
18	Robert	Washington	16 Clinton Ave Rear	Jul-61
19	Wilborne	Easton	8 Clinton Ave	Aug-61
20	Henry	Rumper	8 Clinton Ave	Aug-61
21	Victor	Von	35 Jonathan St	Mar-61
22	Anton	Kriegenbergh	35 Jonathan St	Oct-61
23	Stuart P.	Mutsoarts	32 Jonathan St	Apr-61
24	George	Green	32 Jonathan St	Mar-61
25	Alfred	Watts	66 Tyler St	Apr-61
26	Clarence	Raymond	27 Faith St	Mar-61
27	Milton F.	Butler	37 Faith Street	Jan-61
28	Earl	Washington	50 Tyler St	Jul-61
29	Douglas	Elderkin	91 Vanzandt St	Mar-61
30	Donald H.	Sylvia	91 Vanzandt St	Oct-61
31	Robert A.	Turner	89 Van Zandt St	Oct-61
32	John & Florence	Turner	107 Calhoun Ave	Apr-62
33	Minnie	Santos	2 Clinton St	Apr-61
34	Walter	Louden	2 Clinton St	May-61
35	Abelle	Johnson	15 Pacific Ave	Jul-61
36	Lillian	Mercer	19 Pacific Ave	Feb-61
37	Floyd	Heath	12 Pacific Ave	Mar-61
38	Alex	Smith	70 Burrington St	Mar-61
39	James	Gobern	71 Burrington St	Sep-61
40	Kent G.	Weeden	67 Burrington St	Mar-61
41	Esther	Wilson	59 Burrington St	Mar-61
42	LeRoy	Wooden	55 Burrington St	Mar-61
43	Jesse	Wooden	51 Burrington St	Jan-61
44	Harold L.	Heath	37 Burrington Street	Jun-61
45	Ella	Colbert	26 Burrington St	Jun-61
46	William	Colbert	26 Burrington St	
47	Jerome	Allen	26 Burrington St 11	Jun-61
48	John	Silva	Lowe Ave	May-61
49	Beatrice	Pina	37 Pleasant View Ave 9	Mar-61
50	Nathan	Murray	13 Hamburg Ave	Aug-61
51	Carnetta	Jones	13 Hamburg Ave 13	Mar-61
52	Chester	Ward	Hamburg Ave 17	Mar-61
53	Marcus	Straker	Hamburg Ave 17	Apr-61
54	Edwin	McPherson	Hamburg Ave 21	Jul-61
55	James	Holland	Hamburg Ave 21	Nov-61
56	Walter	Briggs	Hamburg Ave 25	
57	Peter	De Silva	Hamburg Ave 25	May-61
58	William	Conway	Hamburg Ave 29	Apr-61
59	Clara	Colbert	Hamburg Ave 29	Jun-61
60	Joseph	Metts	Hamburg Ave 37	
61	Susan	Tiffany	Hamburg Ave 41	May-61
62	Raymond Gomes	Thatcher	Hamburg Ave 41	May-61
63	Nathaniel	Robertson	Hamburg Ave 30 Pacific Ave	Mar-61
64	Henry	Simmons	13 Tyler St	Jul-61
65	Rexford	Sylvia	8 Tyler St	Mar-61
66	Manuel	Gomes	2 Tyler St	Jul-61
67	Lewis	Smith	63 Vanzandt St	Aug-61
68	Richard	Laughlin	63 Vanzandt St	May-62
69	Elizabeth	Bell	59 Vanzandt St	Feb-61
70	Thomas	Baskins	55 Vanzandt St	Jan-62
71	Ersalin	Tavares	41 Pacific Ave	
72	Gilmore W.	Maynard Sr.	45 Pacific Ave	Oct-61
73	Jerome	Briggs	50 Vanzandt St	Jul-61
74	Evelyn	Jennings	51 Hamburg Ave 50	Mar-61
75	Virgil	Lay	Hamburg Ave 54	May-61
76	James	Fletcher	Hamburg Ave 57	Apr-61
77	Charles	Lemar	Pleasant View Ave 73	May-61
78	Porter	Diggs	Pleasant View Ave 87	Jun-61
79	Ostena	Latham	Pleasant View Ave 98	Mar-61
80	Herbert	Johnson	100 Pacific Ave	Feb-61
81	Romana	Braxton	Pacific Ave 101	Nov-61
82	Robert	Randolph	14 Balch St	Dec-61
83	Carl	Howard	5 Ham St	Jun-61
84	Cordelia	Young	8 Balch St	Nov-61
85	Walter E.	Pendleton	145 Calhoun Ave 142	May-61
86	Mary E.	Caffey	Calhoun Ave 142	Nov-61
87	William	Black	Calhoun Ave	Sep-61
88	Edward	Truell		Apr-62
89	Fred R.	Bassett		Oct-61
90	Belmont	Byers		May-62
91	Pearl	Conn		Jan-62
92	Albert	Belmont		Jul-61
93		Gailloux Anderson		May-61
94	James P.	Lewis	138 Calhoun Ave 138	Jan-62
95	Hubert	McKinnon	Calhoun Ave 136	Feb-61
96	Alphonse E.	Baker	Calhoun Ave 133	Nov-61
97	Christopher	Craighead	Calhoun Ave 133	Feb-61
98	Charlotte	Silvia	Calhoun Ave 129	Apr-61
99	Gerald	Smith	Calhoun Ave 84	Apr-61
100	Alfred	Thompson	Vanzandt St 120	Apr-61
101	Raymond E.	Thomas	Calhoun Ave 82	Dec-61
102	Robert G.	Ferguson	Vanzandt St 88	Jan-62
103	Ellsworth	Lewis	Vanzandt St 54 Faith	May-61
104	Leonard	Blunt	St	Sep-61
105	Charles	Butler	55 Faith St	Apr-61
106	Clarence A.	Butler	59 Jonathan St 64	Jun-61
107	Charles E.	Jennings	Jonathan St 70	Nov-61
108	Clifford	Guy	Jonathan St 70	Oct-61
109	Hannah	Mitchell	Jonathan St 79	Sep-61
110	Charles T.	Johnson	Jonathan St 92	Apr-61
111	William	Manning	Jonathan St 94	Jun-61
112	Herbert C.	Waldron	Jonathan St 104	Oct-61
113	Isaac	Edmondson	Jonathan St 105	Nov-61
114	Moses	Jones	Jonathan St 105	Apr-61
115	Dorothy	Hankinson	Jonathan St 105	Jun-61
116	Clarence	Williams	Jonathan St 108	Nov-61
117	Mary	James	Jonathan St 109	Mar-61
118	Lonny	Ross	Frankfort St 94	Feb-61
119	Isabelle	Manning	Frankfort St 92	Feb-61
120	Herbert C.	Waldron	Faith St 122 Faith St	Oct-61
121	Milton	Davis	185 Calhoun Ave 168	Nov-61
122	Robert	Holston	Aquidneck St 30	Feb-61
123	Ronald F.	Barnett	Binney St 34 Binney	Jul-61
124	Addison	Tapscott	St 29 Binney St 18	Sep-61
125	Rev. Jesse L.	Connor	Dupont St 50 Day St	Aug-61
126	Charles F.	Borge	11 Day St	Feb-61
127	Domingo G.	Adams	11 Day St	Sep-61
128	James	Jennings	7 Day St	Mar-61
129	Margaret	Grenier	791 Cranston St	Apr-61
130	Robert	Fletcher		Aug-61
131	Oscar	Elderkin		Nov-61
132	Thomas	Crowder Jr		Oct-61
133	Charles	Marshall		Mar-61
134	Charles	LeBar		Mar-61
135	George	Barros		Feb-61
136	Dorothy	Roy		Aug-61

A MATTER OF TRUTH

Rise & Fall of Lippitt Hill Black Businesses – A Case Study

Minority businesses suffered from the relocation mandates, too. The Lippitt Hill redevelopment area—bounded by North Main, Doyle, Camp, and Olney Streets—forced dozens of established Black-owned businesses to move. Many of them operated out of homes. A 1960 Providence Journal article outlined the problem for Black business owners:

> *The problem of what to do with the neighborhood small business establishment looms even larger in the Lippitt Hill area, where the big majority of the 42 firms forced to move are businesses with roots deeply in the neighborhood, including food markets, bars, package stores, loan companies and variety of other operations providing various services. The big problem confronting the Family and Business Relocation Service in relocating these small businesses is the lack of space available to them in the general area of Lippitt Hill.*[418]

Black-owned businesses in Lippitt Hill relied on the existing neighborhood for customers. Urban renewal dislocated their storefronts—and their customer base. Charts—and before and after photographs—tell the story of urban renewal or, as James Baldwin would remind us, "Negro Removal."[419]

Lippitt Hill 1952 **Lippitt Hill 1962**

Black Owned Businesses in Lippitt Hill 1949-1950

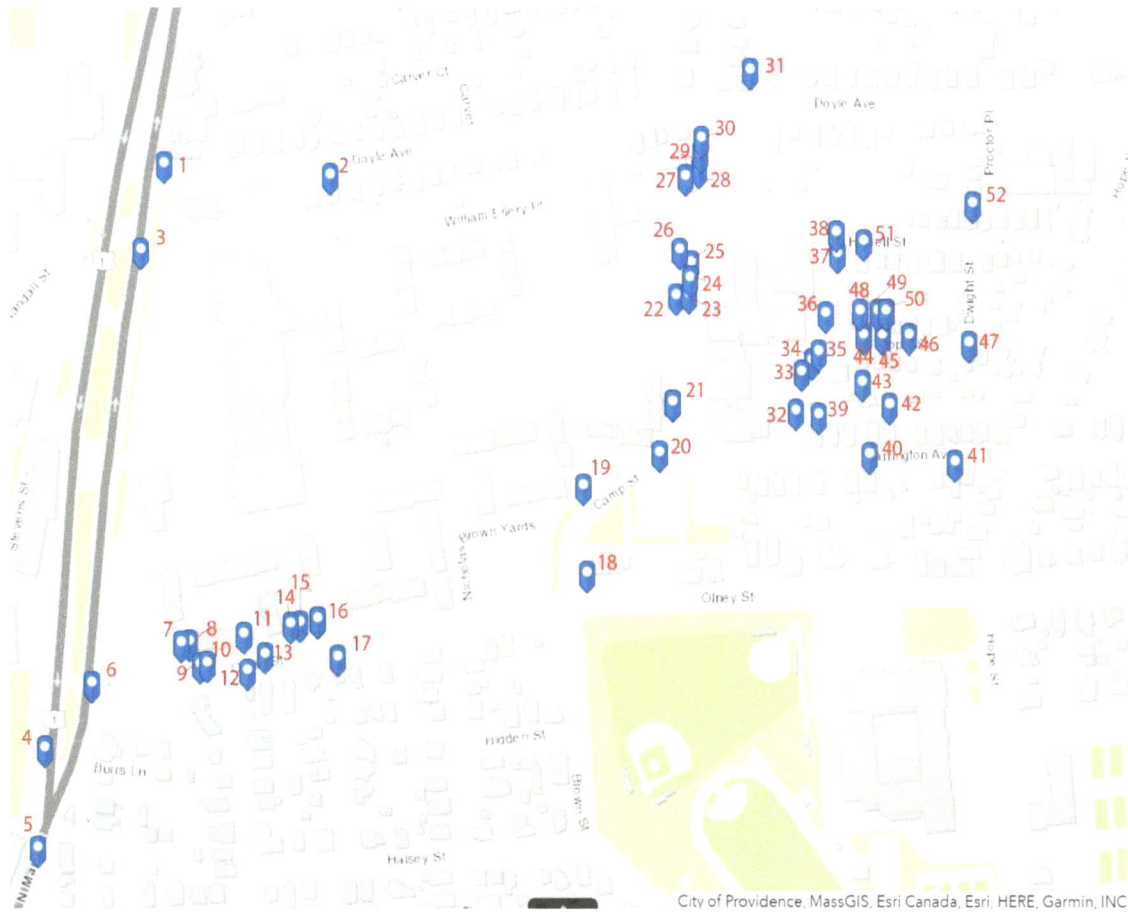

LIPPITT HILL NEIGHBORHOOD BLACK OWNED BUSINESSES 1949-1950

1. **Joe Watts All Stars**
Joseph Watts
3 Doyle Avenue

2. **Furniture Movers**
Manuel Baptista
33 Doyle Avenue

3. **Armory Cleaners**
Alice Barrows
631 North Main Street

4. **Hines Rest Chambers**
464 North Main Street

5. **Frank Gomes Barbershop**
Frank Gomes
419 North Main Street

6. **Ruth's Beauty Salon**
Ruth Bailey
483 North Main Street

7. **Rooming House**
Earl H. Woods
16 Olney Street

8. **Wood's Catering Services**
18 Olney Street

9. **Bailey Funeral Home**
21 Olney Street

10. **Piano Tuning & Repair**
Harry B. Bailey
23 Olney Street

11. **Olney Street Baptist Church**
Reverend Walter Hoard
30 Olney Street

12. **Corria's Market**
Ruth Corria
31 Olney Street

14. **NAACP Providence**
B. Albert Ford
40 Olney Street

15. **Oil Burner Service**
Sidney W. Gaul
42 Olney Street

16. **Mendes Funeral Home**
44 Olney Street
Public Notary
Ambrose C. Mendes
4 4 Olney Street

17. **Thel-Mars Beauty Shop**
Hazel Grimes
51 Olney Street

18. **Dr. Carl Gross**
Medical Doctor
102 Olney Street

19. **Dr. John W. McCrea**
Chiropodist
12 Camp Street

20. **Jacks Barbershop**
Alfred Jacks
23 ½ Camp Street
LaVogue Salon
Elizabeth Graves & Irene Moreineo
23 Camp Street
Carpenter
Harold E. Cromell
23A Camp Street

21. **Dr. Theodore Fleming**
Dentist
28 Camp Street
Piano Teacher
Madeline Genebra
28 Camp Street

22. **Ernest Cary Barbershop**
Ernest Cary
2 Camp Street

23. **Beulah Boy's Beauty Salon**
eulah Jackson
43 Camp Street

24. **Cary's Inn**
45 Camp Street

25. **Exotic Aquarium**
Stanley Frazier
47A Camp Street

27. **Veterans Chorus**
Truman Johnson
58 Camp Street

28. **Fernandez & Ramos Barbershop**
Jose Ramos
59 Camp Street

29. **Carpenter**
Bill Parker
61 Camp Street
The Handy Electrical Service Shop
Joseph R. Pyle
61 Camp Street

30. **Rick's Restaurant**
Richard Troutman Jr.
63 Camp Street

31. **Kirk-Lo Beauty Shop**
Nora Kirkland & Harriett Lopes
118 Doyle Avenue

32. **Electrician**
John Delgardo
23 Howell Street

33. **Furniture Movers**
James E. Gross
87 Howell Street

34. **Cox Beauty Shop**
Doris Cox
107 Howell Street

35. **Dress Maker**
Mildred Brown
117 Howell Street

36. **Salesman**
Myra Noonan
123 Howell Street

37. **Plastering**
Paul Cabral
163 Howell Street

38. **Rubbish Removal**
Pascoe Wallace
171 Howell Street

40. **Jimmie Berry's Orchestra**
49 Carrington Avenue

41. **Salesman**
Lydia Pina
69 Carrington Avenue

42. **Carpenter**
Isaiah Russell
52 Carrington Avenue

43. **Bricklayer**
Preston Read
42 Carrington Avenue

44. **Herbert Hicks**
Automobile Repair
57 Lippitt Street

45. **Wilkins Trucking**
C.L. Wilkins
105 Lippitt Street

46. **Electrician**
William Williams
169 Lippitt Street

47. **Painter**
Theodore J. Ford
209 Lippitt Street

48. **Furniture Movers**
John Martin
50 Lippitt Street

49. **Obe's Place**
Obe Wesley Catlin Jr.
92 Lippitt Street

50. **New England Welding Company**
Fred B. Taylor
112 Lippitt Street

51. **Saggers Inn**
Mr. & Mrs. John W. Saggers
177 Howell Street

52. **The Stompers Band**
206 Howell Street

The College Hill Study 1959

The redevelopment of parts of College Hill, also designated as a blighted area, took a very different path, largely due to the preservation interests of Providence's elite families and institutions. The College Hill neighborhood, part of the city's first and second wards, had always included an African heritage population. For the two centuries between 1770 and 1970, "*it had a proportionately greater share of African Americans in its population than prevailed in the city as a whole. The oldest extant properties on College Hill have strong associations with people of African descent, both enslaved and free.*"[420] This long history of African heritage people living, working, and worshiping in College Hill is reflected today in the number of existing historic properties directly associated with the African heritage experience. But redevelopment undermined that presence. As a 2009 African American Site Survey of College Hill notes:

> *The expansion of Brown University, the development of Pembroke College (originally the Women's College of Brown University) and the Rhode Island School of Design, highway construction and urban renewal, and waves of gentrification undermined the African American presence on College Hill and in some cases erased evidence of the community's historical association with the neighborhood.*[421]

The residents of College Hill faced different pressures than those in other neighborhoods. Between 1940 and 1956, Brown University spent $2.1 million dollars to purchase properties for new dormitories and offices and to clear land for the Wriston Quadrangle.[422] Brown's expansion dramatically accelerated the destabilization of the East Side's communities of color:

> *While Brown did not operate the bulldozers of urban renewal that tumbled the "slum dwellings" adjacent to its campus, as did many of its peer institutions like the University of Chicago, Penn, and Columbia during this era, its presence and participation in East Side urban renewal is undeniable and ubiquitous. First, its pursuit of a residential college ignited the guiding force of renewal on the East Side... Meanwhile, its presence incentivized speculators to see immense profit opportunities inherent in transforming once-low-income East Side neighborhoods to instead meet the needs of the university community. For example, the East Side neighborhood to the north of campus, Lippitt Hill— once home to a plurality of the city's Black population—was replaced by a low-rise, middle-income urban renewal development called "University Heights," specifically targeted towards meeting the housing needs of Brown's growing graduate student population, as the development's name attests.*[423]

In an effort to clean up neighborhoods, officials sometimes razed historic structures. In response, a group of concerned Providence citizens urged city officials to identify historic buildings deemed worthy of rescue and restoration. With a grant from the Urban Renewal Administration and Home Finance Agency (known today as the U.S. Department of Housing and Urban Development), the Providence City Plan Commission and other agencies produced a 1959 report, *College Hill: A Demonstration Study of Historic Area Renewal*.

City officials weren't the only ones interested in identifying the city's early buildings. Founded in 1956, the Providence Preservation Society was started by John Nicholas Brown, Malcolm Chace, Henry Tingley, and Mrs. William Slater Allen.[424] In 1957, the Society partnered with the City of Providence to create what would become the College Hill Study. The plan surveyed 1,500 properties and sites within the College Hill area bounded by Olney Street, Hope Street, Wickenden Street, and the Providence River. It suggested public and private contractors work together.

African heritage residents were not a visible part of the public and private plans. The historic Congdon Street Baptist Church at 17 Congdon Street was not included on the *"First Priority List"* of existing structures of historic interest.[425] Fortunately, a later African American Site Survey of College Hill included African heritage structures past studies failed to report.

Private investors played a major role in the College Hill plan. *"It is recommended that attempts be made to stimulate private investment in College Hill by alerting certain individuals and groups to the opportunities for investment in the area."*[426] Using private, corporate, and institutional money to spur neighborhood renewal and private home restoration proved a sound strategy. But it left out those in the neighborhood with little access to capital. The plan recommended investors take advantage of FHA mortgages and lending programs—the same programs that were denied to previous and existing residents in College Hill. Did the authors of the Plan not read the Home Owner's Loan Corporation 1935 Redline Map of Providence?[427]

The College Hill Plan broke new ground in the fields of community planning and historic preservation. It predated the National Historic Preservation Act of 1966, which helped preserve historic and archaeological sites across the country. While the plan was innovative, it failed to include minorities in the planning and preservation process. It left out those who had endured years of discrimination in education, employment, and housing—those who would have been the most deserving of the innovative programs and services recommended by the plan.

Providence & Model Cities

In 1966, the U.S. Congress passed the Demonstration Cities and Metropolitan Development Act. It provided aid to cities rebuilding blighted areas and provided money to improve the welfare of people living in underdeveloped neighborhoods. The program was carried out by the U.S. Department of Housing and Urban Development (HUD), which replaced the former Urban Renewal Administration.

The Secretary of Housing and Urban Development is authorized to provide grants and technical assistance to help communities of all sizes to plan, develop, and carry out comprehensive city demonstration programs. These are locally prepared programs for rebuilding or restoring neighborhood slums and blighted areas by the concentrated and coordinated use of federal aid and local, private, and governmental resources.

The program will operate in two stages:

> *(1) Assistance will be provided to plan and develop demonstration programs ($12 million for this fiscal year and $12 million for next fiscal year), and (2) after July 1, 1967, assistance will be provided to carry out the programs planned ($400 million for next fiscal year and $500 million for the following fiscal year).*[428]

Providence, under Mayor Joseph Doorley, was one of the first cities to join the federal Model Cities Program. Robert C. Wood, HUD's undersecretary, came to the city on June 25, 1966. He talked about the new federal program to a class of Brown University students at the Graduate School of Savings and Banking, declaring:

> In the next 40 years, the United States will build as many houses and other buildings as they have built in the country's history. The pattern of most of this will be laid out in the form of the "Spread City," a dense core surrounded by suburbs. The answer for Providence lies in the demonstration cities project.[429]

Providence's involvement in the federal project could not have come at a better time for Mayor Doorley, under attack from religious leaders, for building a new civic center in the city's downtown area while ignoring the needs of South Providence.[430] Doorley survived the political storm, thanks to his connections to President Lyndon B. Johnson's administration and his ties to Rhode Island Congressman Fernand J. St. Germain, who sat on the powerful House Subcommittee on Banking and Currency, which handled the Model Cities bill.[431] The need for federal investment in Providence's inner-city neighborhoods was considerable. Federal funding would help programs like the Progress for Providence Youth centers to expand their reach.[432] In 1967, officials relied on the federal program to demolish buildings and designate Upper South Providence as a Model City. Officials adopted a suburban design standard that included flat-roof shopping centers and Cape Cod-style single-family homes. It did not go smoothly. Some residents bridled at the top-down approach to community development.

At the end of 1968, it was reported that there were problems within the city's Model Cities Planning Committee. There was a federal government requirement that called for citizen involvement in the process of renewal in their neighborhoods. The planning committee was originally made up of twenty-eight residents of South Providence. By December of 1968, twelve committee members were suspended for lack of attendance at meetings, and three resigned. The meetings of this committee were not productive because of conflicts among committee members and conflicts between the staff of the Model Cities program and committee members. Model Cities director Richard R. Torchia also clashed with committee members. Many uneducated committee members felt ashamed to speak at committee meetings and did not understand the technical language, zoning laws, and the charts and graphs presented by Torchia and his staff. Committee members felt that they were only there to approve the ideas of the staff and not to participate in the planning process for their neighborhoods.[433]

While the program tried to empower residents through neighborhood revitalization and home ownership, historians consider Model Cities to be the least effective of the Great Society programs due to problems arising from competing local interests, bureaucratic tangles, and insufficient funding. The program was shut down in 1974.[434]

1967 Prairie Avenue Race Riot

As historians note, the "Summer of Love" in the United States occurred alongside rising racial tensions in the nation's major cities. Nearly 160 riots broke out during the hot, tense summer of 1967. The most violent occurred in Newark, New Jersey, and Detroit, Michigan. Government leaders and law enforcement officials blamed the riots on lawlessness protesters, but the unrest was a reaction to a larger American problem. The deep-seated anger and hopelessness simmering in many disenfranchised urban communities had reached a boiling point. "White flight" had reduced the tax base in formerly prosperous cities, causing urban blight, poverty, and racial discord. After decades of urban redevelopment, housing assistance, and blight removal, many urban residents of color did not feel any better off.

On Providence's South side, neighborhood relationships with the police were uneasy. Many residents had painful memories of a police incident in 1962 when 57 men and women were arrested without cause at the popular Blackstone Café at 228 Plain Street during a police search for a stabbing suspect. According to eyewitness accounts provided to the Springfield Sun:

Progress For Providence Worker During South Providence Riot Curfew, UPI Telephoto from Providence TV Outlet, August 3, 1967

Fifty-seven Negroes were rounded up in raid-like fashion while sitting in the Blackstone Café. Police, using their trained dogs, surrounded the café and herded all the occupants into waiting patrol wagons. After spending two hours in the city jail and being subjected to questions establishing their identity, these citizens were released without an explanation as to why they were being detained and inconvenienced. Humiliated couples, pregnant mothers, embarrassed and worried individuals were required to walk from downtown Providence to their homes in South Providence at 2:30 am. Irate citizens, aware of the injustice imposed upon them in this mass arrest, turned to their spokesman in the community, Jack Maddox, candidate for house of representative, to correct this undignified treatment at the hands of law officials. Mr. Maddox appointed Cliff Monteiro to investigate the incident and gather information from the individuals involved. He advised those persons who feel that their rights as citizens have been violated to contact Monteiro as soon as possible. Mr. Monteiro stated that many of the people detained the other night want someone to take action to protect their rights of lawful assembly. After all important facts have been obtained, Mr. Monteiro said they will be turned over to the NAACP.[435]

On August 23, 1962, African heritage community leaders—including George Lima, president of the NAACP, Alton Wiley, NAACP legal redress chair, John Maddox and Cliff Monteiro, NAACP executive committee members, and Jack Warwick of the Urban League—met with Providence Public Safety, Commissioner Francis A. Lennon. They presented Lennon with nineteen statements from victims of the incident. The NAACP recommended the city establish a community liaison to relieve the tension between law enforcement and citizens of color.

Unfortunately, the NAACP leaders walked away from the meeting with no commitment for better community relations. The police roundup at the Blackstone Café was entirely unnecessary. Before everyone had been taken into jail that evening, the police had already learned of a suspect at another location.[436]

On August 1, 1967, during an Emancipation Day celebration, a riot in South Providence was ignited when more than a hundred young white people chanting *"White Power"* attacked Black gangs, throwing rocks and bottles. *"Gunfire was used by both gangs. Providence Police battled sniper fire from behind fire trucks in the Willard Avenue Shopping Center."*[437] Mayor Joseph Doorley ordered a curfew within a boundary of two square miles around Prairie Avenue. African heritage volunteers from Progress for Providence walked the streets urging calm.

After the 1967 race riots in Providence, Rhode Island, U.S. Senator Claiborne Pell promoted a plan for urban revitalization, education, and workforce training that would be designed and led by the African heritage community of Providence.

Brown University – "Our History and Our Guilt"

Amid the racial tensions of the 1960s, Brown University President Ray Lorenzo Heffner delivered the Fall 1967 Convocation address. He called it *"Our History and Our Guilt."* Heffner used the moment —and his platform as president of one of the nation's leading universities— to speak openly and honestly about the racial discrimination faced by African heritage people.

> *The year 1967 is a time of trial for the United States of America. The questions facing us today, just as in 1787 and in 1860, are the fundamental questions: Can we survive and work together as one nation, united in basic principle, though encouraging and protecting all diversity of opinion? It is not too surprising that some Negro Americans and some impoverished slum dwellers of all backgrounds are almost ready to give up on the American Dream. Too often, promises have not been kept. I am convinced that the majority of black Americans and others, who until recently constituted the forgotten in this land of privilege and opportunity, are not yet ready to give up.*

> *We all bear a share of the guilt for this sorry state of affairs: New Englanders and Southerners, Protestants, Catholics, and Jews. We tend even now to equate the Negroes in our large cities with religious and ethnic minorities who have overcome prejudice and won a share of political and economic power in the past. We forget that, through our doing, the Negro had little cultural or religious tradition to sustain him. There were and are, of course, rich cultural traditions in black Africa, but the slave-holding society used every means at its command to cut the American Negro off from these and to see that he got nothing in their place.*

> *I remind us of our history and our guilt in order to suggest what our attitude should be in the latest crisis in race relations, which has developed in 1967. We must remember that black Americans do not beg for our sympathy or indulgence, or toleration when they claim their inherent natural rights. What is needed is a re-dedication to those principles, together with a passionate sense of urgency about putting principles into effective practice. This, too, is what the Charter means when it charges us to take effectual care of the morals of the College.*[438]

President Heffner's words were timely, but it would take a student protest the following year to bring the issue of Black equality vividly home to Brown University. On December 5th, 1968, over 60 African heritage students walked off Brown University's campus to protest the school's lack of commitment to students of color. The students marched to the Congdon Street Baptist Church, the site of Rhode Island's first African heritage congregation. The protest worked.

After three days, President Heffner agreed to take steps to increase African-American admissions and to improve financial aid options. The percentage of Black women admitted would be increased to 12.5% and $1.2 million would be set aside over three years for scholarship and recruitment programs in order to raise the overall percentage of enrolled Black students. In 1969, 128 Black students entered the University.[439]

As President Heffner stated a year before, *"Nothing short of a full national commitment and large dedication of energy and resources will get the job done."* [440]

African heritage students took him at his word and achieved positive change.

One Foot In the Ghetto, One on the Mall

On October 12, 1969, the Providence Journal published a groundbreaking narrative in its Sunday magazine titled *"Our Black Heritage."*[441] It marked the end of a turbulent decade of racial and social unrest in America, a decade that included the Vietnam War, riots, protests, and the assassinations of President John F. Kennedy, his brother Robert, Malcolm X, and the Reverend Martin Luther King, Jr. James N. Rhea, a dynamic African heritage reporter who had covered the Civil Rights movement in the South, had reached out to Fredrick Williamson, Dr. Carl Gross, and James Williams to help shape a series of stories that would accurately reflect African heritage people's experiences in the Ocean State. His Sunday magazine article, *"One Foot in the Ghetto, One on the Mall,"* described life in Rhode Island from an African heritage perspective for a largely white readership who likely had little knowledge of Black life in Rhode Island. Rhea began his piece with a racial snapshot of the state:

> *There were about 25,000 nonwhite persons in Rhode Island in 1965, according to the U.S. Census figures. Of these, some 90 percent were Negroes. Almost 15,000 of the nonwhites lived in Providence. 80 percent of them crowded into nine of the city's 37 census tracts. In the same year, 3,600 of Newport's 47,000 people were nonwhites. There were 12 among Barrington's 14,000 citizens. The range in other cities and towns varied between these two.*[442]

Rhea wrote about the separate and unequal experiences of whites and African-heritage citizens. He described the disparities in employment and poverty between the two groups. He talked about the vastly different experiences he found within housing and neighborhood conditions. *"Eighty-three percent of all housing in Providence is classified as "sound" according to federal standards. But only 55 percent of nonwhite families live in "sound" housing. About 20 percent, or roughly 630 households, live in shelters classified as dilapidated and unsafe. About 2 percent of the white Providence families live in such places."*[443] The years of urban renewal and public housing construction had a little positive impact on the city and the state's largest non-white inhabitants, he concluded.

The magazine series included a history of African heritage people in Rhode Island, with the names of men and women largely unknown at the time. But it was an article by William D. Wiley, a founder of the Providence Urban League and editor of the Providence Chronicle, who wrote a story that resonated with many: *"Why Don't More of My People Go To College."* Wiley pointed out that African-heritage people who dreamed of going to college could find few jobs in Rhode Island. Black college graduates were better off looking for employment in other states, he said. Wiley's article described the challenges of being young, educated, skilled, and Black in Rhode Island. As was the case during the WWII years, employers hired few nonwhites, regardless of their education level or skills. He concluded his article with a plea for action—a plea that resonates today:

> *Therefore, it is going to take a selling job to convince many of the present generations that there are new opportunities and that they should prepare for them. This is a job for all of us, but especially for the whites who still have within their hands so much power to open jobs and opportunities for all.*[444]

Black Self Determination & OIC of Rhode Island

In 1959, Black progressive author Harry Haywood described the *"Great American Migration,"* the move by more than six million African Americans from the rural South to the cities of the North, Midwest, and West. Haywood, who moved to Chicago during the WWI years, experienced first-hand the violent race riots during the "Red Summer" of 1919 when race riots took place in more than three dozen cities across the United States. Later, he wrote an article that described the making of a Black ghetto within urban America:

> *Half a century ago, in 1910, eight out of ten U.S. Negroes resided in one or another of the eleven states of the Old Confederacy. Over 90 percent of these Negroes, moreover, lived in rural areas. Negroes began moving to the North during World War I and continued to move during the 1920s when restrictive legislation slowed down the flow of immigrants from southern and eastern Europe. By 1940 the Negro population in the Old Confederacy had increased only 12 percent, whereas in the same period, the Negro population elsewhere in the U.S. had more than doubled, from 1,900,000 to four million But the Old Confederacy still contained more than two-thirds of all U.S. Negroes. The Negro people who migrated out of the deep South because of the lack of economic, social, and political advancement, generally moved to the twelve largest cities. The freedom that they sought was not in the cards for them. They found themselves crowded in despicable slums with run-down, dilapidated houses generally built around the turn of the century, inadequate, segregated schools, very little in the way of services such as sanitation, hospitals, and police protection. But most of all, they entered an area where there was already mass unemployment among the Negro people, and the prospects of getting work were almost nonexistent. In all of these cities where there has been a mass influx of Negro people, the area of Negro concentration is usually expanded rather than new areas opening up to the newcomers. As a result, the ghettos are intensified.[445]*

Haywood described the creation of *"ghettoized"* urban neighborhoods. Advanced segregation and discrimination became the match that lit the race riot fuses of the 1960s.

It would take a new and innovative approach to solve problems faced by inner-city residents. In an abandoned jailhouse in North Philadelphia, Dr. Leon Sullivan offered one approach: he organized the first Opportunities Industrial Center (OIC) to provide employment training by and for people of color within their impoverished communities. In Providence, a group of African heritage civic, religious, and political activists shared that vision with Senator Claiborne Pell.

Senator Pell, the Newport socialite who would later create *"Basic Educational Opportunity Grants,"* or Pell Grants, pushed for federal funding for an OIC program in the heart of South Providence. Speaking in the Senate in the wake of the 1967 riots, he pointed to news articles from the Providence Journal depicting the South Providence riots. Influenced by Providence's Black leaders, he embraced the plan of *"Black Self-Determination"* through training and employment. Pell's African heritage mentors included Cliff Monteiro, Andrew Bell, and James Williams of the Urban League, young community leader Michael Van Leesten, Reverends Carl Banks of the Pond Street Baptist Church and Arthur Hardge of the Hood Memorial AME Church, and Jewish fair housing leader, Irving Jay Fain.[446] Pell made the case for an OIC agency in Rhode Island in the Senate, stating:

> *Mr. President. I invite the attention of the Senate and the administration to the efforts being made by a group of public-spirited citizens in the capital city of Rhode Island, which is Providence, to train and retrain the unemployed and idle in the Providence area. This group has incorporated themselves under the name of Opportunities Industrialization Center of Rhode Island, Inc.*

He continued, speaking of Providence's inner city:

> *Mr. President, the reasons why I believe the administration should move quickly in this matter are evident, for on August 10th, I spoke on the floor of the Senate regarding the contribution of the OIC employees to the prevention of what could have been a grave disturbance in Providence: in fact, in the very area where the OIC program will be located. This area is one in which there is an aura of pessimism and fatalism amongst the impoverished inhabitants that tend to see life as a fate, an endless cycle from which there is no deliverance, and thereby, they contain the seeds of frustration and depression, which can explode into violence unless the chains of poverty which bind them are not finally broken. Mr. President, we who are not deprived have a responsibility to look through the wall of affluence that surrounds the underprivileged and shields them from us. We know the problem: we believe that through the program that I previously outlined, we have the solution. I believe we can tarry no longer. I urge the administration to implement this program with the utmost speed.*[447]

Later, the U. S. Department of Commerce's Economic Development Administration awarded a $ 4.1-million-dollar grant to the OIC of Rhode Island. The Black-owned training and education institution built a full-service campus in the heart of South Providence on a six-acre parcel on Hilton Street. Michael Van Leesten, a graduate of Hope High School and Rhode Island College and a Providence civil rights activist, would become the new executive director. OIC of Rhode Island later launched the Omni Development Company, an affordable housing and community development corporation, and Peerless Precision Company, which evolved into Banneker Industries, one of the state's leading minority supply chain management companies.

Formation of Citizens United for Urban Enterprises (CURE)

Decades of urban redevelopment programs and federal housing programs had accomplished little in providing safe and affordable housing in Providence's urban neighborhoods. The Model Cities program had some successes, but it was phased out by the early 1970s. In direct response to the lack of steady government support, a new organization was formed to directly take on Providence's affordable housing and community development challenges. The Citizens United Renewal Enterprises, or CURE, was organized on January 6, 1968, as a non-profit corporation. Unlike local, state, and federal programs, CURE built strong neighborhood alliances so that people within the community would have an active stake in their neighborhood futures. It sought large-scale investments to improve the housing conditions of low- and moderate-income families within the former Model Cities area in South Providence. Its formula for success called for:

> **_Neighborhood Involvement:_** *Neighborhood groups would have to be actively engaged in the planning and execution of projects.*
>
> **_Professional Staff:_** *The Corporation would need a highly competent professional staff, knowledgeable*

in planning, finances, and community relations.

General Community Support: *The Corporation would need the full support of public and private resources. This means more than substantial financial support. It also means the active participation of individuals with special professional competencies.*

Cooperation: *The Corporation would need the active cooperation of city and state agencies and leaders.*[448]

The founding members of CURE included many of the most active civil rights leaders in Providence, men who had fought in the trenches for social justice, among them Andrew J. Bell, Charles "Moe" Adams, Albert Carrington, and Cliff Monteiro. CURE's staff included young and future Providence social justice leaders, most notably George Castro and Freeman Soares.[449]

In 1971, Cliff Monteiro traveled to Washington D.C., to testify before a U.S. Senate subcommittee on appropriations (Rhode Island Senator John O. Pastore chaired it) to talk about CURE and request additional federal support for their successful housing development and counseling programs:

Our organization started in 1968 by a group of concerned citizens for the housing plight of low-income families. We were successful in receiving a $100,000 non-interest loan, and funding from the Department of Community Affairs and the New England Regional Commission. This money assisted us in hiring an outstanding staff charged with the responsibility of counseling. In addition to providing new and rehabilitated housing, CURE serves as consultants to other non-profit housing groups.[450]

CURE helped set the standard for Providence's neighborhood-based housing and community development organizations. Later organizations adopted their approach to neighborhood empowerment, including Omni Development, West Elmwood Housing Development Corporation, Women's Development Corporation, and Stop Wasting Abandoned Properties, or SWAP.

PART 6: SCHOOL & COMMUNITY INTEGRATION & TRIBAL SOVEREIGNTY (1970-2020)

Providence Public School Integration Plan

In Providence, Black activists fought for fair and equal housing while well-meaning city officials bulldozed their neighborhoods to make way for superhighways, a park, and more segregated housing. But what about the schools? African heritage citizens won the right to public education after the Civil War. However, their children were assigned to public schools in segregated neighborhoods created by longstanding housing discrimination.

Scholar Carl Antonucci described the situation: *"The housing patterns of Providence caused the neighborhood elementary schools of the city to mirror the ethnic composition of the neighborhoods where they were located and to become segregated. Thus, elementary schools in many neighborhoods had a majority of white students or a majority of African American students depending on the location of the neighborhood where the schools were located."*[451]

Significant population shifts between 1965 and 1975 exacerbated the problem:

> *The total student population of the Providence School District has steadily declined since the early 1960s. The total number decreased from 25,908 in 1966 to 20,680 in 1975, a decrease of 20.2 percent. The number of black students, however, has increased from 4,159 in 1966 to 5,228 in 1975, by which time black students made up 25.3 percent of the student body.*

Although the school district did not collect data on Spanish-speaking background students, information from the U.S. Department of Health, Education, and Welfare (HEW) indicates that Hispanic student enrollment has also increased significantly. The number of Hispanic students increased from 222 (0.9 per cent) in 1970 to 379 (1.7 percent) in 1972 to 646 (3 percent) in 1973.[452]

In 1962, urban renewal plans for Lippitt Hill included the demolition of the Thomas A. Doyle and Jenkins Street elementary schools. A municipal bond was passed to build a new K-6 grade school. Two grassroots organizations, Help Our Public Education and the East Side Neighborhood Council, recognized the new school would create an opportunity for racially integrated classrooms.[453] The Lippitt Hill School, which opened at the start of the 1967 school year, was a "magnet" school with a specialized curriculum that attracted students beyond the neighborhood's boundaries. As reported by the U.S. Commission on Civil Rights:

> *The new Lippitt Hill Elementary School, a citywide magnet school, opened September 7, 1967, 4 years after the Providence School Committee approved a replacement for the Doyle and Jenkins Schools. The kindergarten to third-grade school, which was open to students throughout the city, had a well-publicized, innovative educational program. In the first year, the voluntary open enrollment policy produced a student population that was 65 percent white and 35 percent black (whereas the two schools replaced by Lippitt Hill had been as much as 97. percent black).*[454]

The success of the innovative new school was lost on the rest of the city. School segregation continued to anger parents and students, especially those in Southside Providence. The failure of city officials and school committee members to resolve school segregation issues caused the Providence School Superintendent, Charles A. O'Connor, to call for busing black and white students to achieve a racial balance within Providence's public schools. Known as the *"O'Connor Plan,"* it was supported by newspapers and local and statewide educational, religious, and civil rights organizations, but there was little overall community and political support.[455] There was also opposition from both black and white neighborhood groups that opposed mandatory reassignments, rezoning, and bus trips to schools in other neighborhoods. The busing plan came under immediate fire from all sides. Mayor Joseph Doorley, one of the most vocal critics, opposed compulsory busing of some 1,000 students in South Providence schools.[456]

Seeking to gain control over what had become a highly charged political issue in Providence, Mayor Doorley appointed a 27-member task force to oversee the O'Connor Plan. The busing plan went more smoothy than in neighboring Boston and other cities, where the practice sparked violent protests. It also created a more diversified administration:

> *The desegregation effort also affected the composition of the faculty in the Providence public schools. Prior to 1967, there were no black principals or assistant principals and no blacks in administrative positions. By 1971, there were five black administrators, including one middle school principal and one special assistant for equal educational opportunity. A total of 22 black, 4 Hispanic, and 5 Portuguese teachers were hired between 1969 and 1975.*[457]

School desegregation had a major effect on the Providence school system. Fourteen elementary schools closed while two magnet schools opened. Providence's busing model benefited from the compact nature of the city. Bussed students never traveled more than four miles to new schools. Parents of color achieved some level of parity in public education, regardless of neighborhood location. But the battle for a more diversified faculty wasn't over. According to a U.S. Civil Rights report:

> *One major problem is the continuing underrepresentation of minority teachers in the school system. In 1975 there were 88 black teachers on the faculty of 1,223 persons or 7 percent of the total. There were four Hispanic and five Portuguese teachers.*[458]

1978 Rhode Island Indian Claims Settlement Act

The 1880 detribalization law in Rhode Island hobbled Narragansett tribal authority, but it did not eliminate the people. In 1976, the Nashua Telegraph newspaper revisited the racial stereotypes used against the Narragansett people to strip away their authority. For many Rhode Islanders, the Telegraph said, *"the Narragansett is invisible, mistaken for American Blacks, Latin American, Indians or Cape Verdeans."*[459] The reporter quoted Narragansett Indian Chief Lloyd Wilcox, Eric and Ella Thomas Sekatau, and Everett Weeden, who assured the public that the Narragansetts have and will continue to exist in Rhode Island. They said they would fight to reclaim their stolen land and native identity, *"that cannot be measured in Western thinking."*[460]

In fact, the tribe in 1975 sued the state for 3200 acres of land in Charlestown. Tribal members claimed their ancestral land had been taken by the State of Rhode Island in violation of the Federal Trade and Intercourse Act of 1790. The law said that conveyances of native land are invalid unless approved by the federal government. Lengthy negotiations produced an agreement whereby a Narragansett-controlled corporation received 900 acres of land from the state. The Narragansetts bought another 900 acres of private land with $3.5 million from the federal government. In return, the agreement authorized the extinguishment of all Narragansett claims in Rhode Island. Approved on September 30, 1978[461], the agreement enabled the Narragansetts to reclaim at least 1,800 acres of native land. However, the deal created a new problem for the tribe.

1983 Narragansett Indian Tribe Federal Acknowledgement

After a century of discrimination, and ongoing attempts to break apart the tribe, the Narragansett's received federal recognition on April 11, 1983. The landmark decision by U. S. Secretary of the Interior Ken Salazar and the Bureau of Indian Affairs (BIA) stated, *"We recommend that the Narragansett Indian Tribe be acknowledged as an Indian tribe with a government-to-government relationship with the United States and be entitled to the same privileges and immunities available to other federally recognized tribes by virtue of their status as Indian tribes."*[462] As part of its decision, the BIA cited Rhode Island's attempts to undermine the tribe's authority and take its land as part of the 1880 detribalization act:

> *In 1879, the State Assembly appointed a commission which held three hearings on the questions of whether to abolish tribal relations of the group, make them citizens, and end their relationship with the state. This process is commonly referred to as "detribalization." At those hearings, all five tribal council members opposed any such move. The council did agree to have the school closed. Later, in 1879, the Narragansett council inexplicably voted to sell tribal lands at an undocumented meeting with the commission. There· are indications that the council was unclear about the issues on which they were voting, and they later claimed that they only intended to sell the reservation and not quitclaim any other lands owned by the tribe. There was no vote taken of the tribal membership on the issue, and there was a protest by individual tribal members in 1881. The State Assembly passed legislation in 1880 which purported to abolish tribal authority and tribal relations, declared tribal members citizens, ended the state's relationship with the tribe, and which authorized the sale of all land held in common. The proceeds of the land sale were to be distributed to individual members. Tribal lands held individually were to be deeded to the individual Indian landholders. The state's action was devastating to the tribe, resulting in the loss of virtually all of the approximately 927 acres of remaining tribal land held in common. Only two acres around the Narragansett Church and the church itself were saved for the tribe.*[463]

In 1985, under Rhode Island law (Title 37 - Public Property and Works, Chapter 37-18), the Narragansett Indian Land Management Corporation transferred its land to the now federally recognized tribe:

> *Upon the presentation of federal recognition to the Narragansett Indian land management corporation and the secretary of state, the Narragansett Indian land management corporation shall forthwith transfer and convey to the federally recognized Narragansett Tribe of Indians all powers, authority, rights, privileges, titles, and interest it may possess to any and all real property acquired, owned, and*

> *held for the benefit of those individuals of Indian ancestry set forth in the list established pursuant to P.L. 1880 ch. 800, § 4, and thereafter, the Narragansett Indian land management corporation shall have no further interest in the real property. All real property transferred by the Narragansett Indian land management corporation to the federally recognized Narragansett Tribe of Indians pursuant to this provision.*[464]

After a long struggle, the Narragansett tribe regained its territory and its inherent authority to govern the Narragansett people on their ancestral land.

1997 Senator Chafee Rider

In 1988, the federal government passed the Indian Gaming Regulatory Act to provide a legislative basis for the operation and regulation of Indian gaming. The act's purpose was three-fold:

1. to provide a statutory basis for the operation of gaming by Indian tribes as a means of promoting tribal economic development, self-sufficiency, and strong tribal governments.

2. to provide a statutory basis for the regulation of gaming by an Indian tribe adequate to shield it from organized crime and other corrupting influences, to ensure that the Indian tribe is the primary beneficiary of the gaming operation, and to assure that gaming is conducted fairly and honestly by both the operator and players.

3. to declare that the establishment of independent Federal regulatory authority for gaming on Indian lands, the establishment of Federal standards for gaming on Indian lands, and the establishment of a National Indian Gaming Commission are necessary to meet congressional concerns regarding gaming and to protect such gaming as a means of generating tribal revenue.[465]

Money from Indian casinos and other forms of gaming provided tribes with new sources of revenue. Indian gaming revenues grew from $100 million in 1988, the year of the Indian Gaming Act, to $16.7 billion in 2003. Currently, approximately 350 Indian gaming operations are being conducted by over 220 tribes in 29 states.[466]

In 1992, the Narragansetts announced plans to build and operate a 60,000 to 80,000-square-foot gaming facility on their 1,800-acre tribal land.[467]

That year, the State of Rhode Island gave two existing gaming companies permission to offer slots, video poker, and electronic table games at their sites. Meanwhile, the Rhode Island Attorney General sent a letter of opposition to the Narragansett tribe. A federal law pertaining specifically to the Narragansett tribe placed the tribe under state law, he said. That law required state and local referendums before a casino could be built.[468] The state had interfered in tribal affairs in the 1800s; now, in the 20th century, it was again interfering in tribal land decisions.

The state had powerful friends. In 1997, U. S. Senator John Chafee added a rider to the Omnibus Appropriations Act (P.L. 104-208), stating, "*For the purposes of the Indian Gaming Regulatory Act, settlement lands shall not be treated as Indian lands.*"[469] Native tribes across the county criticized Chaffe's action. The National Congress of American Indians issued a resolution stating:

> **WHEREAS**, the National Congress of American Indians (NCAI) was established in 1944 and is the oldest and largest national organization of American Indian and Alaska Native tribal governments;

and

WHEREAS, *the United States Congress has never acknowledged distinctions in or classifications of inherent sovereignty possessed by federally recognized and acknowledged Indian tribes, which all maintain a government-to-government relationship with the United Sates; and*

WHEREAS, *the 1997 Omnibus Appropriations Act (P.L. 104-208) included a non-germane rider by the late Senator John Chafee of Rhode Island (Chafee Rider) which violated the government-to-government relationship between the Narragansett Indian Tribe (of Rhode Island) and the United States and unilaterally stripped the Narragansett of their sovereign rights by removing them from the Indian Gaming Regulatory Act (IGRA); and*

WHEREAS, *the Chafee Rider was a discriminatory attack upon the Narragansett Tribe and its sovereign rights that violates the United States' trust and fiduciary responsibility to protect the inherent rights and sovereignty of every Indian Nation; and*

NOW THEREFORE BE IT RESOLVED, *that the NCAI does hereby request that the US Congress continue to honor its trust obligations to the Indian Nations and support the government-to-government relationships between the Indian Nations; and*

BE IT FURTHER RESOLVED, *the NCAI also requests that the egregious and discriminatory injustice that is the Chafee Rider be corrected by urging, in the strongest terms possible, the House Resources Committee and the Senate Committee on Indian Affairs pass, Congress support, and the President sign, legislation to repeal the Chafee Rider and to restore the IGRA rights to the Narragansett Tribe in the most expeditious manner possible.*[470]

To directly counter the state's actions, the Bureau of Indian Affairs in March 1998 notified Rhode Island of its intent to take a 31-acre parcel into Federal Trust status. The state appealed this decision to the Interior Board of Indian Appeals, which ruled in favor of the tribe and the BIA.[471] Fearing the Narragansetts would now exercise their new-found authority to develop their land, the state filed more suits to block the action.

Tensions between the state and the tribe increased during the summer of 2003. In July, the tribe began selling untaxed cigarettes out of a Smoke Shop trailer on Route 2. State officials said the store violated state tax laws. On July 14, Rhode Island State Police, with orders from Governor Donald Carcieri, raided the store. A confrontation ensued when Narragansett tribal members resisted the search warrant and fought off officers. Local news stations filmed the melee. In the end, several tribal members were arrested, including Chief Sachem Matthew Thomas. The tribe's inventory was confiscated.[472]

The Narragansetts responded by filing suit in federal district court. They argued the tribe's federal recognition status precluded the state from enforcing its tax laws on the tribe. Eventually, as the suit moved through several state and federal court systems, it was determined the Narragansett tribe voluntarily waived its tribal sovereign immunity when it signed the earlier land settlement act.[473]

Many Rhode Islanders saw the fight for gaming rights and the Smoke Shop raid as a long-standing political fight. But for the Narragansetts, it was another skirmish in a centuries-long battle for self-determination and sovereignty.

2000 Sergeant Cornel Young Jr. Shooting

Sergeant Cornel Young, Jr. was a promising African heritage member of the Providence Police Department when, on January 28, 2000, he was shot and killed by two other police officers who mistook him for a suspect. His death— he had been with the police department for less than three years—sparked outrage and allegations of racial profiling. Hundreds of protestors gathered outside Providence Mayor Vincent A. Cianci, Jr.'s office, chanting, "Stop police brutality." The mayor, however, said *"he had no evidence that racism played a role in the shooting."*[474]

Cornel Young, Courtesy of CBS NEWS

On April 6, Rhode Island Governor Lincoln Almond issued an executive order creating a *"Rhode Island Select Commission on Race and Police-Community Relations."* Young's death, he said, had highlighted *"numerous areas of concern in race relations and the relationship between the police and the community served, not only for Providence but also for communities large and small throughout the state."*[475] In the report, the commission stated, *"We will never know what role, if any, Sergeant Young's race had on the shooting."*[476] The statement came after many citizens had expressed deep concern with discrimination within law enforcement:

> *Throughout the hearing process, Commissioners heard repeated testimony about the existence of 'a sad divide' between the communities served and the police who serve them. This was expressed acutely by African Americans, Latinos, Native Americans, Asians, Caucasians, and extended to all the corners of the state. Transcending race, we also heard similar testimony from the Gay, Lesbian, Transgendered community and from youth to the elderly. Use of force incidents and the Young shooting itself were the source of agony, certainly, but the tales of a steady corrosion of indignities and interruptions by rude or uncivil officers comprised significant portions of the testimony as well. The Select Commission noted painfully the alienation of young Rhode Islanders of all colors evident from the cities to the suburbs.*[477]

While the report recognized significant areas of concern tied to race relations and law enforcement, its recommendations were limited to two brief statements:

CHAPTER FOUR: RACISM

1. *Screening for potential bias must be routinely part of any selection and interview process for police selection and police promotion.*
2. *An affirmative statement regarding nondiscriminatory law enforcement and community service become part of the oath of office for each law enforcement officer within the state.*[478]

City and state officials could have used the Cornel Young, Jr. tragedy to publicly change the uneasy relationship between law enforcement and people of color. Mostly, they wasted that opportunity. While the governor's report recommended enhanced police training, it was largely silent on the issue of racial bias. A wrongful death lawsuit against the City of Providence was dismissed; a federal judge based his decision in part on the fact that a jury previously found the supervisory police officer innocent of violating officer Young's civil rights.[479] The Cornel Young, Jr. case should have been a wake-up call for city and state government officials, a chance to recognize implicit racial bias and its potential effects on law enforcement actions. Instead, the unfinished business of race in Rhode Island was left to simmer and boil over again and again.

Brown University Steering Committee on Slavery and Justice

In 2003, Ruth J. Simmons, Brown University's first and only African-heritage president, appointed a Steering Committee on Slavery and Justice to examine Brown's historical relationship to slavery and the transatlantic slave trade. Brown became one of the first Ivy League schools to look at its dark past. In a Boston Globe opinion piece, President Simmons said the committee *"will investigate and discuss an uncomfortable piece of the University's—and our nation's—history. The Committee's work is not about whether or how reparations should be paid. Rather, it will do the difficult work of scholarship, debate, and civil discourse, demonstrating how difficult, uncomfortable, and valuable this process can be."*[480]

The committee's report documented Brown University's deep ties to African enslavement and the transatlantic slave trade. The report also made a series of recommendations in light of the school's past, many of them tied to student enrollment, memorialization, investment policy, and historical research. Brown also promised to *"use the resources of the University to help ensure a quality education for the children of Rhode Island."*[481] To meet that promise, the university developed an endowment for $10 million to establish a Fund for the Education of the Children of Providence.[482] Brown's recommendations for reparative justice are commendable. However, the university's role in the destabilization of African heritage neighborhoods has yet to be addressed in a similar comprehensive manner.

2009 U.S. Supreme Court Carcieri v. Salazar Ruling

The battle over Narragansett gaming, sovereignty, and land use rights played out in the courts for years. First, the U.S. District Court and the U.S. Court of Appeals for the First Circuit sided with the BIA and the Narragansetts. Then, the State of Rhode Island filed an appeal to the United States Supreme Court.

In a 2009 majority decision led by Supreme Court Justice Clarence Thomas, the high court ruled that to qualify for the Indian Reorganization Act (IRA's) trust-land provisions, a tribe had to have been under federal jurisdiction in 1934—the year Congress enacted the IRA. While the Court did not consider what evidence might prove that a particular tribe was subject to such jurisdiction, it did conclude that the Narragansett tribe had not proved it was under federal jurisdiction in 1934.[483] The decision was devastating not only for the Narragansetts of Rhode Island but for any native tribe who might rightfully seek federal recognition after the 1934 Act. In a dissenting opinion, Justice Stevens stated:

> *Congress has used the term "Indian" in the Indian Reorganization Act of 1934 to describe those individuals who are entitled to special protections and benefits under federal Indian law. The Act*

specifies that benefits shall be available to individuals who qualify as Indian either as a result of blood quantum or as descendants of members of "any recognized Indian tribe now under Federal jurisdiction." 25 U. S. C. §479. In contesting the Secretary of the Interior's acquisition of trust land for the Narragansett Tribe of Rhode Island, the parties have focused on the meaning of "now" in the Act's definition of "Indian." Yet, to my mind, whether "now" means 1934 (as the Court holds) or the present time (as respondents would have it) sheds no light on the question whether the Secretary's actions on behalf of the Narragansett were permitted under the statute. The plain text of the Act clearly authorizes the Secretary to take land into trust for Indian tribes as well as individual Indians, and it places no temporal limitation on the definition of "Indian tribe." Because the Narragansett Tribe is an Indian tribe within the meaning of the Act, I would affirm the judgment of the Court of Appeals.[484]

In allowing recognized tribes to have land held in trust under the IRA, the BIA has embraced the protective principles that have been consistently lacking in the history of the Narragansett Tribe of Rhode Island and the experiences of most other tribes across the country. The ruling in the case now known as Carcieri v. Salazar Supreme Court unraveled the federal-tribe trust relationship that took centuries to achieve. As constitutional lawyer Sarah Washburn puts it:

The Carcieri decision potentially divides American Indian tribes into two classes: those included in the IRA list, and those recognized since 1934 based on traditional recognition methods or the 25 C.F.R. Part 83 process. This division is arbitrary, as each group must meet the same basic criteria for recognition. All federally recognized tribes were under federal jurisdiction in 1934 in the broad sense that federal plenary power and trust relationship principles governed federal relations with existing tribes. To qualify for recognition, tribes must show historical existence as American Indian entities and existence as communities from historical times until the present, and Congress has clearly expressed that such proof satisfies the IRA. If interpreted to exclude such tribes from obtaining these benefits, the Court's decision in Carcieri v. Salazar will contradict the Department of the Interior policies as well as Indian law canons of construction. Such an interpretation will subject tribes to discriminating treatment. In allowing recognized tribes to have land held in trust under the IRA, the Department of the Interior has embraced the protective principles implicit in federal plenary power and the federal-tribal trust relationship. Congress and the courts should act to ensure that Carcieri does not override that policy.[485]

2013 Rhode Island Equity Profile

America and Rhode Island are changing. In the state and in the nation, the question of race is no longer so black or white. Fifty years ago, the census in Rhode Island reported that 90 percent of the nonwhite people in the state were of African heritage. A study conducted in 2013 by Policy Link and the University of Southern California found that communities of color are the driving force behind Rhode Island's population growth.[486] According to the United States Census, the population of people *"who are Two or More Races is projected to be the fastest-growing racial or ethnic group over the next several decades, followed by Asians and Hispanics."*[487] Residents in Rhode Island and especially Providence will see a significant rise in nonwhite population over the next two decades, says Policy Link. By 2040, *"41 percent of Rhode Island's residents will likely be people of color, with Latinos reaching more than a quarter of the total population. The entire state will continue to diversify, and it is expected that Providence will be majority people of color."*[488]

While Rhode Island's population will continue to diversify, with Latinos (representing many different races and ethnicities) leading the growth, these fast-growing populations still face significant socio-economic challenges.

> *More than a quarter of the state's Latinos and 2006-2010 Blacks live below the poverty level—more than triple the rate of whites. Although Rhode Island as a whole maintains a low working poverty rate, Latinos have rates (11.3%) far above the regional and national averages. Whites in the state have the lowest numbers for poverty (8.3%) and working poverty (1.4%).[489]*

2020 COVID-19 & Anti-Racist Majority

The COVID-19 pandemic had disproportionately impacted Rhode Island's growing nonwhite population. Thanks to long-standing systemic health and social inequities, some minority groups are at an increased risk of getting COVID-19. Many experience severe illness, regardless of age, according to the Centers for Disease Control and Prevention. Disturbing infection rates within Black and Latino populations include:

- Non-Hispanic black persons have a rate approximately 5 times that of non-Hispanic white persons.

- Hispanic or Latino persons have a rate approximately 4 times that of non-Hispanic white persons.[490]

Discrimination, which includes racism, can lead to chronic and toxic stress—and place minority groups at increased risk for COVID-19.[491]

In Rhode Island, Latinos are approximately 16 percent of the state's population but comprise about 43 percent of those testing positive for the coronavirus, according to the Rhode Island Department of Health. African Americans and those within urban centers have also experienced higher infection rates.[492]

COVID-19 has devastated the U.S. labor market, and minority workers have suffered the most. According to a Pew Research Center study on the pandemic's impact, "Asian, Hispanic, and Black workers have experienced a greater employment loss than white workers."[493] According to Ira Wilson, chair of Health Services, Policy, and Practice at Brown University's School of Public Health, minority workers face greater risks:

> *People of color are more likely to have low-wage service jobs that are deemed essential, such as "driving buses, working in hospitals and working in grocery stores," according to Ira Wilson, chair of health services, policy, and practice at the School of Public Health. These jobs are much more likely to cause exposure to COVID-19, he added. Data from The Bureau of Labor Statistics shows that 29.9 percent of white workers and 37 percent of Asian workers have the ability to work from home in the United States. Only 19.7 percent of Black or African American workers and 16.2 percent of Hispanic or Latinx workers have that option.[494]*

To take advantage of a growing, diverse population and build a more equitable economy, Rhode Island must **take steps to better connect its communities of color to jobs, housing, and quality education—even more important in a COVID-19 environment.** Policy Link would make several recommendations for future public policy considerations in building a more equitable and sustainable economy and health population that remain salient today, particularly in a post-COVID-19 Rhode Island environment:

> ***Bridge the Racial Generation Gap.*** *The divergent trends in population by age and race highlight the need to support strong public schools for all children and to otherwise commit to ensuring that the next generation of workers is well-equipped to succeed. To address the rapidly increasing racial generation gap, Rhode Island must plan for complete, multigenerational communities, which are accessible, safe, and inclusive for all ages and racial groups. This will allow the elderly to age in place at the same time as providing safe and healthy environments for families to raise children. By identifying infrastructure investments that suit these needs, Rhode Island can create built environments with appropriate community facilities and public spaces.*
>
> ***Grow Good Jobs.*** *With historically slow job growth, Rhode Island must focus workforce development toward growing jobs in high-opportunity sectors. By identifying quality jobs and economic development strategies to grow wages—wage contracting, minimum wage increases, among other strategies—the state's economy will be both robust and equitable. Additionally, public infrastructure investments throughout the state present an opportunity to build bridges out of poverty.*
>
> ***Connect Unemployed and Low-Wage Workers to Careers in High-Growth Industries***. *It is vital for Rhode Island to connect its strong industries with middle-skill jobs that pay good wages and could provide economic mobility for workers without college degrees while also ensuring that all workers—including those who face high barriers to employment—can get the advanced training or education they need to succeed.*
>
> ***Identify Educational Pathways.*** *Education attainment for African Americans and Latinos is a critical issue, even as progress has been made over the last few decades to close racial gaps. The persistently high number of Latino youths not in school or work highlights the importance of increasing access to quality secondary education throughout the state.*
>
> ***Create Healthier Communities***. *By making neighborhoods healthier—with complete streets, access to healthy food, and community design—the state can create a supportive built environment for reducing persistent health gaps.*
>
> ***Expand Transportation Choices and Mobility.*** *Rhode Island must focus its public transportation investments to connect employment centers with housing for all incomes, ensuring affordable housing development and preservation are co-located with multi-modal transportation investments. To create a sustainable state, Rhode Island must coordinate transportation, housing, and economic development investments to address concentrated poverty, segregation, housing, and transportation burdens—all of which have disproportionately negative effects on communities of color.*[495]

What do state and national demographic trends mean for Providence and the nation? The most hopeful outcome would be an anti-racist majority in Providence and America. **This anti-racist majority, if organized, will advance a new level of health, economic, and educational equity that has been absent since the very settlement of the city, state, and country.**

The Summer of Black Lives Matter Movement

The summer of 2020 witnessed the largest social movement since the 1960s. Back then, the social and political movements were anchored around civil rights, anti-war demonstrations, environmentalism, and the early fight for women's rights. The 2020 protests focused on fighting racism, police brutality and winning equal rights for African heritage people in America. The Black Lives Matter (BLM) movement, which attracted from 15 million to 26 million in the U.S. Protesters demonstrated over the death of George Floyd and other Black men and women.[496] According to interviews with scholars and crowd-counting experts, these figures made the BLM protests the largest social movement in the country's history.

In the Providence and across Rhode Island, crowds of protesters joined the BLM movement, calling for an end to systematic racism and police brutality and advancing criminal justice reform and economic empowerment. On June 6, more than 10,000 participants gathered in Providence and marched to Rhode Island State House.[497] Over the summer, Black Lives Matter Rhode Island worked with the Rhode Island State Police to establish programs, including a civilian oversight board to review the department's actions and bring awareness to issues like abuse of power and systemic racism.[498] Simultaneously, on July 15, 2020, Mayor Jorge O. Elorza signed an Executive Order that identified and created a process of Truth, Reconciliation, and Municipal Reparations to address institutional and systemic bias and racism affecting Black, Indigenous people, and people of color within the City of Providence.[499]

There were missteps, too, said the Rhode Island ACLU. The State Attorney General's office issued an Access to Public Records Act (APRA) opinion, making it more difficult for the public to monitor allegations of misconduct by police officers in the state.[500] In the wake of the summer protests, some groups are doing the hard work of building coalitions. Public policies and private business practices are necessary to meet the needs of African heritage and people of color who have endured centuries of structural discrimination and isolation. Said Alicia Garza, an African heritage civil rights activist and co-founder of the international Black Lives Matter movement, *"I believe that Black communities have the potential to unlock a new democracy, a new civil society, and a new economy in the United States. I believe that Black communities have the power not just to save the country but to lead the country."*[501]

Black Lives Matter Rally, June 1, 2020, Photograph by Keith Stokes

PART 7: CONTINUING LEGACY (2020 & Beyond)

Inclusive Rhode Island History – K-12 Curriculum

Whenever there has been a major social protest or civil rights movement in America, there has always been a call for more classes in Black and ethnic history. The Black Lives Matter protests renewed those calls for the inclusion of Black and multicultural history in the nation's schools. Once again, there is a heightened interest in the history of people who have been a part of the American fabric since the beginning. Many believe that an understanding of America's past will advance racial relations and healing. No one has played a greater role in emphasizing the value of African heritage and history than Carter G. Woodson, the individual who created Negro History Week in February 1926. Woodson would often recite the most important reason to embrace a comprehensive history in U.S. classrooms: *"Those who have no record of what their forebears have accomplished lose the inspiration which comes from the teaching of biography and history."*

To date, only six states have legislative mandates to establish African heritage history at various school curriculum levels. At the municipal level, the Philadelphia school district has made a yearlong African American history course a requirement for high school graduation. In many cases, the programs are not comprehensive, even though K-12 Black history is as important as ever, given the impact of the Black Lives Matter movement. None of the above-mentioned programs attempt to expand African Heritage history into other parts of the educational curriculum, including literature, art, and the sciences, along with civic and social studies. Even more concerning, Black History programs are largely available to students not as part of their required learning objectives but as elective courses.

In honor of Black History Month 2021 in Rhode Island, Anastasia P. Williams, a Providence state representative, has submitted legislation (H-5697) that would require education courses in African American history in elementary and secondary schools in Rhode Island commencing in the 2022-2023 school year. This effort will recognize Rhode Island as one of the nation's first states to provide a comprehensive African heritage and history curriculum for K-12 public schools. Walmart Corporation, as part of its corporate investment efforts to advance racial equity, has contributed a $50,000 grant to Rhode Island to help in the design of the curriculum.[502]

Rhode Island is in a unique position to include African heritage and Indigenous history in its school curriculum. With a rich collection of documents and artifacts spanning nearly four centuries of African heritage and Indigenous history, Rhode Island can create a broad curriculum that recognizes the vital contributions these fellow Rhode Islanders have made to our state and also our nation, and the world. A more inclusive history does not change how history is taught but instead augments and enriches what students learn. The history of African heritage and Indigenous people is the story of Rhode Island; it touches every part of the state's unique history. Most importantly, students of color represent a rapidly growing population in Rhode Island's K-12 public schools, particularly the Providence School System, the state's largest.

Rhode Island can lead the nation on how we tell the story of all Americans by advancing public education and accelerating the inclusion of African heritage and Indigenous peoples' history and their important contributions to Rhode Island and American history. Above all, reconciliation and healing start with education and learning, and we will learn more when we learn together.

Indigenous Peoples Sovereignty Today & Tomorrow

School Begins, Puck Magazine, January 25, 1899

> Take up the White Man's burden—
> Send forth the best ye breed— Go
> send your sons to exile
> To serve your captives' need
> To wait in heavy harness
> On fluttered folk and wild—
> Your new-caught, sullen peoples,
> Half devil, and half child.[503]

Rudyard Kipling was an English journalist, poet, and novelist best known for his collection of stories, *The Jungle Book*. He wrote the poem *"The White Man's Burden: The United States and the Philippine Islands"* to encourage American colonization and annexation of the Philippine Islands, a Pacific Ocean archipelago conquered in the three-month Spanish-American War. The poem suggests that the white race is morally obliged to civilize the nonwhite people of the world. The English colonists in early America held a similar view. Taking land and subjugating people was their divine right, a part of "God's Will." The ongoing burden was how best to civilize and control the Indigenous people.

The Narragansett tribe in Rhode Island did not share the colonists' view of history. They chafed under laws that tried to control their land, and they fought against rules designed to determine their identity—who was native and who was not. White laws favored the colonizers:

> *The conquest of the earth is not a pretty thing when you look into it too much. The history of the American Indian in Western legal thought reveals that a will to empire proceeds most effectively under a rule of law. In the United States, and in the other Western settler-colonizer states, that rule begins with the Doctrine of Discovery and its discourse of conquest, which denies fundamental human rights and self-determination to Indigenous tribal people.[504]*

If history can teach us anything, it is the Indigenous people of Rhode Island and America may be some of the most resilient people who have ever walked the earth. Despite the best efforts of the early Rhode Islanders to disband their tribe and deny their selfhood, the Narragansetts have maintained their identity as the first people of Rhode Island. This is a civil rights issue.

Many of the rights secured by the Narragansett people were won through continuous efforts over generations. Going forward, state and federal authorities must strengthen laws that enable native people to continue to reclaim their ancestral land and, most importantly, advance their rights of self-determination.

As noted by Robert A. Williams Jr., a leading legal scholar in the field of federal native law:

> *The federal trust responsibility has evolved from a paternalistic obligation to care for Indian people to a tool protecting the boundaries of tribal governmental authority to provide that care itself. But the evolution is incomplete. Moreover, new conflicts and questions are inevitable as the power of tribal governments grows, and tribes flex more governmental authority. As the formerly paternalistic trust responsibility gives way to a new federal policy favoring tribal self-governance, the role of the federal government on Indian reservations will continue to be debated and modified. During the coming decades, federal policymakers and courts will be forced to decide, in a range of areas, whether the federally supported tribal renaissance justifies more federal oversight of tribal decisions or, in the alternative, stronger allegiance to norms of respect for tribal sovereignty.*[505]

On January 26, 2021, President Joseph R. Biden issued a memorandum to all federal agencies announcing his administration's commitment to honoring tribal sovereignty. *"The head of each agency shall submit to the Director of the Office of Management and Budget (OMB), within 90 days of the date of this memorandum, a detailed plan of actions the agency will take to implement the policies and directives of Executive Order 13175. The plan shall be developed after consultation by the agency with Tribal Nations and Tribal officials as defined in Executive Order 13175."*[506] Municipal and state officials need not wait. They can meet with tribal leaders now to organize an advocacy plan in support of President Biden's recognition of tribal sovereignty and self-governance.

Criminal Justice Reform

On June 11, 2009, former U. S. Senator Jim Webb appeared before a Senate subcommittee on Crime and Drugs. Committee members had gathered for a judiciary hearing on his proposed National Criminal Justice Commission Act. Webb opened his remarks with some sobering statistics: *"We (United States) have 5% of the world's population but 25% of the world's known prison population. 7.3 million Americans are incarcerated, on probation, or parole. 2.38 million Americans are in prison - five times the world's average incarceration rate."*[507] A decade later, the U.S. continues to lead the world in prison population rates. Blacks and Hispanics make up a large part of the prison population. A recent U. S. Department of Justice report provides a clear look at the racial disparities in the criminal justice system:

> *At year-end 2019, there were 1,096 sentenced black prisoners per 100,000 black residents, 525 sentenced Hispanic prisoners per 100,000 Hispanic residents, and 214 sentenced white prisoners per 100,000 white residents in the U.S. Among sentenced state prisoners at year-end 2018 (the most recent data available), a larger percentage of black (62%) and Hispanic (62%) prisoners than white prisoners (48%) were serving time for a violent offense. Black males age 18 to 19 were 12 times as likely to be imprisoned as white males of the same ages, the highest black-to-white racial disparity of any age group in 2019.*[508]

The over-representation of African heritage men within the American criminal justice system is well documented. According to a 2017 report by the Economic Progress Institute, *"Black Rhode Islanders in the Ocean State cities face arrest rates that range from 3.4 times to 9.1 times non-Black arrest rates. The Black arrest rate in five cities – Newport, Middletown, South Kingstown, and Warwick – exceeds 300 per 1000 residents. These disparities, while noteworthy, are largely consistent with national patterns."*[509] Implicit bias—an unconsciously-held set of attitudes and stereotypes about a people—is deeply rooted in the criminal justice and law enforcement system, according to experts and studies.

The best available evidence shows that police bias toward Black Americans increases the likelihood of negative Black-and-white encounters—encounters ending in stops, searches, use of force, and arrest. Poverty further increases that risk.[510]

African heritage people have endured unjust legal punishments for hundreds of years, starting with Rhode Island's 18th-century slave codes, its later 19th-century disorderly house charges, and finally, its vagrancy laws well into the 20th century. This history has been well documented:

> *Racial disparities in the criminal justice system have deep roots in American history and penal policy. In the South, following Emancipation, black Americans were specific targets of unique forms of policing, sentencing, and confinement. Laws that capitalized on a loophole in the 13th Amendment that states citizens cannot be enslaved unless convicted of a crime intentionally targeted newly emancipated black people as a means of surveilling them and exploiting their labor. In 1865 and 1866, the former Confederate legislatures quickly enacted a new set of laws known as the Black Codes to force former slaves back into an exploitative labor system that resembled the plantation regime in all but name. Although these codes did recognize the new legal status of black Americans, in most states, newly- freed people could not vote, serve on juries, or testify in court. Vagrancy laws at the center of the Black Codes meant that any black person who could not prove he or she worked for a white employer could be arrested. These "vagrants" most often entered a system of incarceration administered by private industry. Known as convict leasing, this system allowed for the virtual enslavement of people who had been convicted of a crime, even if those "crimes" were for things like "walking without a purpose" or "walking at night," for which law enforcement officials in the South aggressively targeted black people. Northern states also turned to the criminal justice system to exert social control over free black Americans. Policymakers in the North did not legally target black Americans as explicitly as did their southern counterparts, but disparate enforcement of various laws against "suspicious characters," disorderly conduct, keeping and visiting disorderly houses, drunkenness, and violations of city ordinances made possible new forms of everyday surveillance and punishment in the lives of black people in the Northeast, Midwest, and West.*[511]

Systematic discrimination—a discriminatory act or set of actions that become embedded in a society—is the challenge that people of color generally, and African heritage people specifically, have faced since the earliest days of America. Fortunately, the American Civil Liberties Union (ACLU) has launched the Criminal Law Reform Project (CLRP) to confront systematic discrimination within the criminal justice and law enforcement system. The ACLU has advanced innovative policies and procedures that prevent mass incarceration and overcriminalization at the "front end" of the system.[512] This innovative approach includes:

> *Creating robust statewide indigent defense systems to ensure that people charged with a crime have access to effective assistance of counsel; ending unnecessary and unjust pretrial detention through bail reform and other abusive pretrial practices; reforming unconstitutional and racially biased*

police practices; challenging prosecutorial abuses of power that result in or enable regressive and unconstitutional practices; reforming our nation's punitive drug policies, which have failed to achieve public safety and health while eroding constitutional rights and criminalizing unprecedented numbers of people, particularly people of color; and reclaiming equal protection of the laws and guaranteeing substantive and procedural due process protections at each stage of the arrest-to-sentencing process of criminal cases. CLRP works closely with the ACLU's Campaign for Smart Justice, which collaborates with partners to build a movement for social change, promote racial justice, and win state-based reforms needed to cut the size of our nation's incarcerated population by 50 percent.[513]

Another front-end opportunity to reduce overcriminalization is for municipal and state policymakers to review the thousands of criminal statutes enacted by legislatures, particularly those that carry criminal penalties. It is the responsibility of elected officials to carefully consider what infractions can result in a criminal conviction and prison time.[514]

The City of Providence, known as the *"Creative Capital,"* has the opportunity to creatively partner with the Providence Branch NAACP, ACLU of Rhode Island, Mayor Elorza's African American Advisory Group, Providence Police Department, Providence Human Relations Commission, and other community stakeholders to engage with outstanding think-tank organizations such as the Urban Institute's Justice Policy Center and implement a series of strategies to reduce criminalization at the front end.[515]

Immigration Reform

The Colony of Rhode Island was uniquely founded under the radical principles of religious and civil liberties. It attracted a diverse population of early immigrants, differing in race, religion, class, and ethnicity. This early settlement pattern enabled the colony to participate in the transatlantic maritime economy—including the slave trade. For some, particularly persecuted religious minorities, Rhode Island has been a welcoming place. The irony? The colony that valued freedom also waged war against the Native people and kept enslaved African men, women, and children in their homes and on their farms.

Rhode Island's history of diversity accelerated during the 19th century amid an early industrial economy sparked by Samuel Slater and his water-powered cotton-spinning mill in Pawtucket in 1790. A few years later, Slater began hiring families from the surrounding area, including children, to work the spinning machines.[516] Immigrant laborers from Europe created a new working class. These workers helped drive the industrial revolution in 19th-century Rhode Island.

Today, Rhode Island has a comparatively large community of immigrants, many of them from Latin America. As reported in an Equity Profile of Rhode Island, *"Over the last 30 years, the state has gone from being seven percent to 24 percent people of color. In just the last decade, Rhode Island's Latino population grew 44 percent, adding almost 40,000 residents. The Asian and African American populations also grew by 28 and 23 percent, respectively. But, the non-Hispanic white population shrunk by six percent."*[517] The Immigration of Spanish-speaking people dates back to a group of Sephardic Jewish families who arrived in search of religious toleration in the mid-17th century. The most consistent wave of Latino immigrants into Providence occurred during the 1960s and 1970s, a group largely made up of Puerto Rican and Dominican people:

In 1965, the most recent ethnic migration into South Providence began. At about this time, the first large influx of Spanish-speaking Americans arrived, settling near Prairie Avenue and Oxford Street. In the last decade, the Spanish speaking community has grown significantly and is now widely settled throughout South Providence. Many of the new residents from New York City and other northeastern industrial centers have been drawn to Providence by the lure of home ownership and the promise of a better way of life than they had known in more congested urban areas. The presence of this new faction in the community is manifested in the numerous Spanish-speaking commercial establishments that have appeared in South Providence and in the new Spanish Catholic portion of the congregation at Saint Michael's Church.[518]

According to the 2010 Census, the total Latino (Hispanic) population in Rhode Island was 120,586. The four largest Latino ethnic groups included Dominicans (33,879), Puerto Ricans (29,904), Guatemalans (18,125), and Columbians (9,998).[519] According to Data USA, in 2018, 43% of the people in Providence were Latino. Nearly 30% of Providence's residents were born outside of the United States, a number higher than the national average of 13.7%.[520] As reported by the Federal Reserve Bank of Boston, the cities of Boston and Providence are the top two destinations in New England for immigrants, with foreign-born residents comprising one-quarter of each city's population.[521]

Rhode Island continues to benefit from immigrant workers, *"who comprise nearly two-fifths of workers in production occupations and one-third of workers in healthcare support occupations. As neighbors, business owners, taxpayers, and workers, immigrants are an integral part of Rhode Island's diverse and thriving communities and make extensive contributions that benefit all."*[522] In greater Providence, 29 percent of the region's small businesses are immigrant-owned.[523]

The new arrivals are helping *all* workers. According to the Brookings Institution, *"economists find that, on average, previous waves of immigrants tended to boost American wages."*[524] As immigration continues at the national, state, and municipal levels, many municipal governments have adopted policies to manage immigration and maximize their contributions to the community's economic and social well-being. Policies and programs include the following suggestions:

- Create a mayor's office for immigrant affairs or new Americans
- Reassert municipal law enforcement's commitment to public safety
- Develop programs to support undocumented residents
- Implement municipal ID programs
- Explore strategic priorities with city council members, such as tax credits for businesses offering English as a Second Language classes for workers[525]

Providence has a long history of welcoming newcomers. Embracing immigration reform not only makes good business sense but helps all citizens to realize the ideals of Providence's first immigrant, Roger Williams.

Urban Public Education Funding

A zip code address should not determine a child's access to a quality education. The educational achievement gaps between urban students and suburban students—and the achievement gaps between African heritage, Latino, and white students—may well be one of the most important civil rights issues of the 21st century. In many cases, these gaps are tied to neighborhood and school locations. As noted by the Economic Policy Institute:

> *Social and economic disadvantage – not only poverty, but a host of associated conditions – depresses student performance. Concentrating students with these disadvantages in racially and economically homogenous schools depresses it further. Schools that the most disadvantaged black children attend are segregated because they are located in segregated high-poverty neighborhoods, far distant from truly middle-class neighborhoods. Living in such high-poverty neighborhoods for multiple generations adds an additional barrier to achievement, and multigenerational segregated poverty characterizes many African American children today.*[526]

Providence and Rhode Island integrated their public schools in 1866 and reduced neighborhood school segregation through busing and student integration policies in the 1960s and 1970s. Today, data suggests that little has changed. An immigration surge, coupled with white flight into the suburbs and private schools, has made the situation worse in some places. Consider this 2018 U.S. News & World Report article:

> *Consider the City of Providence, R.I. In 2000, just over a third, or 36 percent, of the district's 55 public schools, were at least 90 percent minority – black, Hispanic, or Asian. Fifteen years later, almost three-quarters, or 74 percent, of the schools were 90 percent or more non-white. At first glance, that might look like a dramatic resegregation. It was the biggest jump in non-white schools of any district in the nation, according to Meredith Richards, an expert in school segregation at Southern Methodist University, who calculated these figures for The Hechinger Report.*[527]

Many academics and researchers agree that urban school districts like Providence face numerous challenges, including the overdependence and inadequacy of funding municipal education through property taxes. In 2018, the U.S. Commission on Civil Rights noted that too often, low-income Black and Latino students end up in schools with crumbling walls, old textbooks, and unqualified teachers. Such inequities *"are caused by the fact that schools are most funded with state and local tax dollars."* More than 92 percent of funding comes from nonfederal sources, the Commission said.[528]

In 1954, the U.S. Supreme Court in *Brown v. Board of Education* ruled that racial segregation of children in public schools was unconstitutional. Many praised the decision as an end to school desegregation, but as scholars have pointed out, the ruling offered no deadline.[529] While desegregation of schools was painfully slow after the Brown decision, neighborhoods largely remained segregated, resulting in Black-only schools in some places. This is the unrealized civil rights issue that faces cities like Providence today:

> *The schools black children attend today, in North and South, East and West, are segregated mostly*

because their schools are located in segregated neighborhoods. In some small cities and towns, schools can be integrated by adjusting attendance zones, establishing magnet schools, or implementing controlled choice programs. But in major metropolitan areas, places like Atlanta, Baltimore, Chicago, Cleveland, Detroit, New York, St. Louis, and so on, distances between ghetto and suburb are too great, and school district jurisdictional lines too established, for these methods to accomplish significant integration. Schools cannot be integrated unless the neighborhoods where they are located are integrated; in particular, by making housing opportunities for low-income, black, urban residents available in white middle-class suburbs.[530]

"Schools alone can't fix this," says Sheneka Williams, an expert in school desegregation history at the University of Georgia. *"Housing is a place to start. There has to be a federal incentive with housing. If the nation is interested in integrating schools, you have to incentivize people to live together."*[531] The path forward is clear: integrated schools call for integrated neighborhoods, towns, and cities. Historically, the City of Providence has provided a diverse and affordable housing stock. However, other Rhode Island municipalities have not met the challenge. A state-wide effort is needed. In 2004, the state addressed the issue with two measures—the Rhode Island Comprehensive Housing Production and Rehabilitation Act and the Rhode Island Low and Moderate-Income Housing Act (Rhode Island General Laws 45-5). The laws required cities and towns to set aside 10% of their housing stock as "affordable."[532]

Unfortunately, many Rhode Island municipalities, particularly suburban and rural towns and cities, have not done so. New legislation could offer financial incentives to those communities that meet the 10% affordable housing minimum and penalties for those that don't. Anything thing less continues the *"separate and unequal"* Jim Crow policies that still plague us today,

Health Equity Post COVID-19

As COVID-19 swept the nation and the world, systematic health inequalities drove its disproportionate impact on communities of color. As reported by the American Medical Association on July 28, 2020, *"Marginalized and minoritized patients have and will suffer disproportionally during the COVID-19 crisis due to the inequities in society perpetuated by systematic practices."*[533] According to another report, *"African Americans are overrepresented among reported coronavirus disease 2019 (COVID-19) deaths in the United States."* Factors that may explain the disparities in COVID-19 deaths include health conditions such as hypertension and cardiovascular disease, barriers to health-care access, and differences in cultural attitudes. *"While these individual-level factors predictably contribute to disparate COVID-19 outcomes, systematic and structural factors have not yet been reported."*[534]

Other agencies and authors agree. According to the Centers for Disease Control and Prevention, *"Long-standing systemic health and social inequities have put many people from racial and ethnic minority groups at increased risk of getting sick and dying from COVID-19."*[535] In urban Rhode Island:

> 59 percent of positive test cases where race was reported, Hispanic or Latinx residents comprise 44 percent of positive COVID-19 coronavirus test cases in the state, and non-Hispanic Black or African

American residents comprise 13 percent. These residents are also disproportionately represented in COVID-19-related hospitalizations, though they make up only 15 percent and 6 percent of the population of Rhode Island respectively.[536]

Recent COVID-19 tracking data has found that *"the race and ethnicity data reported by states shows declining — but persistent—inequities. 1 in 6 Latinx people in Rhode Island and Utah has tested positive for COVID-19 since the pandemic began."*[537] The impact of the COVID-19 pandemic has been severe across the world. In America and Rhode Island, people of color have been hit especially hard:

Moving forward, we must apply a health equity lens ... explicitly for African Americans, as well as other populations at risk for biased treatment in the health-care system, including women and non- gender confirming sexual minorities, incarcerated and other institutionalized persons, the disabled, the elderly, non-native English speakers, undocumented residents—the list is endless. The health-care system and all of its agents, policy makers, and elected officials are all accountable to ensure that our social and political determinants of health no longer disproportionately burden the groups most at risk for unfair or inequitable treatment but strive to deliver our systems best care. The bridge between public health and medicine also needs to be strengthened such that the findings of population studies can be more readily translated to improve our current health-care delivery system. Or…maybe we are okay with the alarming rate of COVID-19 deaths among African Americans, applying our usual explanations that they are sicker, poorer, and have less access to care. Maybe health disparities are the inalienable truth and status quo in America. Accepting this reality will not increase the capacity of well-meaning medical staff to help all people fairly and belies the self-evident principles on which this country was founded. We (a collective of African American physicians and public health professionals) are sounding the alarm that we seize this opportunity to address the health disparities and systematic inequities that continue to result in premature mortality and shortened life expectancy among African Americans and other disadvantaged, disenfranchised, and already marginalized populations.[538]

Closing the Wealth Gap

"The 400 richest American billionaires have more total wealth than all 10 million Black American households combined." -Vanessa Williamson [539]

Centuries of discrimination and exploitation have left African-heritage Americans much poorer than white Americans. As the Brookings Institution notes:

The median white household has a net worth of $171,000, 10 times the net worth of the median Black household, $17,100, In other words, Black households are overrepresented among the poor and working class, and underrepresented among the upper-middle class and the wealthy. The poorest 20% of American households have a net worth of less than $4,700; many of these households have a negative wealth due to debt. Of these households, 26% identify as Black. The richest 20% of American households have a net worth of more than about $500,000; 3% of these households identify as Black.[540]

In Rhode Island, the disparity between Black and white wealth is vast. According to a 2017 study by the Economic Progress Institute:

- Black overall poverty and child poverty rates are much higher than the corresponding White rates. Since 2007, the Black poverty rate has been nearly 3 times the White poverty rate, while the Black child poverty rate has been more than 3 times higher than the White child poverty rate.

- Black Rhode Islanders comprise 6.5 percent of the population but 23.8 percent of the homeless population.

- The Black median household income consistently trails the White median income; from 2005 to 2015, for every dollar in median income in a White-headed household, the Black median household saw only fifty-seven cents.

- Black households remain furthest behind in recovering from the impact of the Great Recession on household incomes.[541]

For years, African-heritage Americans have been denied or given limited access to loans, mortgages, insurance, and other finance-building instruments. Many of these financial programs were initiated, operated, and guaranteed by public authorities. These barriers to wealth creation have been dramatically described by McKinsey & Company:

Equity capital, liquid savings, credit, and access to investable assets are key to a stable base of family wealth. Black families have uneven access to each of these components, which constrains their ability to develop material and diversified asset portfolios. Black families begin with lower levels of wealth: only 8 percent of black families receive an inheritance, compared with 26 percent of white families. When an inheritance does come, it is 35 percent of the value of that of a white family. This difference in "starter" wealth also affects other components of the wealth-generation process: recent research shows that black college graduates' wealth declines after graduation because they are more likely than white college graduates to support their parents financially instead of the other way around.[542]

The Brookings Institution has a solution: progressive tax policies.

A first step would be to reverse the slide toward regressivity that has characterized the American tax code in recent decades. Top marginal income tax rates have fallen from a peak of 92% in the early 1950s to 37% today. The income tax rewards wealth over work by taxing income from ownership at much lower rates than income from salaries and wages. State and local taxes, moreover, are generally regressive. In sum, the tax code is only somewhat progressive for those between the poor and the upper-middle class, and tax rates actually go down for the very rich.[543]

The most consistent path to family wealth and economic security has been homeownership and steady employment. Both conditions depend on the ability to build credit and save money. Unfortunately, these basic components of the American Dream have been denied to African heritage and people of color because of publicly sanctioned policies of discrimination. And while local, state, and federal laws have been enacted to combat bias in employment, housing, and financing, they have only existed since the latter part of the 20th century. They have yet to catch up to nearly four centuries of discrimination and socioeconomic isolation.

While there are numerous public policy and private investment strategies to help close the wealth gap, an important starting point, particularly in Providence and Rhode Island, would be to recognize our shared history of complicity. The colony's early settlers flourished, in part, because they paid little or nothing for native land. They paid no wages for the African labor that produced the products and services that created white wealth. This history is important, not only because it tells us about the past but because it helps us understand its impact on the state's minority population today.

Tackling Racial Inequalities in Housing & Neighborhoods

The bias directed towards people of color is clearly evident in the inequalities seen in Rhode Island's homes and neighborhoods. As noted by the Brookings Institution, *"More than half of black or white residents in 70 of the 100 largest U.S. metro areas would need to move to a different census tract in order to integrate the metro. At the rate of progress we've seen since the 70s, 268 of our metro areas will not be integrated until the year 2120. Younger black city-dwellers (born between 1985 and 2000) are just as likely to live in a high-poverty neighborhood as the previous generation (born between 1955 and 1970)."*[544]

The causes of residential segregation are complex, enduring, and overlapping, Brookings says. Among the factors contributing to segregation, five stand out:

> **Zoning**. *Even in the post-civil rights era, many forms of land use regulation have perpetuated segregation. Complex webs of covenants and zoning ordinances across U.S. cities—in particular for low-density development—superimposed on already highly-segregated neighborhoods have slowed integration. When there are wide economic gaps by race, as we have in the U.S., exclusionary land-use policies based on families' economic circumstances entrench racial segregation.*
>
> **Transportation**. *Highways and runways have often damaged or cut off black neighborhoods. "Highways cut the heart out of poor areas," as Transportation Secretary Anthony Foxx observed. Meanwhile, public transit investments often fail to connect minority communities to opportunities for education and employment.*
>
> **Steering**. *Black and other minority homebuyers and renters receive different treatment from realtors and agents. In 2012, white and black "homebuyers" (in fact, actors) were sent to 8,000 randomly selected realtors. Black home-seekers were shown 18% fewer homes. There are some signs that realtors "steer" by race with reference to local schools.*
>
> **Credit**. *After being denied home loans before the civil rights era, black Americans have continued to be denied affordable credit and have been pushed towards sub-prime loans. SunTrust, Wells Fargo, and Bank of America have, in recent years, settled with the Justice Department (for $21 million, and $175 million and $335 million, respectively) for pushing black homebuyers into subprime mortgage deals, overcharging them for home loans, and other breaches.*
>
> **Attitudes**. *Although harder to pinpoint, the attitudes and preferences of individuals and families likely play a role too. Attitudes are shifting but remain heavily influenced by race. Many white Americans strongly prefer to live with only a minority of black neighbors, up to roughly 20 percent of the neighborhood. Black Americans, meanwhile, prefer "50-50" neighborhoods, and are averse to homogeneous neighborhoods.*[545]

African heritage people, Indigenous people, and people of color in Providence have endured all of the root causes of segregation and discrimination. To name a few: urban redevelopment practices, exclusionary zoning, the I-95 and I-195 highways that cut off neighborhoods of color, the steering of homebuyers and renters of color away from white neighborhoods, the denial of home loans through redlining, and the years of racist attitudes and stereotypes fueled by centuries of racial separation. *"The past is never dead,"* said the novelist William Faulkner. *"It's not even past."* But cities like Providence can end discriminatory laws and practices by adopting progressive policies that will repair centuries of inequities. Innovative partnerships and public policies coupled with private investment strategies can help close gaps in health, education, and wealth equity.

Dr. Dannie Ritchie and her Brown University student researchers have proposed one such strategy:

> *In addition to addressing student housing, we hold that Brown should be involved in the production of low-income housing through direct investment upwards of 10 million dollars. Brown University can emulate Harvard's 20/20/2000 program, leveraging its financial resources to create a revolving loan program to finance the production and maintenance of low-income housing opportunities across Providence. In keeping with the justice-oriented framework we recommend, decision-making for this program would be decided through the co-led partnership that we've outlined, including nonprofit developers.*[546]

The *"Big Ideas"* that arise from progressive thinking by community, academic, business, and political leaders need a platform for implementation. Despite the barriers to innovation in the public sector, the City of Providence has initiated the process of generating policies that will repair past transgressions and give all of its citizens a shot at prosperity. The first part of this process has been a thorough examination of Providence's and Rhode Island's past, a search for historical Truth through the Mayor's 2020 Executive Order, which calls for *"detailed instructions on how evidentiary documents shall be compiled and made available for public interpretation and future policy-making efforts."*

Providence can move the socioeconomic needle by building on successful models of citizen engagement, such as Mayor Elorza's African American Advisory Group. City officials should consider establishing a *"Blue Ribbon Commission On Racial Equity."* The Commission would be charged with researching, documenting, and recommending measurable policies and programs that the mayor and city council can use to build an equitable, diverse, and inclusive city for all citizens. Recognizing that the city alone cannot accomplish everything, Commission members would include government agencies, nonprofit organizations, and private sector companies, along with state officials tied to housing, business, workforce development, education, transportation, and healthcare. Funding would come from a partnership of public and private sources to employ staff and support work products that reflect the highest public policy research and program planning standards.

Most importantly, the Commission's composition and work would require active Providence citizen involvement in all aspects of strategic development and implementation. This is what reparations could look like in the City of Providence, where all citizens have the earned right to prosper, regardless of race, ethnicity, religion, national origin, and sexual orientation. This would make Roger Williams proud and honor the African heritage and Indigenous people on whose shoulders we stand today.

V. THE RESOURCES: Contributing Historical Institutions & Libraries

This research was made possible through the generous time, consideration, and contributions from the following Providence and Rhode Island institutions and their collections. A historical narrative review and editing contribution were by historical author W. Paul Davis.

Primary Research Repositories
- Rhode Island Black Heritage Society
- Rhode Island Historical Society
- Rhode Island Historical Preservation & Cultural Commission
- Rhode Island State Archives
- Providence Preservation Society
- Newport Historical Society
- Special Collections, Adams Library, Rhode Island College
- Special Collections, Phillips Memorial Library, Providence College
- Special Collections, Providence City Archives
- Special Collections, Newport Public Library
- Special Collections, Providence Public Library
- Stokes Family Collection

Online Research Sources
- JSTOR Digital Library — https://www.jstor.org/
- Ancestry.com — https://www.ancestry.com/
- Newspapers.com — https://www.newspapers.com/
- Genealogy Bank — https://www.genealogybank.com/
- NewsBank — https://www.newsbank.com/
- Slave Voyages — https://www.slavevoyages.org/
- National Archives — https://www.archives.gov/
- New England Indian Papers — https://web.library.yale.edu/collection/new-england-indian-papers-series
- John Carter Brown Library — https://jcblibrary.org/collection/themes/slavery-and-slave-trade
- HathiTrust Digital Library — https://www.hathitrust.org/
- Small State/Big History — http://smallstatebighistory.com/

Endnotes

1. *Indian New England Before the Mayflower*, Howard S. Russell, University Press of New England, 1980, pp.32
2. New England Native American Group, National Geographic Encyclopedia, 2019
3. *A History of the Narragansett Tribe of Rhode Island*, Robert A. Geake, The History Press, 2011, pp. 2
4. *Guns, Germs & Steel: The Fates of Human Societies*, Jared Diamond, W. W. Norton Press, 1997, pp. 97
5. *1491: New Revelations of the Americas Before Columbus*, Charles C. Mann, Alfred & Knopp, New York, 2006, pp. 54
6. "The Significance of Disease in the Extinction of the New England Indians," Sherburne F. Cook, Human Biology, Vol. 45, No. 3 (September 1973), pp. 485-508
7. *The Boisterous Sea of Liberty: A Documentary of America from Discovery Through the Civil War*, Brion Davis and Steven Mintz, Oxford University Press, 1998, pp. 69
8. *A Key into the Language of America*, Roger Williams, Edited by Howard M. Chapin, Applewood Books, 1936, pp. 196
9. *Terra Nova*, Cynthia Huntington, Southern Illinois University Press, 2017, pps. 61-62
10. *The New England Soul: Preaching & Religious Culture in Colonial New England*, Henry S. Stout, Oxford University Press, 1986, pp. 54
11. *Sovereignty and the Sacred: Secularism and the Political Economy of Religion*, Robert A. Yale, University of Chicago Press, 1992, pp.129
12. *God, War, and Providence: The Epic Struggle of Roger Williams and the Narragansett Indians against the Puritans of New England*, James A. Warren, Scribner, 2018, pp. 4
13. *An Historical Discourse on the Civil and Religious Affairs of the Colony of Rhode Island*, John Callender, Second Edition, by Romeo Elton, Knowles, Vose & Company, 1838, pp. 88
14. *Indian Legends*, Johanna R.M. Lyback, Lyons and Carnahan Publishers, 1925, pp. 4-5
15. *Memoir of Roger Williams*, James D. Knowles, Lewis & Penniman Press, 1833, pp. 95
16. *Roger Williams and the Creation of the American Soul*, John M. Barry, Penguin Books, 2011 pp. 206
17. Ibid., pp. 102-106
18. Aquidneck Island Land, Deed, Receipt and Agreement, 1637, Rhode Island State Archives
19. The Tenure of the Lands of Aquethneck, 1641, Rhode Island State Archives
20. An Act for the permitting of Illegal and Clandestine Purchases of the Native Indians in this Colony, March 1, 1663, Rhode Island State Archives
21. *Atlas of Indian Nations*, Anton Treuer, National Geographic, 2016
22. "The Charter of 1663, Major Milestone on the Road to Religious Liberty," *A Lively Experiment: Reflections on the Charter of 1663*, Rhode Island Council for the Humanities, 2013
23. A Parliamentary Patent, 1643, Rhode Island State Archives
24. Colony of Rhode Island Royal Charter, 1663, Rhode Island State Archives

25   *Property Rights in Transition*, Edited by Donn A. Derr and Leslie Small, Arno Press, 1977, pp. 107

26   *West Africa Before the Colonial Era: A History to 1850*, Basil Davidson, Routeledge Press, 2014, pp. 9-10

27   *Black Yankees: The Development of an Afro-American Subculture in Eighteenth Century New England*, William D. Piersen, University of Massachusetts Press, 1988, pp. 3

28   *Transformations in Slavery: A History of Slavery in Africa*, Paul E. Lovejoy, Cambridge University Press, 2012, pp. 9

29   *Strange New Land: Africans in Colonial America*, Peter H. Wood, Oxford University Press, 1996, pp. 25

30   Emory Center for Digital Scholarship, https://www.slavevoyages.org/

31   "The Constitution and Finance of the Royal African Company of England From its Founding Till 1720," W.R. Scott, American Historical Review, Vol VIII, No 2, (January 1903), pp. 242

32   "Slavery, Sovereignty, and "Inheritable Blood": Reconsidering John Locke and the Origins of American Slavery," Holly Brewer, The American Historical Review, Volume 122, Issue 4, (October 2017), pp. 1038–1078

33   "The Changing Nature of Indian Slavery in New England, 1670–1720," Margaret Ellen Newell, Colonial Society of Massachusetts, Vol. 7, (April 2003) pp. 107-136

34   *Slaves and Englishmen: Human Bondage in the Early Modern Atlantic World*, Michael Guasco, University of Pennsylvania Press, 2014, pp. 186

35   *The History of the State of Rhode Island and Providence Plantations, Volumes I-V*, Thomas Williams Bicknell, American Historical Society, 1920, vol. 2, pp.501

36   An Act Prohibiting Black Mankind Slavery, Rhode Island State Archives

37   *The Economic and Social History of New England: 1620-1789*, William B. Weeden, Houghton, Mifflin and Company, 1891, pp. 444

38   *The History of the King Philip's War*, Increase Mather, J. Munsell, Editor, 1862 Edition, pp. 9

39   "'We Are All the Sachems from East to West': A New Look at Miantonomi's Campaign of Resistance," Michael Leroy Oberg, The New England Quarterly, Vol. 77, No. 3 (September 2004), pp. 478-499

40   *The Red King's Rebellion: Racial Politics in New England*, Russell Bourne, Oxford University Press, 1991, pp. 99

41   "'We Chuse to Be Bounded': Native American Animal Husbandry in Colonial New England," David J. Silverman, The William and Mary Quarterly, Vol. 60, No. 3 (Jul. 2003), pp. 511-548

42   "A Relation of the Indian War, by Mr. Easton of Rhode Island 1675," Paul Royster, Editor, University of Nebraska-Lincoln Publications, 2006, pp. 3-4

43   *The History of the State of Rhode Island and Providence Plantations, Volumes I-V*, Thomas Williams Bicknell, American Historical Society, 1920, vol. 2, pp. 446-447.

44   *Native American Almanac: More Than 50,000 Years of the Cultures and Histories of Indigenous peoples*, Yvonne Wakim Dennis, Arlene Hirschfelder, and Shannon Rothenberger Flynn, Visible Ink Press, 2016

45   "The Long Wake of the Pequot War," Katherine A. Grandjean, Early American Studies, Vol. 9, No. 2, Special Issue: The Worlds of Lion Gardiner, ca. 1599—1663: Crossings and Boundaries (Spring 2011), pp. 379-411

46   "'Why shall see have peace to bee made slaves': Indian Surrenderers During and After King Philip's War," Linford D. Fisher, Ethnohistory, Volume 64, Issue 1 (January 2017) pp. 91-114

47   *Records of the Colony of Rhode Island and Providence Plantations in New England*, Edited by John Russell Bartlett, 1865, Vol. III. pp. 389

48   Proclamation of the Plymouth Colony Council, To The Elders Of The [Churches Of] Plymouth, Colonial Society of Massachusetts, Vol. 79, Section Three, King Philip's War 1675–1676, pp. 108

49   *King Philip's War: The History and Legacy of America's Forgotten Conflict*, Eric B. Schultz and Michael J. Tougias, The Countryman Press, 1999, pp. 244-249

50   Ibid., pp. 264

51   *Memoir of Roger Williams*, James D. Knowles, Lewis & Penniman Press, 1833, pp. 347-348

52   "Indian Slaves of the King Philip's War," James G. Vose, Publications of the Rhode Island Historical Society, Volume 1, 1893

53   *Brethren By Nature: New England Indians, Colonists, and the Origins of American Slavery*, Margaret E. Newell, Cornell University Press, 2015

54   "Our Hidden History: Roger Williams and slavery's origins," Margaret Newell, Providence Journal Special Section, August 29, 2020

55   The American Universal Geography, or a View of the Present Sate of all the Empires, Kingdoms, States and Republics, and of the United States of America, Part I, Jedidiah Morse, (June 1802) pp. 318

56   *A Statement of the Case of the Narragansett Tribe of Indians, As Shown in the Manuscript Collections of Sir William Johnson*, James N. Arnold, Mercury Publishing, 1806, pp. 3

57   Ibid., pp. 4

58   Ibid., pp. 5

59   *Minutes of the African Union Society of Newport 1787-1824*, Special Collections, Newport Historical Society

60   "Slavery, Emancipation and Black Freedom in Rhode Island, 1652-1842," Christy Clark-Pujara, Thesis and Dissertation, University of Iowa, (Fall 2009) pp. 27

61   *A Forgotten History: The Slave Trade and Slavery in New England*, Choices Program, Watson Institute for International Studies, Brown University (June 2005) pp. 3

62   *New England Bound: Slavery & Colonization in Early America*, Wendy Warren, W.W. Norton & Company, 2016

63   *Records of the Colony of Rhode Island and Providence Plantations in New England*, Edited by John Russell Bartlett, 1865, Vol. III. pp. 308

64   *Early Rhode Island: A Social History of the People*, William B. Weeden, Grafton Press, 1910, pp. 187

65   An Act For laying A Duty On Negro Slaves That Shall Be Imported Into This Colony, February 27, 1711, Rhode Island State Archives

66   *Records of the Colony of Rhode Island and Providence Plantations in New England*, Edited by John Russell Bartlett, 1865, Vol. III. pp. 492

67   Rhode Island Colony Act To Prevent all Persons Keeping House within Colony from Entertaining Indian, Negro or Mulatto Servants or Slaves, Stokes Family Collection, 1757

68   Records of the Colony of Rhode Island and Providence Plantations in New England, Edited by John Russell Bartlett, 1865, Vol IV, pp. 415

69 *Gender and Law Policy*, Katherine T. Bartlett, Et Al., Wolters Kluwer Publishing, 2021

70 An ACT for the More Effectual Punishment of Negroes that Shall Attempt to Commit a Rape on any White Woman, August 23, 1743, Rhode State Archives

71 *Disowning Slavery: Gradual Emancipation and Race in New England*, Joanne Pope Melish, Cornell University Press, 2015, pp. 2

72 *The Notorious Triangle: Rhode Island and the African Slave Trade, 1700-1807*, Jay Coughtry, Temple University Press, 1981

73 Slave Voyages, Emory Center for Digital Scholarship, University of California at Irvine, https://www.slavevoyages.org

74 "Rhode Island and the Slave Trade," J. Stanley Lemons, Rhode Island Historical Society, Vol. 60, No. 4, (Fall 2002), pp. 97

75 *The Slave Trade*, Hugh Thomas, Simon & Schuster, 1997, pp. 520

76 *The Notorious Triangle: Rhode Island and the African Slave Trade, 1700-1807*, Jay Coughtry, Temple University Press, 1981, pp.174

77 *Early Rhode Island: A Social History of the People*, William B. Weeden, Grafton Press, 1910, pp. 189

78 "American Rum, African Consumers, and the Transatlantic Slave Trade," Sean M. Kelley, University of Essex, African Economic History, Volume 46, Number 2, (2018), pp. 1-29

79 *Where the Negroes Are Masters: An African Port in the Era of the Slave Trade*, Randy J. Sparks, Harvard University Press, 2014, pp. 165

80 *The Notorious Triangle: Rhode Island and the African Slave Trade, 1700-1807*, Jay Coughtry, Temple University Press, 1981, pp.88

81 Letter From Governor Josias Lyndon to British Lord Commissioners for Trade & Plantations, January 26, 1764, Rhode Island State Archives

82 *The Works of John Adams: The Second President, Vol. 10 (Letters 1811-1825)*, Charles Francis Adams, Little Brown and Company, 1851

83 *Runaway Slaves: Rebels on the Plantation*, John Hope Franklin and Loren Schwinger, Offord University Press, 1999, pp. 3

84 *New York Burning: Liberty, Slavery, and Conspiracy in Eighteenth-Century Manhattan*, Jill Lepore, Vintage Books, 2006

85 *Black Jacks: African American Seamen in the Age of Sail*, W. Jeffery Bolster, Harvard University Press, 1988, pp. 5-6

86 *The Notorious Triangle: Rhode Island and the African Slave Trade, 1700-1806*, Jay Coughtry, Temple University Press, 1981, p. 60

87 Reading Between the Lines of Slavery: Examining New England Runaway Ads for Evidence of an Afro-Yankee Culture, Lauren Landi, Senior Thesis, Salve Reginal University, 2012, pp. 29

88 Creative Survival: Africans as Mariners in Colonial Rhode Island, Keith W. Stokes, Small Sate, Big History: The Online Review of Rhode Island History, http://smallstatebighistory.com/, February 2020

89 Shining in Borrowed Plumage: Affirmation of Community in the Black Coronation Festivals of New England (c. 1750-c. 1850) Melvin Wade, Western Folklore, Vol. 40, No. 3 (July 1981), pp. 211-231

90 *Celebrating Ethnicity and Nation: American Festive Culture from the Revolution to the Early 20th Century*, Genevieve Fabre, Berghahn Books, 2001, pp. 92

91 *Black Yankees: The Development of an Afro-American Subculture in Eighteenth-Century New England*, William D. Piersen, University of Massachusetts Press, 1988, pp. 124

92 "African Institutions in America," Hubert H. S. Aimes, The Journal of American Folklore, (March 1905), Vol. 18, No. 68, pp. 16

93 *An Imperfect Union: Slavery Federalism, and Comity, Paul Finkelman*, The Lawbook Exchange, 2000, pp. 79

94 *The Slave Trade: The Story of the Atlantic Slave Trade 1440-1870,* Hugh Thomas, Simon & Schuster, 1997, pp. 520
Journal of the Slave Ship Mary, Digital Georgetown University, Georgetown University Library, https://repository.library.georgetown.edu/handle/10822/1055276

95 An Act Authorizing the Manumission of Negros, Mulattoes and Others, February 25, 1784, Rhode Island State Archives

96 The Origins Debate: Slavery and Racism in Seventeenth-Century Virginia, Alden T. Vaughan, The Virginia Magazine of History and Biography, Vol. 97, No. 3, (July 1989), pp. 324

97 "Slavery, Sovereignty, and "Inheritable Blood": Reconsidering John Locke and the Origins of American Slavery," Holly Brewer, The American Historical Review, Volume 122, Issue 4, (October 2017), pp. 1038– 1078

98 "Sexual Racism: A Legacy of Slavery," Kenneth James Lay, UCLA National Black Law Journal, Vol. 13, (1993) pp. 165-183

99 *Public Laws of the State of Rhode Island and Providence Plantations,* Printed at Providence by Carter and Wilkinson, 1798

100 "The Proceedings of the Free African Union Society and the African Benevolent Society," William H. Robinson, Rhode Island College, 1976, pp. 26-27

101 "Black Founders: The Free Black Community in the Early Republic," Richard S. Newman, The Library Company of Philadelphia, 2008, pp. 37

102 The Life of William J. Brown of Providence, RI, Books for Libraries Press, 1971, pp. 84

103 Dictionary of Afro-American Slavery, Edited by Randall M. Miller and John David Smith, Greenwood Press, 1997, pp. 324.

104 The Life of William J. Brown of Providence, RI, Books for Libraries Press, 1971, pp. 5.

105 The Works of Samuel Hopkins, D.D., A Memoir of His Life and Character, Sewall Harding, Doctrinal Tract and Book Society, Vol I, 1854, pp. 133

106 In Hope of Liberty: Culture, Community and Protest Among Northern Free Blacks, 1700-1860, James Oliver Horton & Lois E. Horton, Oxford University Press, 1997,

107 "Cesar Lyndon's Lists, Letters, and a Pig Roast: A Sundry Account Book," Tara Bynum, Early American Literature Vol. 53, No. 3 (2018), pp. 839-849

108 *The System of Doctrines, Contained in Divine Revelation*, Samuel Hopkins, D.D. Isaiah Thomas & Ebenezer T. Andrews Printers, 1793

109 *An Historical Discourse on the Civil and Religious Affairs of the Colony of Rhode Island*, John Callender,

Second Edition, by Romeo Elton, Knowles, Vose & Company, 1838, pp. 87

110 *Changes in the Land: Indians, Colonists, and the Ecology of New England*, William Cronon, Hill & Wang, 1983, pp. 56

111 An CT for the permitting of Illegal and Clandestine Purchases of the Native Indians in this Colony, March 1, 1663, Rhode Island State Archives

112 An ACT to prevent Indians being abused and wronged by designing and ill-minded Persons, in making them Servants, June 3, 1730, Rhode Island State Archives

113 An ACT enabling George Ninigret Indian Sachem, to sell some Lands in the Narragansett Country, for the Payment of his just Debt, February 15, 1741, Rhode Island State Archives

114 "Indian Labor in Early Rhode Island," John A. Sainsbury, New England Quarterly, Vol. 48, Np. 3 (September 1975) pp. 379

115 *Narragansett Tribe of Indians: Report of the Committee of Investigation, A Historical Sketch and Evidence Taken*, House of Representatives, January Session 1880, E.L. Freeman & Company Printers, 1880, pp. 16

116 "Death of Thomas Ninigret, Sachem," Boston Evening Post, December 4, 1769

117 Tobias Shattock Letter, Great Britain Indian Department Collection, Manuscripts Division, William L. Clements Library, University of Michigan, 1997. M-4653, https://quod.lib.umich.edu/c/clementsead/umich-wcl-M-4653gre?view=text

118 Narragansett Tribe of Indians: Report of the Committee of Investigation, A Historical sketch and Evidence Taken, House of Representatives, January Session 1880, E.L. Freeman & Company Printers, 1880, pp.53

119 Rethinking Schooling and Literacy in Eighteenth Century Algonquian Communities in Southern New England, Alanna Rice, American Indian Culture and Research Journal, No. 34:3, 2010, pp.47

120 A Statement of the Case of the Narragansett Tribe of Indians, James N. Arnold, Mercury Publishing, 1806, pp. 9

121 An ACT Impowering the Town Council of each respective Town, to prevent Disorderly Indian Dances, June 23, 1729, Rhode Island State Archives

122 *Bodies Politic: Negotiating Race in the Ameican North, 1730-1830*, John Wood Sweet, University of Pennsylvania Press, 2003, pp. 54

123 *Narragansett Tribe of Indians: Report of the Committee of Investigation, A Historical sketch and Evidence Taken*, House of Representatives, January Session 1880, E.L. Freeman & Company Printers, 1880, pp. 19

124 The Afro-Yankees: Providence Black Community in the Antebellum Era, Robert J. Cottrol, Greenwood Press, 1982, pp. 41

125 The Proceedings of the Free African Union Society and the African Benevolent Society, William H. Robinson, Rhode Island College, 1976, pp. 20

126 "History of Free and Accepted Masons, (Prince Hall) in Rhode Island: 'From Whence We Came,'" Dr. Carl Russell Gross, (1971), Dr. Carl Russell Gross Collection, Rhode Island College Archives

127 The Proceedings of the Free African Union Society and the African Benevolent Society, William H. Robinson, Rhode Island College, 1976, pp. 16

128 White Americans in Black Africa: Black and White American Methodist Missionaries in Liberia, 1820-1875, Eunjin Park, Routledge Publishing, 2001, pp. 9

129 "The Providence African Society's Sierra Leone Emigration Scheme, 1794-1795: Prologue to the African Colonization Movement," George E. Brooks, Jr., The International Journal of African Historical Studies, Vol. 7, No. 2 (1974), pp. 196

130 Newport Gardner (1746-1826), The Black Perspective in Music, Vol. 4, No. 2, Bicentennial Number (Jul., 1976), pp. 207

131 Christian Slavery: Conversion and Race in the Protestant Atlantic World, Katharine Gerbner, University of Pennsylvania Press, 2018, pp. 11

132 The Life of William J. Brown of Providence, R.I., Books for Libraries Press, 1971, pp. 46

133 The Life of William J. Brown of Providence, R.I., Books for Libraries Press, 1971, pp. 41

134 A Short History of the African Meeting House and School House, Brown & Danford, 1821, pp. 4

135 Ibid., pp. 5

136 Ibid., pp. 28

137 The Life of William J. Brown of Providence, R.I., Books for Libraries Press, 1971, pp. 83

138 A Heritage Discovered: Blacks in Rhode Island, Rowena Stewart, Rhode Island Black Heritage Society, 1984, pp. 52 139   Ibid., pp. 59

140 "Strange Bedfellows: The Politics Of Race In Antebellum Rhode Island," Erik J. Chaput and Russell J. DeSimone, Common Place: The Journal of American Life, Issue 10.2 (January, 2010)

141 The Definitive Journals of Lewis & Clark, Joseph Whitehouse, Volume 11, University of Nebraska Press, 2001, pp. 30

142 Jim Crow North: The Struggle for Equal Rights in Antebellum New England, Richard Archer, Oxford University Press, 2017, pp. 16

143 The Life of William J. Brown of Providence, R.I., Books for Libraries Press, 1971, pp. 89

144 Warning Out in New England, 1656-1817, Josiah Henry Brenton, W.B. Clarke Company, 1911, pp. 10

145 The Afro-Yankees: Providence Black Community in the Antebellum Era, Robert J. Cottrol, Greenwood Press, 1982, pp. 52

146 Ibid., pp. 54

147 Providence Gazette Newspaper, July 7, 1824, https://www.genealogybank.com/

148 The Life of William J. Brown of Providence, R.I., Books for Libraries Press, 1971, pp. 89

149 American Work: Four Centuries of Black and White Labor, Jacqueline Jones, W.W. Norton & Company, 1998, pp. 247

150 Memoirs of Elleanor Eldridge, Frances H. Green, B.T. Albro, Providence, 1838, pp. 36

151 Creative Survival: The Providence Black Community in 19th Century Providence, Rhode Island Black Heritage Society Exhibit and Publication, 1988, pp. 45

152 The Life of William J. Brown of Providence, R.I., Books for Libraries Press, 1971, pp. 89

153 History of the Providence Riots, From September 21 to September 24, 1831, Providence Committee, H.H. Brown, 1831, pp. 18

154 Creative Survival: The Providence Black Community in 19th Century Providence, Rhode Island Black Heritage Society Exhibit and Publication, 1988, pp. 60

155 Rhode Island American Newspaper, October 11, 1831, https://www.genealogybank.com/

156 Rhode Island Patriot Newspaper, October 1, 1831, https://www.genealogybank.com/

157 Independent Inquirer Newspaper, December 30, 1824, https://www.genealogybank.com/

158 Cities in American Political History, Richardson Dillworth, Editor, CQ Press, 2011, pp.207

159 Creative Survival: The Providence Black Community in 19th Century Providence, Rhode Island Black Heritage Society Exhibit and Publication, 1988, pp. 45

160 Creative Survival: The Providence Black Community in 19th Century Providence, Rhode Island Black Heritage Society Exhibit and Publication, 1988, pp. 47

161 "Encouraging Faithful Domestic Servants: Race, Deviance, and Social Control in Providence," Jane Lancaster, Rhode Island History, Vol. 51, No. 3, pp. 72

162 Creative Survival: The Providence Black Community in 19th Century Providence, Rhode Island Black Heritage Society Exhibit and Publication, 1988, pp. 46

163 The Irish Bridget: Irish Immigrant Women in Domestic Service in America, 1840-1930, Margaret Lynch-Brennan, Syracuse University Press, 2009, pp. 22

164 "Reluctant Charity: Poor Laws in the Original Thirteen States," William P. Quigley, University of Richmond law review, Vol. 31, Issue 1, 1997 pp. 137

165 Dark Work: The Business of Slavery in Rhode Island, Christy Clark-Pujara, New York University Press, 2016, pp. 99

166 Disorderly House Keepers: Poor Women in Providence, Rhode Island, 1781-1832, Andrew T. Polta, Master Theses, University of Rhode Island, 2018, pp.63

167 Down and Out in Early America, Billy G. Smith, Pennsylvania State University Press, 2004, pp. 53

168 Women and Freedom in Early America, Larry L. Eldridge, New York University Press, 1997, pp. 272

169 Disorderly House Keepers: Poor Women in Providence, Rhode Island, 1781-1832, Andrew T. Polta, Master Theses, University of Rhode Island, 2018, pp.12

170 Providence Town Council Minute Book, Providence City Archives (hereafter PTC), 9A:182-183. Disorderly House Keepers: Poor Women in Providence, Rhode Island, 1781-1832, Andrew T. Polta, Master Theses, University of Rhode Island, 2018, pp.9

171 Dr. Carl Russell Gross Collection, Jane P. Adams Library, Rhode Island College, Manuscript D, pp. 16

172 Women and Freedom in Early America, Larry L. Eldridge, Editor, New York University Press, 1997, pp. 284

173 The Free African American Cultural Landscape: Newport, RI, 1774-1826, Akeia A. F. Benard, Dissertation – University of Connecticut, 2008, pp. 224

174 Record 7:549, Providence City Archives. Providence Town Council. "Providence Town Council Records Book," 1800. 1789-1801 [7:549]. Providence City Archives)

175 Minutes of the African Union Society of Newport 1787-1824, Special Collections, Newport Historical Society

176 "Colonizing the Children: Indian Youngsters in Servitude in Early Rhode Island," Ruth Wallis Herndon and Ella Wilcox Sekatau, Colonial Society of Massachusetts, Vol. 7, (April 2003) pp. 138

177 Ibid., pp.139

178 "Indian Labor in Early Rhode Island," John A. Sainsbury, New England Quarterly, Vol. 48, Np. 3,

(September 1975) pp. 378

179 Indian Slavery in Colonial America, Alan Gallay, Editor, University of Nebraska Press, 2010, pp.58

180 "Miscegenation and Acculturation in the Narragansett County of Rhode Island, 1771—1790," Rhett S. Jones, Trotter Review, Vol. 3, Issue 1, Article 4, (1989), pp. 10

181 Ibid., pp. 10

182 History of Providence County, Vol I & II, Ed. by Richard M. Bayles; W.W. Preston & Co., NY. 1891, pp.197

183 "Social Turmoil and Governmental Reform in Providence, 1820-1832," Howard P. Chudacoff and Theodore C. Hirt, Rhode Island History, Vol. 31, No. 1, (February 1972), pp. 21

184 History of Providence County, Vol I & II, Ed. by Richard M. Bayles; W.W. Preston & Co., NY. 1891, pp.200

185 "Encouraging Faithful Domestic Servants: Race, Deviance, and Social Control in Providence," Jane Lancaster, Rhode Island History, Vol. 51, No. 3 (August 1993) pp. 85

186 Charter of the City of Providence, And the Act of the General Assembly for Organizing the Government Under the Name, Passed at October Session, 1831, Also the Mayor's Address to the City Council, June 4, 1832, Printed by the Order of the City Council, William Marshall and Company Printers, 1832, City of Providence Archives, pp. 21

187 Ibid., pp. 27

188 Ibid., pp. 27

189 The Providence Plantations for 250 Years: A Historical Review of Foundation, Rise and Progress of the City of Providence, J.A. & R.A. Reid Publishers, 1886, pp. 114-115

190 "Social Turmoil and Governmental Reform in Providence, 1820-1832," Howard P. Chudacoff and Theodore C. Hirt, Rhode Island History, Vol. 31, No. 1, (February 1972), pp. 28

191 King's Pocket-Book of Providence, R.I., Moses King, Cambridge, Mass., Tibbitts, Shaw & Co., Providence, RI, 1882, pp. 105

192 New England Artisan, and Laboring Man's Repository, Thursday, Jun 07, 1832, Providence, RI, https://www.genealogybank.com/

193 "Miscegenation and Acculturation in the Narragansett County of Rhode Island, 1771—1790," Rhett S. Jones, Trotter Review, Vol. 3, Issue 1, Article 4, (1989), pp. 10

194 U.S. Federal Census, 1790, Smithfield, RI, pp. 218

195 MSS452S6B14, Part F, 1833, Rhode Island Historical Society

196 "'Neither Justice nor Mercy": Public and Private Executions in Rhode Island, 1832–1833, Stephen Chambers, The New England Quarterly, Vol. 82, No. 3 (September 2009), pp. 437

197 Providence Industrial Sites, Statewide Historical Preservation Report, P-P-6, Rhode Island Historical Preservation Commission, (July 1981), pp. 5

198 "The Business of Slavery and Antislavery Sentiment: The Case of Rowland Gibson Hazard – An Antislavery "Negro Cloth" Dealer," Christy Clark-Pujara, Rhode Island History Journal, Vol 71, (Summer/ Fall 2013), pp. 35

199 Robert Stafford of Cumberland: Growth of a Planter, Mary R. Bullard, University of Georgia Press, 1995, pp. 276

200 Providence Patriot Newspaper, June 19, 1822, https://www.genealogybank.com/

201 An ACT Incorporating Certain Person by the Name of the Providence Society for the Abolition of

Slavery, June 1790, Rhode Island State Archives

202 "Rhode Island and the Slave Trade," J. Stanley Lemons, Rhode Island Historical Society, Vol. 60, No. 4, (Fall 2002), pp. 97

203 Providence Daily Journal, November 4, 1835, https://www.genealogybank.com/

204 Ibid.

205 "The Business of Slavery and Antislavery Sentiment: The Case of Rowland Gibson Hazard – Antislavery "Negro Cloth" Dealer," Christy Clark-Puara, Rhode Island History Journal, Vol 71, (Summer/Fall 2013), pp. 50

206 Charter of Harmony Lodge in Providence, December 20, 1826, Rhode Island Black Heritage Society

207 The Proceedings of the Convention with Their Address to The Free Persons of Color in the United States, J.W. Allen Printers, 1831

208 A Short History of the African Meeting House and School House, Brown & Danford, 1821, pp. 4 209
The Afro-Yankees: Providence's Black Community in the Antebellum Era, Robert J. Cottrol, Greenwood Press, 1982, pp. 8

210 Petition of the Coloured People for Relief Against Taxes, July 11, 1831, Rhode Island State Archives.

211 The Life of William J. Brown of Providence, RI, Books for Libraries Press, 1971, pp.86

212 The "Mustard Seed": Providence's Alfred Niger, Antebellum Black Voting Rights Activist, C.J. Martin, Small State Big History, August 1, 2020, http://smallstatebighistory.com/the-mustard-seed-providences-alfred-niger-antebellum-black-voting-rights-activist/

213 "Strange Bedfellows: The Politics of Race In Antebellum Rhode Island," Erik J. Chaput and Russell J. DeSimone, Common Place: The Journal of American Life, Issue 10.2 (January, 2010)

214 "Proslavery and Antislavery Politics in Rhode Island's 1842 Dorr Rebellion," Erik J. Chaput, The New England Quarterly, Vol. 85, No. 4 (December 2012), pp. 659

215 The Afro-Yankees: Providence's Black Community in the Antebellum Era, Robert J. Cottrol, Greenwood Press, 1982, pp. 73

216 Creative Survival: The Providence Black Community in 19th Century Providence, Rhode Island Black Heritage Society Exhibit and Publication, 1988, pp. 58

217 The Afro-Yankees: Providence's Black Community in the Antebellum Era, Robert J. Cottrol, Greenwood Press, 1982, pp. 73-74

218 New Age Constitutional Advocate Newspaper, October 22, 1841, Providence, RI. https://www.genealogybank.com/

219 Ibid.

220 The Tide Taken at Flood: The Black Suffrage Movement During the Dorr Rebellion in the State of Rhode Island, Caleb T. Horton, Providence City Archives, pp.4

221 The Afro-Yankees: Providence's Black Community in the Antebellum Era, Robert J. Cottrol, Greenwood Press, 1982, pp.76

222 The Life of William J. Brown of Providence, RI, Books for Libraries Press, 1971, pp. 160
Press, 1982, pp.77

223 The Afro-Yankees: Providence's Black Community in the Antebellum Era, Robert J. Cottrol, Greenwood

224 The Life of William J. Brown, Books for Libraries Press, 1971, pp. 58

225 "A Heritage Discovered: Blacks in Rhode Island," Rhode Island Black Heritage Society, 1988, pp.19

226 Anglo African Newspaper, Vol. II, No. 37, Published by Robert Hamilton, New York, April 11, 1863, Stokes Family Collection

227 "Will the General Assembly Put Down Caste Schools?" George T. Downing, 1857, Cornell University Digital Reprint, 1992, pp. 7

228 Life of George Henry: Together with a Brief History of the Colored People in America, George Henry, H.I. Gould & Company, 1894, pp.67

229 The Afro-Yankees: Providence's Black Community in the Antebellum Era, Robert J. Cottrol, Greenwood Press, 1982, pp. 91

230 Petition Asking for Equal School Rights, January 15,1862, Rhode Island State Archives

231 Notable Black American Women, Book II, Jessie Carney Smith, Editor, Gale Research Inc., 1996, pp.417

232 "The End of School Segregation in Rhode Island," Erik Chaput & Russell J. DeSimone, Small State, Big History: The Online Review of Rhode Island History, (August 2016) http://smallstatebighistory.com/ end-school-desegregation-rhode-island/

233 Dr. Carl Russell Gross Collection, Jane P. Adams Library, Rhode Island College, Manuscript D, pp. 20

234 "A Heritage Discovered: Blacks in Rhode Island," Rowena Stewart, Rhode Island Black Heritage Society, 1984, pp. 24

235 Creative Survival: The Providence Black Community in 19th Century Providence, Rhode Island Black Heritage Society Exhibit and Publication, 1988, pp.58

236 Ibid., 65

237 "The African Repository," Vol. 35, 1859, American Colonization Society, C. Alexander, Printer, 1859, pp. 303

238 Providence Directory and Rhode Island Business Directory, No. XLIX, Sampson, Murdock, & Company, 1889, pp. 773

239 An Act to Secure To All Persons Within The Sate Their Civil Rights, January Session, A. D. 1884, State of Rhode Island and Providence Plantations, Rhode Island State Archives.

240 New York Age Newspaper, April 26, 1890, https://www.genealogybank.com/

241 "The Negro in Rhode Island: His Past, Present and Future," Reverend Mahlon Van Horne, Stokes Family Collection and Rhode Island Black Heritage Society, 1887

242 "Scattered to the Winds of Heaven: Narragansett Indians, 1676-1880," Glenn LaFantaisie and Paul Campbell, Rhode Island History (August 1978) pp.67

243 Parsons Daily Eclipse Newspaper, Parsons, Kansas, August 21,1891, Newspapers.com, https://www.newspapers.com/image/419139525/

244 "Scattered to the Winds of Heaven: Narragansett Indians, 1676-1880," Glenn LaFantaisie and Paul Campbell, Rhode Island History (August 1978) pp. 76

245 Becoming Brothertown: Native American Ethnogenesis and Endurance in the Modern World, Graig N. Cipolla, University of Arizona Press, 2013, pp. 170

246 "Scattered to the Winds of Heaven: Narragansett Indians, 1676-1880," Glenn LaFantaisie and Paul Campbell, Rhode Island History (August 1978) pp. 77

247 Moses Stanton Correspondences, MSS629SG3S1, 1842-1843, Rhode Island Historical Society

248 Newport Mercury Newspaper, August 19, 1843, Genealogy Bank, https://www.genealogybank.com/

249 Common Houses in America's Small Towns: The Atlantic Seaboard to the Mississippi Valley, John A. Jakle & Robert W. Bastian, Georgia Press, 1989, pp. 29

250 An Act the speedier Trial of such Negro and Indian Slaves, May 7, 1718, Rhode Island State Archives

251 "Miscegenation and Acculturation in the Narragansett Country of Rhode Island, 1771—1790," Rhett S. Jones, Trotter Review, Vol. 3, Issue 1, Article 4, (1989), pp.10

252 Public Laws of the State of Rhode Island and Providence Plantations, Printed at Providence by Carter and Wilkinson, 1798

253 Legal History of the Color Line: The Rise and Triumph of the One-Drop Rule, Frank W. Sweet, Backintyme Books, 2005, pp. 11

254 Democratic and Weekly Sentinel, Burlington, Vermont, August 23, 1879, https://www.newspapers.com/

255 "The Last Chief: Head of the Narragansett Tribe of Indians is Dead," Providence Evening Bulletin, December 4, 1899, https://www.genealogybank.com/

256 Report of Commission on the Affairs of the Narragansett Indians Made to the General Assembly, E.L. Freeman & Company, January Session, 1881, pp. 59-61

257 An ACT to abolish the tribal authority and tribal relations of the Narragansett Tribe of Indians, January Session, A.D. 1880, Rhode Island State Archives

Acts, Resolves and Reports of the General Assembly of the State of Rhode Island and Providence Plantations, Part I, E.L. Freeman & Company Printers, 1880 pp.101-103

258 Supreme Court of Rhode Island at Providence, The Narragansett Indians, 20 R.I. 715 (R.I. 1898), 40 A. 347, Decided Feb 24, 1898

259 *An Expression From The Oppressed*, Pamphlet, March 12, 1902, Newport, Rhode Island, Stokes Family Collection

260 "Against Southern Outrages," New York Freeman, December 14, 1889, https://www.genealogybank.com/

261 *African American Civil Rights: Early Activism and the Niagara Movement*, Angela Jones, Praeger Books, 2011, pp. 87

262 *The Encyclopedia of African American History 1896 to the Present*, Paul Finkelman, Editor, Vol. I, A-C, Oxford University Press, 2009, pp. 26

263 Dr. Carl Russell Gross Collection, Jane P. Adams Library, Rhode Island College, Manuscript D, pp. 26

264 Ibid., pp.27

265 From Immigrant to Ethnic: Interview with Joseph LeCount by Joseph Conforti, Rhode Island Ethnic Studies Project, Oral Interview #15, Tape 1, Side 1, May 14 1976

266 The Story of a Sub-Pioneer, Sara M. Algeo, Snow & Farnham Company, 1925, pp. 162

267 The Formation of the NAACP Providence Branch, Edward K. Hooks, Rhode Island Black Heritage Society, 2013, pp. 4

268 The Crisis: A Record of the Darker Races, James W. Ivy, Editor, Vol. 65, No. 10, (December 1958), pp. 635 269 The Birth of a Nation and the Making of the NAACP, Stephen Weinberger, Journal of American Studies

Vol. 45, No. 1, (February 2011), pp. 78

270 Providence Evening Bulletin, "Record Price Paid for Birth Of A Nation," August 28, 1915, https://www.genealogybank.com/

271 New York Age, "Providence Preachers Make Denial," November 4, 1915, https://www.newspapers.com/

272 Providence Evening Bulletin, "Record Price Paid for Birth Of A Nation," August 28, 1915, https://www.genealogybank.com/

273 *African Americans Confront Lynching: Strategies of Resistance from the Civil War to the Civil Rights Era*, Christopher Waldrep, Rowman & Littlefield Publishers, Inc., 2009, pp. 55

274 *Providence Evening Bulletin*, "Negroes Do Not Care For Their Own Race," March 3, 1904, https://www.newspapers.com/

275 *Providence Evening Bulletin*, "Boy Killed, Negro Is Hunted By Mob," July 5, 1913, Stokes Family Collection

276 Newport Mercury, "Murder Verdict In Smith Case," January 24, 1914, https://www.newspapers.com/

277 W.E.B. DuBois: A Biography, David Levering Lewis, Henry Holt and Company, LLC, 2009

278 Pre-Drive Meeting of the Providence Branch, NAACP, April 15, 1920, Pamphlet, Collections of Rhode Island Black Heritage Society

279 *Providence Evening Bulletin*, "Lawton Attacked In Negro Meeting For His Attitude," April 16, 1920, https://www.newspapers.com

280 "Urges Enactment of Ant-Lynching Law," *Newport Mercury*, October 17, 1930, https://www.newspapers.com/

281 *New York Age*, "Colored Women Denied Work in Rhode Island," November 9, 1918, https://www.newspapers.com/

282 Dr. Carl Russell Gross Collection, Jane P. Adams Library, Rhode Island College, Manuscript D, pp. 26
Ibid., pp.29

283 The Crisis: A Record of the Darker Races, Vol. 17, No. 1, "The Colored Woman In Industry," Mary E. Jackson, (September 1918), pp.12-16

284 Association Monthly Magazine, Vol. XII, No. 10, "Colored Girls in the Second Line of Defense," Mary E. Jackson, (October 1918), pp. 363-364

285 The Crisis: A Record of the Darker Races, Vol. 18, No. 1, (May 1919), pp.13-15

286 *Red Summer: The Summer of 1919 and the Awakening of Black America*, Cameron McWhirter, Henry Holt and Company, 2011, pp. 253

287 *Providence Journal*, "Protest Parade By 1000 Negroes," October 15, 1917, https://www.newspapers.com/

288 *They Called Themselves the K.K.K: The Birth of an American Terrorist Group*, Susan Campbell Bartoletti, Houghton Mifflin Harcourt, 2010, pp. 13

289 Ibid., pp. 40

290 "The Klu Klux Klan in Rhode Island," Norman W. Smith, Rhode Island History, Vol. 37, No. 2, (May 1978), pp. 40

291 *Newport Mercury*, "Alleged Klan Meeting," March 8, 1924, https://www.newspapers.com/

292 The Ku Klux Klan in Rhode Island, Norman W. Smith, Rhode Island History, Vol. 37, No. 2, (May 1978), pp. 40 Ibid., pp. 40

293 *A State-by-State History of Race and Racism in the United States*, Patricia Reid-Merritt, Editor, ABC-CLIO, Incorporated, 2018, pp.772

294 *Buffalo Truth News*, Buffalo, New York, "KKK Charter in RI," September 17, 1925, https://www.newspapers.com/

295 Jews in Cape Verde: The Rhode Island Connection, Richard A. Lobban, Jr., Ph.D., Rhode Island Jewish Historical Notes, Volume 12, No. 3, (November 1997), pp. 343

296 *The Forgotten Diaspora: Jewish Communities in West Africa and the Making of the Atlantic World*, Peter Mark and Jose Da Silva Horta, Cambridge University Press, 2011, pp. 52

297 *Cape Verdeans in Rhode Island: A Brief History*, Waltraud Berger Coli and Richard A. Lobban, Rhode Island Ethnic Heritage Pamphlet Series, Rhode Island Publications Society, 1990, pp. 4

298 *Between Race and Ethnicity: Cape Verdean America Immigrants, 1860-1965*, Marilyn Halter, University of Illinois Press, 1993, pp. 4

299 *The Forgotten Diaspora: Jewish Communities in West Africa and the Making of the Atlantic World*, Peter Mark and Jose Da Silva Horta, Cambridge University Press, 2011, pp. 37.

300 *Cape Verdeans in Rhode Island: A Brief History*, Waltraud Berger Coli and Richard A. Lobban, Rhode Island Ethnic Heritage Pamphlet Series, Rhode Island Publications Society, 1990, pp. 21

301 *The Crisis: Record of the Darker Races*, Vol. 49, No. 3, (March 1942), pp.101

302 *Cape Verdeans in Rhode Island: A Brief History*, Waltraud Berger Coli and Richard A. Lobban, Rhode Island Ethnic Heritage Pamphlet Series, Rhode Island Publications Society, 1990, pp. 31

303 Forgotten Fox Point, Remembering Race at Brown Blog Series, Mia Gold, (November 2014) https://blogs.brown.edu/ethn-0790d-s01/2014/11/12/forgotten-fox-point-an-examination-of-the-expansion-of-brown-university-and-the-development-of-the-cape-verdean-fox-point-community/

304 *Final Environmental Impact Statement & Final Section 4(f)/6(f) Evaluation: Improvements to I-195, Providence, Rhode Island*, Rhode Island Department of Transportation, Lincoln Almond Governor, (August 1996), pp. 3-88

305 *Black Republicans and the Transformation of the GOP*, Joshua D. Farrington, University of Pennsylvania Press, 2016, pp. 11

306 *Encyclopedia of the Harlem Renaissance*, Cary D Wintz and Paul Finkelman, Editors, Vol. 2, K-Y, Routledge Press, 2004, pp.954

307 New York Age, "Providence Citizens in New Political Club," February 25, 1922, https://www.newspapers.com/

308 Ibid.

309 Dr. Carl Russell Gross Collection, Jane P. Adams Library, Rhode Island College, Manuscript D, pp. 33

310 Who's Who of the Colored Race: A General Biographical Dictionary of Men and Women of African Descent, Frank Lincoln Mather, 1915

311 *Providence Evening Bulletin*, January 28, 1921, https://www.genealogybank.com/

312 "Monster Mass Meeting, Providence Colored Democratic Club, November 5, 1934," Pamphlet, Rhode Island Black Heritage Society Collections

313 *An Assessment of Life in Rhode Island as an African American in the Era from 1918 to 1993*, Andrew J. Bell, Vantage Press, 1997, pp. 54

314 The New Deal and American Indian Tribalism: The Administration of the Indian Reorganization Act, 1934-45, Graham D. Taylor, University of Nebraska Press, pp. 1

315 *The Narragansett Dawn*, Princess Redwing, Editor, Vol. 2, No. 5, (September 1936), pp.2

316 Ibid., pp. 2

317 Act of June 18, 1934, (Indian Reorganization Act), Chapter 576 of the 73rd Congress, Approved June 18, 1934, Section 19

318 Federalism and the State Recognition of Native American Tribes: A Survey of State-Recognized Tribes and State Recognition Processes across the United States," A. Koenig and J. Stein, Santa Clara Law Review, vol. 48, no. 1, pp. 77–153, 2008.

319 *The Color of Law: A Forgotten History of How Our Government Segregated America*, Robert Rothstein, Liveright Publishing Corporation, 2017, pp.64

320 Federal Housing Administration, Marie Justine Fritz, Encyclopedia Britannica, https://www.britannica.com/topic/Federal-Housing-Administration

321 FHA Underwriting Manual, 1936, Section 233, http://wbhsi.net/~wendyplotkin/DeedsWeb/fha36.html

322 "Homeownership Loan Corporation Redlining Maps: The Persistent Structure of Segregation and Economic Inequality," Bruce Mitchell and Juan Franco, NCRC Research, 2018, pp.4

323 Homeowners Loan Corporation Map, City of Providence, 1935, Providence City Archive

324 Housing Act of 1959, Hearings Before the Committee on Banking and Currency, United States Senate, Eighty-Sixth Congress, First Session, January 22-28, 1959, pp. 818

325 The Providence Survey: A Study in Community Planning, Community Chests & Councils of America, Inc. (May 1936) p. 75

326 Rhode Island General Laws, Title 45 - Towns and Cities, Chapter 45-25 - City Housing Authorities, Section 45-25-2 - Declaration of Necessity

327 *World War II Rhode Island*, Christian McBurney, History Press, 2017, pp. 91

328 "Last Hired, First Fired: Black Women Workers During World War II," Karen Tucker Anderson, Journal of American History, Vol. 69, Issue 1 (June 1982) pp. 82

329 "James N. Williams to Speak on Race Relations," *The Archway Newspaper*, Bryant University, Vol. XXII, No. 12, (April 1961)

330 *A Community of Spirit: People of Color in Providence, Rhode Island, 1870-1950*, Jan Armstrong, Rhode Island Black Heritage Society, 1998, pp. 190-193

331 Ibid., pp. 197

332 "The Hosts Of Black Labor," W. E. Burghardt Du Bois, *The Nation*, Vol. 116 (May 9, 1923), pp. 539-41.

333 *Report of the Commission on the Employment Problems of the Negro*, Governor's Commission To Employment Problems of the Negro, (May 1943), Rhode Island State Archives

334 Ibid.

335 Ibid. pp. 5

336 Ibib., pp. 25-27
337 Ibid., pp. 46
338 Ibid., pp. 48
339 R.I. Governor Asks FEP Act, Burlington Daily News, January 6, 1948
340 Rhode Island Public Law, 1949, TITLE 28, Labor and Labor Relations, CHAPTER 28-5, Fair Employment Practices, SECTION 28-5-1
341 CHAPTER 28-5, Fair Employment Practices, SECTION 28-5-13
342 CHAPTER 28-5, Fair Employment Practices, SECTION 28-5-8
343 Fair Employment Practice Legislation in the United States, Federal, State, Municipal, W. Brooke Graves, Library of Congress Legislative Reference Service, April, 1951, pp. 81
344 Annul Report of the R.I. Commission Against Discrimination, State of Rhode Island, March 10, 1953, pp. 20 345   The Ships from Field's Point Providence, RI 1942-1945, Dorrance Publishing, C. Roger Wallin, 2017, pp. 5 346   "Nearly 700 Negroes Hired in 3 Month By Bridgeport Firm," New York Age, April 17, 1943, https://www.newspapers.com/
347 "African-American Led Worker Solidarity in WW2 Providence: The Story of Boilermakers Local 308," Patrick Crowley, Secretary-Treasurer, RHODE ISLAND AFL-CIO, 40th Annual North American Labor History Conference, (Oct 2018), pp. 1
348 "Suit Against Jim Crow Boilermaker Union in Rhode Island Continues, New Cases Heard," *New York Age*, June 10, 1944, https://www.newspapers.com/
349 Urban League of Rhode Island Collections, April 7, 1944, Phillips Memorial Library, Providence College
350 Ibid., November 21, 1944, Phillips Memorial Library, Providence College
351 Ibid.
352 *Opportunity: A Journal of Negro Life*, Vol. XXIII, No. 1, Winter Issue (Jan.-Mar 1945), pp. 110
353 *An Assessment of Life in Rhode Island as an African American in the Era from 1918 to 1993*, Andrew J. Bell, Vantage Press, 1997, pp. 67
354 Urban Renewal: Title I of the Housing Act of 1949, Department of Housing and Urban Development, Maurice Parkings Associates, P.C., Washington, D.C., 1968
355 *Native American Archaeology In Rhode Island*, Rhode Island Historical Preservation & Heritage Commission, 2002, pp. 55
356 *Native Providence: Memory, Community and Survivance in the Northeast*, Patricia Rubertone, University of Nebraska Press, 2020
357 *Report of Commission on the Affairs of the Narragansett Indians Made to the General Assembly*, E.L. Freeman & Company, January Session, 1881, pp. 133-141
358 "Race and the Census: The "Negro" Controversy," D'Vera Cohn, Pew Research Center, Social and Demographic Trends, January 21, 2010, https://www.pewsocialtrends.org/2010/01/21/race-and-the- census-the-negro-controversy/
359 *Report of Commission on the Affairs of the Narragansett Indians Made to the General Assembly*, E.L. Freeman & Company, January Session, 1881, pp. 133-141

360   Ibid., pp.75

361   United States Census, 1870, 1880, 1885 https://www.ancestry.com/

362   "Indigenous Identity: What Is It, and Who Really Has It?," Hilary N. Weaver, *American Indian Quarterly*, Vol. 25, No. 2 (Spring, 2001), pp. 249

363   "The South in the North," William Dykeman and James Stokely, *New York Times*, April 17, 1960, Section SM, Page 8

364   *Jim Crow America: A Documentary History*, Edited by Catherine M. Lewis and J. Richard Lewis, University of Arkansas Press, 2009, pp. 2

365   "How Free Are We?" *Providence Journal*, James N. Rhea, December 13, 1950, https://www.genealogybank.com/

366   *The Color of Law: A Forgotten History of How Our Government Segregated America*, Richard Rothstein, Liveright Publishing Corporation, 2017, pp.31

367   *A Community Apart - a History Of Public Housing In Providence and The Providence Housing Authority*, Paul Campbell, The Rhode Island Publications Society, 2007, pp. 76

368   Ibid., pp.56

369   *Opportunity: A Journal of Negro Life*, Vol. XXL, No. 3, (July 1943), pp.132

370   *A Community Apart - a History Of Public Housing In Providence and The Providence Housing Authority*, Paul Campbell, The Rhode Island Publications Society, 2007, pp. 96

371   "Any Housing Bans Decried By Mayor," *Providence Journal*, January 7, 1950, https://www.newspapers.com/

372   *Towards Equal Opportunity: The Story of the Providence Urban League of Rhode Island in the 1940's*, Richard F. Irving, Thesis at Brown University, Providence Urban League, 1974, pp. 15

373   "Let's Have No Color Line in Public Housing," *Providence Journal*, Urban League of Rhode Island Collections, Phillips Memorial Library, June 22, 1956, Providence College

374   "Anti-Segregation Weighed," *Providence Journal*, June 22, 1956, https://www.newspapers.com/

375   Ibid., "Urban League Set to Aid Suits on Housing" *Providence Journal*, May 16, 1956

376   Ibid., "Governor Lists Total Integration Housing Policy," *Providence Journal*, September 21, 1956

377   "Irving Fain and the Fair Housing Movement in Rhode Island, 1958-1970," Joseph Conforti, Rhode Island History, Vol. 45, No. 1, (February 1986), pp. 24

      "Rhode Island Lost A Great Citizen: Irving Jay Fain," Joan Nathan Gerson, Rhode Island Jewish Historical Notes, Vol. 8, No. 3, pp. 379

378   *An Assessment of Life in Rhode Island as an African American in the Era from 1918 to 1993*, Andrew J. Bell, Vantage Press, 1997, pp. 77

379   Citizens United for a Fair Housing Law in Rhode Island, Membership List, January 7, 1959, Special Collections, Jane P. Adams Library, Rhode Island College

380   "Fair Housing Law Would Benefit Rhode Island," *Providence Journal*, January 18, 1959, https://www.genealogybank.com/

381   "Law Should Include Private Housing, "Urban League of Rhode Island Collections, January 1959, Phillips Memorial Library, Providence College

382   "500 Jam House Chamber To Hear Opponents of Fair Housing Law," Newport Daily News, February 21,

1959, https://www.newspapers.com/

383 "What is the Case For Fair Housing?" *Providence Journal* advertisement, March 29, 1960, https://www.genealogybank.com/

384 Providence Board of Realtors, March 6, 1962 Letter in Opposition to Fair Housing, Irving Jay Fain Papers, Special Collections, Jane P. Adams Library, Rhode Island College

385 "Doorley Pledges To Promote Fair Housing Bill," Providence Journal, February 16, 1965, https://www.newsbank.com/

386 Ibid

387 "Housing Is Made Law By Chafee," April 12, 1965, *Newport Daily News*, https://www.newspapers.com/ 388 Chapter 34-37, Rhode Island Fair Housing Practices Act, Section 34-37-1

389 Highway Revenue Act of 1956, Hearings Before the Committee On Ways and Means, House of Representatives, Eighty-Fourth Congress, Second Session, February 14-21, 1956, pp. 538

390 *Interstate: Highway Politics and Policy Since 1939*, Mark H. Rose and Raymond A. Mohl, University of Tennessee Press, 2012, pp. 111

391 *South Providence, Providence: A Statewide Historical Preservation Report*, Rhode Island Historical Preservation Commission, (September 1978), pp. 7

392 Ibid., pp 37-38

393 Ibid., pp. 42

394 *South Providence*, Patrick T. Conley and Paul Campbell, Arcadia Publishing, 2020, pp. 59

395 City of Providence Geographic Information System (GIS) Portal, https://www.providenceri.gov/planning/gismaps/

396 *South Providence, Providence: A Statewide Historical Preservation Report*, Rhode Island Historical Preservation Commission, (September 1978), pp.45

397 *You Don't Have A Problem Until You Do: Revitalization and Gentrification in Providence*, Fay Strongin, HousingWorksRI at Roger Williams University, 2017, pp. 3

398 "Missing The Point," *Brown Political Review*, Mitchell Johnson, March 12, 2015, https://brownpoliticalreview.org/2015/03/missing-the-point/

399 *Providence: A Citywide Survey of Historic Resources*, William McKenzie Woodward and Edward F. Sanderson, Rhode Island Historical Preservation Commission, 1986, pp. 17

400 James Baldwin Interview, *Perspectives: the Negro and the American Promise*, 1963

401 "Citizens' Views on Urban Revitalization: The Case of Providence, Rhode Island," Marion Orr and Darrell M. West, Urban Affairs Review, Vol. 37, No. 3, (January 2002), pp. 401

402 "A Study in Contradictions: The Origins and Legacy of the Housing Act of 1949," Alexander von Hoffman, Housing Policy Debate, Vol. 11, Issue 2, Fannie Mae Foundation (2000) pp. 310

403 Rhode Island General Law, Chapter 45-31, Redevelopment Agencies, Section 45-31-5

404 Ibid., Section 45-31-8

405 Housing and Displacement on Providence's East Side and Beyond, Dr. Dannie Ritchie with contributions from others, Brown University, (October 2020), pp. 10.

406 "Discrimination Keeps Negros in Lippitt Hill," *Providence Journal*, October 8, 1959, https://www.

genealogybank.com/

407   Social Plan For Community Renewal of the City of Providence, Rhode Island, Rhode Island Council for Community Services, Sidney Dillick, Ph.D., M.S.W., Executive Director and Charles R. Wood, Urban Renewal Coordinator, 1964, pp. 17

408   "The Culture of Race, Class, and Poverty: The Emergence of a Cultural Discourse in Early Cold War Social Work (1946-1963), Laura Curran, Rutgers University, The Journal of Sociology & Social Welfare, Vol. 30, Issue 3, (September 2003), pp 33

409   "We Gon' Be Alright," Jeff Chang, Picador Publishers, 2016, pp. 3

410   "The Public Menace of Blight: Urban Renewal and the Private Uses of Eminent Domain," Wendell E. Pritchett, Yale Law & Policy Review, Vol. 21, No. 1 (Winter, 2003), pp.2

411   "Negro Housing Crux Of Lippitt Hill Job," *Providence Journal*, October 25, 1959, https://www.genealogybank.com/

412   *An Assessment of Life in Rhode Island as an African American in the Era from 1918 to 1993*, Andrew J. Bell, Vantage Press, 1997, pp. 81

413   *Elmwood, Providence*, Statewide Historical Preservation Report, Rhode Island Historical Preservation Commission, (June 1979), pp. 4

414   "Industrial Park OKd For Mashapaug Pond," *Providence Journal*, May 6, 1960, https://www.genealogybank.com/

415   "Human Values Stressed In Mashapaug Pond Area Plan," The Evening Bulletin, September 20, 1960, https://www.genealogybank.com/

416   *Mashapaug Pond Redevelopment Plan for the Huntington Expressway Industrial Park*, Providence Redevelopment Agency, City of Providence, Rhode Island, 1960

417   *Remembering West Elmwood: Before & After Displacement*, Lucy Asako Boltz, An Oral History Collection Project, Ebenezer Baptist Church, Providence, RI, May 7, 2016, pp. 24

418   "City Relocates Firms," Providence Journal, January 31, 1960, https://www.genealogybank.com/

419   City of Providence Geographic Information System (GIS) Portal, https://www.providenceri.gov/planning/gismaps/

420   African American Site Survey of College Hill, Rhode Island Historical & Preservation Commission & Rhode Island Black Heritage Society, U.S. Department of Interior, National Park Service Grant, 2009, Section 8, Page 1

421   Ibid., Section 8, Page 3

422   Machine Politics and Urban Renewal in Providence, Rhode Island: The Era of Mayor Joseph A. Doorley, Jr., 1965-74, Carl Antonucci, History and Classics Dissertations and Masters Theses, Providence College, (May 2012) pp. 94

423   "Student Housing Choices and Neighborhood Change: Brown University 1937–1987," Nathaniel Philip Pettit and Marijoan Bull, MDPI, Published: 8 November 2020, pp. 7

424   *College Hill: A Demonstration Study of Historic Area Renewal*, Providence City Plan Commission, Providence Preservation Society, City Plan Commission, Providence, Rhode Island, 1967

425   Ibid., pp. 192

426   Ibid., 195

427 Homeowners Loan Corporation Map, City of Providence, 1935, Providence City Archive

428 Demonstration Cities And Metropolitan Development Act of 1966, Public Law 89-754, 89th Congress, 2nd Session, November, 4, 1966

429 "Providence Seen Ideal For Core City Project," *Providence Journal*, June 25, 1966, https://www.genealogybank.com/

430 "Doorley Defends His Thinking on Arena, S.P.," *Evening Bulletin*, March 7, 1966, https://www.newsbank.com/

431 *Machine Politics and Urban Renewal in Providence, Rhode Island: The Era of Mayor Joseph A. Doorley, Jr., 1965-74,* Carl Antonucci, History and Classics Dissertations and Masters Theses, Providence College, (May 2012) pp. 194

432 *Profile of Youth-1966: A Report Prepared at the Request of Senator Claiborne Pell of Rhode Island for the Subcommittee on Employment, Manpower and Poverty, of the Committee on Labor and Public Welfare,* United States Senate, U.S. Government Printing Office, (August 1966), pp. 764

433 *Machine Politics and Urban Renewal in Providence, Rhode Island: The Era of Mayor Joseph A. Doorley, Jr., 1965-74,* Carl Antonucci, History and Classics Dissertations and Masters Theses, Providence College, (May 2012) pp. 127

434 "Revealing the Empowerment Revolution: A Literature Review of the Model Cities Program," Brett Webber, Journal of Urban History, No. 38, (2012), pp. 173-192

435 "South Providence Negroes Aroused By Police Treatment," *Springfield News*, August 9, 1962, Original Transcript, Urban League of Rhode Island Collections, Phillips Memorial Library, Providence College

436 "Negro Leaders Still Differ With Police," *Providence Journal*, August 24, 1962, Urban League of Rhode Island Collections, Phillips Memorial Library, Providence College

437 *Machine Politics and Urban Renewal in Providence, Rhode Island: The Era of Mayor Joseph A. Doorley, Jr., 1965-74,* Carl Antonucci, History and Classics Dissertations and Masters Theses, Providence College, (May 2012) pp. 129

438 "Our History and Our Guilt," The Convocation Address of President Heffner, Brown Alumni Monthly, October 1967, pp. 5-8

439 "1968 Walkout," Protest & Perspectives: Students at Brown 1960s -90s, Brown University Library, https://library.brown.edu/create/protest6090/1968-walkout/

440 "Our History and Our Guilt," The Convocation Address of President Heffner, Brown Alumni Monthly, October 1967, pp. 5-8

441 "Our Black Heritage," *The Rhode Islander Sunday Magazine*, Providence Journal Company, October 12, 1969, Stokes Family Collection.

442 Ibid., pp. 6

443 Ibid., pp. 15

444 Ibid., pp. 33

445 For a Revolutionary Position on the Negro Question, Harry Haywood, Liberator Press, 1975

446 *An Assessment of Life in Rhode Island as an African American in the Era from 1918 to 1993*, Andrew J. Bell, Vantage Press, 1997, pp.94

447 Congressional Record: Proceedings and Debates of the 90th Congress, First Edition, Tuesday, August 22, 1967, pp. 24801- 24807

448 Ibid.

449 Ibid.

450 Statement of Mr. Clifford Monteiro, Citizens United Renewal Enterprises of Rhode Island, Inc., Hearings Before A Subcommittee of the Committee on Appropriations, United States Senate, Ninety-Second Congress, First Session on H.R.9382, Act Making Appropriations for the Department Of Housing and Urban Development, Washington, 1971, pp. 749

451 *Machine Politics and Urban Renewal in Providence, Rhode Island: The Era of Mayor Joseph A. Doorley, Jr., 1965-74*, Carl Antonucci, History and Classics Dissertations and Masters Theses, Providence College, May 2012, pp. 134

452 *School Desegregation in Providence*, Rhode Island, U.S. Department of Health, Education & Welfare, National Institute of Education, and Staff Report of the U.S. Commission of Civil Rights, October 1977, pp. 3

453 *The Bus Stops Here: A Study of School Desegregation in Three Cities*, Anna Holden, Agathon Press, 1974, pp. 168 454 *School Desegregation in Providence, Rhode Island*, U.S. Department of Health, Education & Welfare, National Institute of Education, and Staff Report of the U.S. Commission of Civil Rights, October 1977, pp. 8

455 Ibid., pp.9

456 "School Busing Plan Approved," Fitchburg Sentinel, October 7, 1966, https://www.newspapers.com/

457 *School Desegregation in Providence*, Rhode Island, U.S. Department of Health, Education & Welfare, National Institute of Education, and Staff Report of the U.S. Commission of Civil Rights, October 1977, pp.15

458 Ibid., pp. 21

459 "Too Many in R.I. Narragansett Invisible," Nashua Telegraph, May 10, 1976, https://www.newspapers.com/

460 Ibid

461 An Act to Settle Indian Land claims within the Rhode Island and Providence Plantations, PL 95-395, 95th Congress, September 30, 1978

462 Memorandum, Deputy Assistant Secretary – Indian Affairs, United States Department of the Interior, Burau of Indian Affairs, July 29, 1982, pp. 1

463 Ibid., pp.4

464 Rhode Island General Laws, Title 37 - Public Property and Works, Chapter 37-18
http://www.nigc.gov/Reading_Room/Bulletins/Bulletin_No._2004-2.aspx

465 Narragansett Justice Act, 105th Congress, 2nd Session, Report 105-692, September 9, 1998

466 National Indian Gaming Commission, Bulletin No. 04-2, 2004, https://web.archive.org/web/20120316101447/ 467 "Narragansett Leaders List Plans For Rhode Island Casino," *Hartford Courant*, July 17, 1992, https://www. newspapers.com/ 468 Ibid.

469 Public Law 104–208,104th Congress, September. 30, 1996

470 "Repeal Chafee Rider to Support Restoring IGRA Rights to the

Narragansett Tribe,"The National Congress of American Indians, Resolution #FTL-04-103, 10-15, 2004 471

Town of Charlestown v. E. Area Dir., Bureau of Indian Affairs, 35 IBIA 93 (2000)

472 "Narragansett's Smoke Shop Raid: Narragansett Indian Tribe Of Rhode Island V. The State Of Rhode Island," Charles Hickox Andrew Laviano, and Katherine Elisabeth Kosterlitz, *Northeast Journal of Legal Studies*, Vol. 18, Article 6, Fall 2009.

473 Ibid.

474 "Race Eyed in Fatal Shooting of Black Cop," *UPI*, February 4, 2000, https://www.upi.com/Archives/2000/02/04/Race-eyed-in-fatal-shooting-of-black-cop/8542949640400/

475 *The Report of Rhode Island Select Commission on Race and Police-Community Relations*, Executive Summary, May 2001

476 Ibid., pp V.

477 Ibid., pp. VI.

478 Ibid.

479 "Lawsuit Dismissed In Officer's Death," Richard Lewis, *Associated Press*, November 5, 2003

480 "Slavery and Justice: We seek to Discover the Meaning of our Past," Ruth J. Simmons, *Boston Globe*, April 28, 2004

481 *Slavery and Justice: Report of the Brown University Steering Committee on Slavery and Justice, University Steering Committee on Slavery and Justice*, Brown University, pp 85

482 Slavery and Justice Update, March 18, 2011, http://brown.edu/Research/Slavery_Justice/report/update.html

483 "Distinguishing Carcieri v. Salazar: Why the Supreme Court Got It Wrong and How Congress and the Courts Should Respond to

Preserve Tribal and Federal Interests in the IRA's Trust-Land Provisions," Sarah Washburn, Washington Law Review, Vol. 85, No. 3, 2010, pp. 604

484 Carcieri, Governor Of Rhode Island, Et Al. V. Salazar, Secretary of The Interior, Et Al., United States Supreme Court

(2009), No. 07-526, Argued: November 3, 2008, Decided: February 24, 2009

485 "Distinguishing Carcieri v. Salazar: Why the Supreme Court Got It Wrong and How Congress and the Courts Should Respond to Preserve Tribal and Federal Interests in the IRA's Trust-Land Provisions," Sarah Washburn, Washington Law Review, Vol. 85, No. 3, 2010, pp. 646

486 *An Equity Profile of Rhode Island*, Policy Link and University of Southern California Program for Environmental & Regional Equity, February 19, 2013, pp. 9

487 *Demographic Turning Points for the United States: Population Projections for 2020 to 2060*, United States Department of Commerce, U.S. Census Bureau, Jonathan Vespa, Lauren Medina, and David M. Armstrong, Issued March 2018, Revised February 2020

488 *An Equity Profile of Rhode Island*, Policy Link and University of Southern California Program for Environmental & Regional Equity, February 19, 2013, pp. 19

489 Ibid., 31

490 Health Equity Considerations & Racial & Ethnic Minority Groups, Centers For Disease Control and Prevention, National Center for Immunization and Respiratory Diseases (NCIRD), Division of Viral Diseases, July 24, 2020

491 Ibid.

492 "Latinos hit hardest by coronavirus in Rhode Island need 'tailored approach,' officials say," NBC News, Nicole Acevedo, May 27, 2020, https://www.nbcnews.com/news/latino/latinos-hit-hardest-coronavirus-rhode-island- need-tailored-approach-officials-n1215001

493 "Hispanic women, immigrants, young adults, those with less education hit hardest by COVID-19 job losses," Pew Research Center, Fact Tank/News in the Numbers, Rakesh Kochhar, June 9, 2020

494 "R.I. Department of Health data shows people of color are overrepresented in positive test cases for COVID-19," *Brown Daily Herald*, Corey Gelb-Bicknell, May 1, 2020, https://www.browndailyherald.com/2020/05/01/r-department-health-data-shows-people-color-overrepresented-positive-test-cases-covid-19/

495 *An Equity Profile of Rhode Island*, Policy Link and University of Southern California Program for Environmental & Regional Equity, February 19, 2013, pp. 80-81

496 "Black Lives Matter May Be the Largest Movement in U.S. History," Larry Buchanan, Quoctrung Bui and Jugal K. Patel, New York Times, July 3, 2020, https://www.nytimes.com/interactive/2020/07/03/us/george-floyd- protests-crowd-size.html

497 "Protest for Black Lives Matter in Providence is Massive -- and Peaceful," Amanda Milkovi, Boston Globe, June 6, 2020, https://www.bostonglobe.com/2020/06/06/metro/massive-protest-black-lives-matter-providence- starts-peacefully-ends-with-some-ignoring-curfew/

498 "Black Lives Matter and RI State Police Working Together for Peaceful Change,"WLNE ABC 6 News, Sam Cook, September 24, 2020, https://www.abc6.com/black-lives-matter-and-ri-state-police-working-together-for- peaceful-change/

499 City of Providence, Truth, Reconciliation and Reparations, https://www.providenceri.gov/community-relations/trr/

500 "In Era Of Black Lives Matter, Rhode Island Attorney General Opinion Allows Police To Hide Records Of Misconduct," ACLU, Rhode Island, August 26, 2020, https://www.aclu.org/press-releases/era-black-lives- matter-rhode-island-attorney-general-opinion-allows-police-hide

501 The Purpose of Power: How We Come Together When We Fall Apart, Alicia Garza, Penguin Random House, 2020, pp. 268

502 "Walmart Donates $50,000 to Create Black history Curriculum in RI schools," Providence Journal, February 25, 2021

503 *White Man's Burden: Slogans of Poetry By Rudyard Kipling*, Lulu Publishing, 2008

504 *The American Indian in Western Legal Thought: The Discourses of Conquest*, Robert A. Williams, Jr., Oxford University Press, 1990, pp. 325

505 "What The Future Holds: The Changing Landscape Of Federal Indian Policy," Kevin K. Washburn, Harvard Law Review, Vol. 130, No. 6, (April, 2017), pp. 231

506 Memorandum on Tribal Consultation and Strengthening Nation-to-Nation Relationships, President Jospeh R. Biden, Jr., January 26, 2021, https://www.whitehouse.gov/briefing-room/presidential-actions/2021/01/26/memorandum-on-tribal-consultation-and-strengthening-nation-to-nation-relationships/

507 Remarks of Senator Jim Webb, Subcommittee on Crime and Drugs U.S. Senate Committee on the Judiciary Hearing on the National Criminal Justice Commission Act of 2009, June 11, 2009

508 *U.S. Department of Justice, Office of Justice Programs, Bureau of Justice Statistics, Prisoners 2019 Summary*, E. Ann Carson. Emily Buehler, Stephanie Mueller, Danielle Kaeble, NCJ 255115, October 2020.

509 "The State of Black Families In Rhode Island," Economic Progress Institute, May 2017, http://www.economicprogressri.org/wp-content/uploads/2017/05/SOBRI2017_Final_digital.pdf

510 "An Unjust Burden: The Disparate Treatment of Black Americans in the Criminal Justice System," Elizabeth Hinton, Assistant Professor, Department of History and Department of African and African American Studies, Harvard University, LeShae Henderson, Special Assistant, Research, Vera Institute of Justice, and Cindy Reed, Senior Editor, Vera Institute of Justice, Vera Institute of Justice, *For the Record*, May, 2018, pp. 7

511 Ibid., pp. 2

512 ACLU Criminal Law Reform Project, American Civil Liberties Union, 2020, https://www.aclu.org/other/aclu-criminal-law-reform-project

513 Ibid.

514 Cato Institute Handbook for Policy Makers, Tim Lynch, 8th Edition, (2017)

515 Urban Institute, Urban Policy Center, https://www.urban.org/policy-centers/justice-policy-center

516 Selected Articles on Child Labor, Edna D. Bullock, H.W. Wilson Company, 1911, pp. 8-9

517 *An Equity Profile of Rhode Island, Policy Link and University of Southern California Program for Environmental & Regional Equity*, February 19, 2013, pp. 14

518 *South Providence, Providence: A Statewide Historical Preservation Report*, P-P-2, Rhode Island Historical Preservation Commission, September 1978, pp. 49

519 *Latino History in Rhode Island: Nuestras Raices,* Marta V. Martinez, History Press, 2014, pp. 25

520 Data USA, Deloitte, Datawheel, 2018, https://datausa.io/profile/geo/providence-ri/#demographics

521 "Who Are New England's Immigrants?" Mamie Marcuss and Ricardo Borgos, Federal Reserve Bank of Boston, Communities & Banking, (January 2004), pp. 12

522 "Immigrants in Rhode Island," American Immigration Council, 2020, pp. 1, https://www.americanimmigrationcouncil.org/sites/default/files/research/immigrants_in_rhode_island.pdf

523 Ibid., pp. 5

524 "What New Immigrants Could Mean For American Wages," The Hamilton Project, Brookings Institution, (August 2013) pp 2

525 "Want Immigration Reform? Look to Cities," Bloomberg City Lab, Juliana Kerr, January 23, 2018, https://www.bloomberg.com/news/articles/2018-01-23/9-ways-to-build-a-more-welcoming-city-for-immigrants

526 "The Racial Achievement Gap, Segregated Schools, and Segregated Neighborhoods – A Constitutional Insult," Richard Rothstein, Economic Policy Institute, Race and Social Problems Vol. 6, No. 4, December 2014, https://www.epi.org/publication/the-racial-achievement-gap-segregated-schools-and-segregated-neighborhoods-a-constitutional-insult/

527 "Evenness Vs. Isolation In Schools: The City Of Providence Illustrates How Segregation Gauges Can Move In Opposite Directions," Jill Barshay, U.S. News & World Report, June 2018, https://www.usnews.com/news/

education-news/articles/2018-06-25/the-complicated-facts-of-modern-school-segregation

528 "Poverty, segregation persist In US schools, report says," Maria Danilova, The Associated Press, January 11, 2018, https://www.providencejournal.com/news/20180111/poverty-segregation-persist-in-us-schools-report- says

529 U.S. Supreme Court Brown v. Board of Education of Topeka, 347 U.S. 483 (1954), Decided May 17, 1954, https://supreme.justia.com/cases/federal/us/347/483/

530 "Brown v. Board at 60: Why Have We Been So Disappointed? What Have We Learned?," Richard Rothstein, Economic Policy Institute, April 17, 2014,

531 "Evenness Vs. Isolation In Schools: The City of Providence illustrates how segregation gauges can move In opposite directions," Jill Barshay, U.S. News & World Report, June 2018, https://www.usnews.com/news/ education-news/articles/2018-06-25/the-complicated-facts-of-modern-school-segregation

532 Rhode Island General Law, CHAPTER 45-53:P Low and Moderate Income Housing, http://webserver.rilin.state.ri.us/Statutes/TITLE45/45-53/INDEX.HTM

533 "COVID-19 FAQs: Health equity In a pandemic," American Medical Association, July 28, 2020, https://www.ama-assn.org/delivering-care/health-equity/covid-19-faqs-health-equity-pandemic?gclid=CjwKCAiAsaOBBhA4EiwAo0_AnGeeDmlpG2wlCmQcmMaBmNIxJA1kC6tpsiG0wAAAsIvTGlPc0GFqIxoC1YEQAvD_BwE

534 "Are Clinicians Contributing to Excess African American COVID-19 Deaths? Unbeknownst to Them, They May Be," Adam J. Milam et al. 2020, Mary Ann Liebert, Inc., Health Equity, Volume 4.1, 2020, pp. 139-141

535 "Health Equity Considerations and Racial and Ethnic Minority Groups," Centers for Disease Control and Prevention, Feb. 12, 2021, https://www.cdc.gov/coronavirus/2019-ncov/community/health-equity/race-ethnicity.html

536 "R.I. Department Of Health Data Shows People Of Color Are Overrepresented In Positive Test Cases For COVID-19," Corey Gelb-Bicknell, Brown Daily Herald, May 1, 2020, https://www.browndailyherald.com/2020/05/01/r- department-health-data-shows-people-color-overrepresented-positive-test-cases-covid-19/

537 The COVID Tracking Data Project, The Atlantic, February 12, 2021, https://covidtracking.com/data/state/rhode-island

538 "Are Clinicians Contributing to Excess African American COVID-19 Deaths?, Adam J. Milam, et.al., Health Equity, Vol. 4.1, 2020, https://www.liebertpub.com/doi/pdfplus/10.1089/heq.2020.0015

539 "Closing the racial wealth gap requires heavy, progressive taxation of wealth." Vanessa Williamson, Brookings Blueprints for American Renewal & Prosperity Project, Wednesday, December 9, 2020, https://www.brookings.edu/research/closing-the-racial-wealth-gap-requires-heavy-progressive-taxation-of-wealth/

540 Ibid.

541 *The State of Black Families In Rhode Island*, The Economic Progress Institute, May 2017, http://www.economicprogressri.org/wp-content/uploads/2017/05/SOBRI2017_Final_digital.pdf

542 "The economic impact of closing the racial wealth gap," McKinsey & Company, August 13, 2019, https://www.mckinsey.com/industries/public-and-social-sector/our-insights/the-economic-impact-of-closing-the-racial-wealth-gap#

543 "Closing the racial wealth gap requires heavy, progressive taxation of wealth," Vanessa Williamson, Brookings

Blueprints for American Renewal & Prosperity Project, Wednesday, December 9, 2020, https://www.brookings.edu/research/closing-the-racial-wealth-gap-requires-heavy-progressive-taxation-of-wealth/

544 "Time for justice: Tackling race inequalities in health and housing," Dayna Bowen Matthew, Edward Rodrigue, and Richard V. Reeves, Brookings Institution, Wednesday, October 19, 2016, https://www.brookings.edu/research/time-for-justice-tackling-race-inequalities-in-health-and-housing/

545 Ibid.

546 "Housing and Displacement on Providence's East Side and Beyond," Dr. Dannie Ritchie with contributions from others, Brown University, (October 2020), pp. 151-152

Truth Phase Selected Bibliography & Sources
© 1696HeritageGroup 2021

PRIMARY SOURCES

Archival Records & Collections, Government Documents,
Oral History Interviews, Pamphlets & Personal Papers.

17ᵀᴴ & 18ᵀᴴ CENTURIES

1. Land Deed, Receipt and Agreement, 1636-1637 Between Roger Williams, Caunonnicus and Miantunnomu, Rhode Island State Archives
2. Propositions Relating To Indians By Governor William Coddington and Sachem Miantonomi, 1640, Rhode Island State Archives
3. Laws Relating to Property, Hunting and Harvesting, 1641, Rhode Island State Archives
4. The Parliamentary Patent of 1643 Uniting the Towns of Providence, Portsmouth, and Newport, Rhode Island State Archives
5. Act Forbidding Forced Covenant Bond, 1652, Rhode Island State Archives
6. The Royal Charter of King Charles the II of 1663 Granted for the Colony of Rhode Island and Providence Plantations, Rhode Island State Archives
7. The Royal Charter of 1663 Granted to the Royal African Company by King Charles II, National Archives of United Kingdom
8. An Order by General Assembly of Rhode Island to Draw and Quarter the Body of Late Slave of Mr. Thomas Mumford, Abstract From Rhode Island Colonial Records, May 28, 1707, Rhode Island State Archives
9. An Act for Laying a Duty on Negro Slaves that Shall Be Imported Into This Colony, General Assembly of Her Majesty Colony of Rhode Island and Providence Plantations, February 27, 1711, Rhode Island State Archives
10. An Act for Negro and Mulatto Slaves Not Be Carried Over Ferries, General Assembly of Her Majesty Colony of Rhode Island and Providence Plantations, October 1714, Rhode Island State Archives
11. An Order by General Assembly of Rhode Island to Brand on the Forehead With the Letter R an Indian Boy Name Peter, Abstract from Rhode Island Colonial Records, June 13, 1727, Rhode Island State Archives
12. An Act Related to the Freeing of Molatto & Negro Slaves, General Assembly of Her Majesty Colony of Rhode Island and Providence Plantations, February 1728, Rhode Island State Archives
13. An Act for the Deposing of Money Raised in this Colony on Importing Negro Slaves, General Assembly of Her Majesty Colony of Rhode Island and Providence Plantations, June 3, 1729, Rhode Island State Archives
14. Testimony of George Scott of Newport, Master of the Slaving Sloop Little George, 1730, MSS 17 Box 2, Folder: 1730 "Narrative of Slave Revolt on Ship off Africa," Rhode Island Historical Society Archives
15. Colony of Rhode Island Petition of Joseph Whipple and Trustees of Indian Land of Thomas Ninigret, 1747, Rhode Island State Archives
16. An Act To Prevent All Persons Keeping House Within This Colony, From Entertaining Indian, Negro or Mulatto

Servants or Slaves, General Assembly of Colony of Rhode Island, 1755, Stokes Family Collection.

17. Letter From Rhode Island Governor Josias Lyndon to Lord Commissioners for Trade and Plantations, January 26, 1764, Rhode Island State Archives

18. Resolution To Consider the Petition of Quakers to Abolish Slavery, 1783, Rhode Island State Archives

19. An Act Authorizing the Manumission of Negroes, Mulattoes and Others, and for the Gradual Abolition of Slavery, The General Assembly of the Governor and Company of the State of Rhode Island and Providence Plantations, February 1784, Rhode Island State Archives

20. An Act to Prevent the Slave-Trade and to Encourage the Abolition of Slavery, The General Assembly of the Governor and Company of the State of Rhode Island and Providence Plantations, October 1787, Rhode Island State Archives

21. Heads of Families of the First Census, Rhode Island - 1790, National Archives

22. Deed of Ninigret Chief Sachem of Narragansett Tribe, 1790, Rhode Island State Archives

23. An Act to Incorporate Certain Persons by the Name fo the Providence Society for Promoting Abolition of Slavery, for the Relief of persons unlawfully Held in Bondage and for Improving the Conditions of the African Race, The General Assembly of the Governor and Company of the State of Rhode Island and Providence Plantations, June 1790, Rhode Island State Archives

24. Examination Jack and Phillis Wanton, December 27, 1792, Record 7:549, Providence City Archives. Providence Town Council. "Providence Town Council Records Book," 1800. 1789-1801 [7:549]. Providence City Archives

25. An Act for No White Person To Be Married to a Negro, Indian or Mulatto, The General Assembly of the Governor and Company of the State of Rhode Island and Providence Plantations, September 1796, Rhode Island State Archives

19TH CENTURY

26. Examination Jack and Phillis Wanton, December 27, 1792, Record 7:549, Providence City Archives. Providence Town Council. "Providence Town Council Records Book," 1800. 1789-1801 [7:549]. Providence City Archives

27. Examination of Betsey Blanchard and Her Child Eliza, Providence Town Council Records Book, July 29, 1807, City of Providence Archives

28. Charter of Harmony Lodge in Providence, December 20, 1826, Rhode Island Black Heritage Society

29. Petition of the Colored People for the Relief of Taxes, January 11, 1832, Rhode Island State Archives

30. Rhode Island vs. Thomas Walmsley, 1833, MSS 452 S6, Box 14, Folder 3, Rhode Island Historical Archives

31. Rhode Island State Constitution, November 1842, Rhode Island State Archives

32. Moses Stanton Letter, 1842 MSS 629, Series 1, Box1, Folder 7, Rhode Island Historical Society Archives

33. Moses Stanton Letter, Undated, MSS 629, SG3, Series 1, Box 1, Folder 7, Rhode Island Historical Society Archives

34. Moses Stanton Letter, June 5, 1843, MSsS629, Series 3, Series 1, Box 1, Folder 8, Rhode Island Historical Society Archives

35. Letter from Moses Stanton (Narragansett) regarding petitions to sell land so he can move to Green Bay, MSS

629 SG3 Series 1, Box 1, Folder 8: 1843, January-July, Rhode Island Historical Society Archives

36. Foster & Waterman Day Book, MSS 900-F, Rhode Island Historical Society Archives

37. George T. Downing Papers, Rhode Island Black Heritage Society Collections, Stokes Family Collections, 1850-1900

38. Colored Citizens of Providence Petition Against the Fugitive Slave Law, 1851, Rhode Island State Archives

39. Thomas & Frederick Williams Papers, Stokes Family Collections, 1855-1910

40. Pamphlets & Political Flyers, 1850-1930, Stokes Family Collections

41. Records of the Colony of Rhode Island and Providence Plantations, in New England: Printed by order of the General Assembly, Ed. by John Russell Bartlett, Secretary of State, 1857

42. Petition Asking for Equal Public-School Rights, January 15, 1862, Rhode Island State Archives

43. John C. Minkins Papers, Rhode Island Black Heritage Society Collections, 1869-1959

44. Church Records, Union Colored Congregation Church, (1850 -1900) Newport, Rhode Island Black Heritage Society Collections & Stokes Family Collections

45. Van Horne Family Papers, Rhode Island Black Heritage Society Collections, Rhode Island State Archives, Stokes Family Collection, 1869-1935

46. Church Records, Onley Street Baptist Church, (1870-1950) Providence, Rhode Island Black Heritage Society Collections

47. Church Records, Winter Street AME Church, (1890-1950) Providence, Rhode Island Black Heritage Society Collections

48. Church Records, Mt Zion AME Church, (1845-1910) Newport, Rhode Island Black Heritage Society Collections

49. Church Records of Pond Street (Free Will) Baptist Church, (1842-1900) Rhode Island Black Heritage Society Collections,

50. An Act to Secure All Persons Their Civil Rights, Rhode Island General Assembly, Rhode Island State Archives, 1884

51. The Negro in Rhode Island: His Past, Present and Future, Rev, Mahlon Van Horne, Rhode Island Black Heritage Society & Stokes Family Collections, 1887

52. Supreme Court of Rhode Island, The Narragansett Indians, 20 R.I. 715: 40 A. 347, Decided February 24, 1898

53. Formation of the Charles Sumner Political Club, George T. Downing, M. A. Van Horne, et.al, Stokes Family Collection, January 30, 1898

54. Charter of the City of Providence, And the Act of the General Assembly for Organizing the Government Under the Name, Passed At October Session, 1831, Also the Mayor's Address to the City Council, June 4, 1832, Printed by the Order of the City Council, William Marshall and Company Printers, 1832, City of Providence Archives

55. The Providence Plantations for 250 Years: A Historical Review of Foundation, Rise and Progress of the City of Providence, J.A. & R.A. Reid Publishers, 1886

56. The Proceedings of the Convention With Their Address to The Free Persons of Color in the United States, J.W. Allen Printers, 1831

57. Acts, Resolves and Reports of the General Assembly of the State of Rhode Island and Providence Plantations, Part I, E.L. Freeman & Company Printers, 1880

20TH CENTURY

58. An Expression from the Oppressed, William Robinson, A. Van Horne, Fred Williams, George T. Downing, Stokes Family Collections, March 12, 1902

59. Bertha G. Higgins Papers, Rhode Island Black Heritage Society Collections, 1910-1935

60. William A. Heathman, Esq. Papers, Rhode Island Black Heritage Society Collections, 1915-1960

61. History of African Americans in Rhode Island, 1918-1993, Andrew J. Bell, Rhode Island Black Heritage Society Collections

62. Colored Girls in the Second Line of Defense, Mary E. Jackson, The Association Monthly, Vol XII, No. 10, (October 1918) pp. 363-365

63. Andrew J. Bell Papers, Rhode Island Black Heritage Society Collections, 1920-1993

64. Joseph G. LeCount, Esq. Papers, Rhode Island Black Heritage Society Collections, 1930-1980

65. A Study of the Negro in Rhode Island: His Contributions and Needs, Rhode Island Inter-Racial Conference, February 11-12, 1940, Rhode Island Black Heritage Society

66. A Study of Recreational Opportunities For Negroes in Providence, Rhode Island, Ernest T. Atwell, Bureau of Colored Work, National Recreation Association, June, 1941

67. Anti-Negro Petition from Tomony Hill Housing Project, Special Collections, Phillips Memorial Library, Providence College, 1942

68. Report of the Commission on the Employment Problems of the Negro, State of Rhode Island, May 1943, Rhode Island State Archives

69. Rhode Island Hospital Letter on Negro Nurses, Special Collections, Phillips Memorial Library, Providence College, April 19, 1944

70. Woonsocket Brush Company Letter & Federal Council of Churches Letter, Special Collections, Phillips Memorial Library, Providence College, June 18, 1948

71. List of Negro Owned Business in Lippett Hill, Rhode Island Black Heritage Society Collections, 1949-1950

72. The Negro Community in Rhode Island, Urban League of Rhode Island, Special Collections, Adams Library, Rhode Island College, 1950

73. Annual Report of the Rhode Island Commission Against Discrimination, State of Rhode Island, 1952, Rhode Island State Archives

74. Narraganset History Summary, Dr. Grace H. Sherwood, Librarian and State Records Commissioner, State of Rhode Island, 1955, Rhode Island State Archives

75. 18 Providence Journal Editorials on Housing Discrimination, Special Collections, Phillips Memorial Library, Providence College, July 23, 1956

76. Urban Renewal Pamphlet, Federal Housing and Home Finance Agency, Rhode Island State Archives, 21. Rhode Island Can Lead the Way in Integration, Providence Visitor, Special Collections, Adams Library, Rhode Island College, December 11, 1958

77. Catholic Interracial Council of Rhode Island, Special Collections, Adams Library, Rhode Island College, 1958-1960.

78. Temple Emanu-EL Resolution on Discrimination in Housing, Special Collections, Adams Library, Rhode Island College, January 12, 1959
79. Citizens United for a Fair Housing Law in Rhode Island, Special Collections, Adams Library, Rhode Island College, 1959-1964
80. Relocation Information Pamphlet for Lippitt Hill Families 1960, Rhode Island State Archives
81. Annual Reports, Providence Redevelopment Agency, Special Collections, Adams Library, Rhode Island College, 1960-1969
82. Annual Report of the Rhode Island Commission Against Discrimination, State of Rhode Island, 1962, Rhode Island State Archives
83. Providence Board of Realtors Letter on Fair Housing, Special Collections, Adams Library, Rhode Island College, March 6, 1962.
84. Police Witness Statements on Blackstone Café Incident, Special Collections, Phillips Memorial Library, Providence College, August 2 & 3 1962
85. Providence Journal Articles on Blackstone Café Incident, Special Collections, Phillips Memorial Library, Providence College, August 24, 1962
86. Meeting Minutes Providence Branch NAACP, Discussions on Lippitt Hill Redevelopment, November 25, 1963, Special Collections, Phillips Memorial Library, Providence College
87. Report of the Governor's Civil Rights Task Force, State of Rhode Island, January 3, 1964, Rhode Island State Archives
88. College Hill: A Demonstration Study of Historic Area Renewal, by Frank H. Malley, 2nd ed. Providence City Plan Commission, (Providence, Rhode Island: City of Providence, 1967)
89. Community Involvement in School Desegregation: The Story of the MLK School Providence, Center for Urban Education, 1967, Rhode Island State Archives
90. Citizens United Renewal Enterprises (CURE), Special Collections, Adams Library, Rhode Island College, 1969-1971

91. The Urban Coalition of Rhode Island, Special Collections, Adams Library, Rhode Island College, 1970-1971
92. Sketches of Negroes and Events in Rhode Island by Dr. Carl Gross, Special Collections, Adams Library, Rhode Island College, 1971
93. An Act to Settle Indian Land Claims Within the State of Rhode Island and Providence Plantations, Public Law 95-395, 95th United States Congress, September 30, 1978
94. South Providence Survey, Rhode Island Historical Preservation & Heritage Commission, 1978, Rhode Island State Archives
95. Elmwood Survey, Rhode Island Historical Preservation & Heritage Commission, 1979, Rhode Island State Archives
96. Recommendation and Summary of Evidence for Proposed Findings for Federal Acknowledgement of the Narragansett Indian Tribe Rhode Island Pursuant to 25 CFR 83, United States Department of the Interior, Bureau of Indian Affairs, July 29, 1982
97. Narragansett Justice Act, H.R. 1983, 105th Congress – Second Session, September 9, 1998
98. Recommendation and Summary Evidence for Proposed Finding for Federal Acknowledgement of the

Narragansett Indian Tribe of Rhode Island, United States Department of the Interior, Bureau of Indian Affairs, 25 CFR 83, 1983

99. Providence A Citywide Survey of Historic Resources, William McKenzie Woodward & Edward F. Sanderson, Rhode Island Historical Preservation Commission, 1986

100. Oral History Interview Tapes: Providence Civil Rights- 1995, Providence City Archives Special Collections

101. Dr. Carl Russell Gross Collection, Jane P. Adams Library, Rhode Island College, Manuscript A,B, C & D

102. Final Environmental Impact Statement & Final Section 4(f)/6(f) Evaluation: Improvements to I-195, Providence, Rhode Island, Rhode Island Department of Transportation, Lincoln Almond Governor, (August 1996),

103. Social Plan For Community Renewal of the City of Providence, Rhode Island, Rhode Island Council for Community Services, Sidney Dillick, Ph.D., M.S.W., Executive Director and Charles R. Wood, Urban Renewal Coordinator

104. Annul Report of the R.I. Commission Against Discrimination, State of Rhode Island, March 10, 1953

21ST CENTURY

105. Rhode Island Select Commission on Race and Police-Community Relations, Executive Order 00-3 by Governor Lincoln Almond on April 6, 2000.

106. The Report of Rhode Island Select Commission on Race and Police-Community Relations, State of Rhode Island, Executive Summary, May 2001, Rhode Island State Archives

107. Carcieri, Governor of Rhode Island, ET AL, Vs. Salazar, Secretary of the Interior, ET Al, Supreme Court of the United States, No. 07-526, Argued November 3, 2008, Decided February 24, 2009

108. An Equity Profile of Rhode Island, Policy Link, USC Program for Environmental & Regional Equity, February 19, 2013

109. Hardscrabble and Snowtown Transportation Enhancement and Historical Preservation Transportation Improvement Program Proposal, January 2, 2016, Rhode Island Black Heritage Society

110. Survey Report: African American Struggle for Civil Rights in Rhode Island, The Twentieth Century, Statewide Survey and National Register Evaluation, Public Archeology Laboratory, National Park Service Historic Preservation Fund, January 2020

111. Oral History Interviews: Rhode Island Black Heritage Society, 2018/2020

112. Resolution Recognizing and Honoring African American History in Rhode Island and urging the adoption of African American Education in Rhode Island's K-12 Schools starting in the 2021-2022 Academic Year, Providence City Council Resolution, June 18, 2020

A MATTER OF TRUTH

113. <u>Removal of the Term Plantations From the City of Providence Documents and Ceremonies</u>, Mayor Executive Order, June 19, 2020, City of Providence

SECONDARY SOURCES

Books, Journals, Articles, & Dissertations

AFRICAN HERITAGE & HISTORY

114. <u>Memoirs of Elleanor Eldridge</u>, Frances H. Green, B.T. Albro, Providence, 1838
115. <u>From Slave to Citizen: The Story of the Negro in Rhode Island,</u> Irving Bartlett, 1954
116. <u>Our Black Heritage,</u> Rhode Island Sunday Journal Magazine, October 12, 1969
117. <u>Building the Democratic Party: Black Voting in Providence in the 1930's</u>, Rhode Island History, Volume 44, Number 3, August, 1985
118. <u>A Heritage Discovered: Blacks in Rhode Island,</u> Rowena Stewart, Rhode Island Black Heritge Society, 1984
119. <u>We Went South, James Rhea, Providence Journal Reporter,</u> Rhode Island Black Heritage Society Collections, October 20-30, 1957.
120. <u>The Minkins Sisters: To Be Young, Black, and Female at Brown in the 20's and 30's,</u> Brown Alumni Monthly, May 1982
121. <u>From Immigrant to Ethnic: Interview with Joseph LeCount,</u> Rhode Island College Ethnic Studies Project, May 1976
122. <u>Voices of Civil Rights Lawyers: 1964-1980</u>, Malcolm Farmer Interview, University of Florida Press, 2017
123. <u>Along the NAACP Battlefront: The Boilermaker Suit in Rhode Island Goes On,</u> Crisis Magazine (NAACP), July 1944
124. <u>Minutes of the African Union Society of Newport 1787-1824</u>, Special Collections, Newport Historical Society
125. <u>Will The General Assembly Put Down Caste Schools?</u> George T. Downing, 1857, Cornell University Library Digital Reprint, 1992
126. <u>The Providence Black Community in the 19th Century,</u> The Rhode Island Black Heritage Society, 1984
127. <u>African Americans in Newport</u>, Richard Youngken, Rhode Island Black Heritage Society and Rhode Island Historical Preservation & Heritage Commission, 1998
128. <u>Rhode Island's Freedom Trail,</u> Carl Senna, Rhode Island Black Heritage Society, 1986
129. <u>The Life of William J. Brown of Providence</u>, RI, Books for Libraries Press, 1971
130. <u>We Were Here Too: Selected Stories of Black History in North Kingstown</u>, Timothy Cranston, 2005
131. <u>George T. Downing and Desegregation of Rhode Island Public Schools, 1855-1866</u>, Lawrence Grossman, Rhode Island History, Volume 36, November, 1977
132. <u>Then Why the Negroes: The Nature And Course of the Anti-Slavery Movement in Rhode Island: 1637-1861</u>, Arline Ruth Kiven, Funded through the Dorothy H.W. Hunt Fund, Urban League of Rhode Island, 1973

133. Historical Sketch of the Shiloh Baptist Church at Newport, RI, Reverend H. N. Jeter, R. W. Pearce Printer, 1891
134. Rhode Island and the Slave Trade, J. Stanley Lemons, Rhode Island Historical Society, Vol. 60, No. 4, (Fall 2002), pp. 95-105
135. Negroes on the Island of Rhode Island, Charles Battle, Privately Published, 1932
136. Afro Yankees: Providence Black Community in the Antebellum Era, Robert J. Cottrol, Greenwood Press, 1982
137. Disfranchisement of Negroes in New England, James Truslow Adams, The American Historical Review, Vol. 30, No. 3, April 1925
138. The Negro's Struggle for Freedom in Its Birthplace, Charles H. Wesley, The Journal of Negro History, Vol. 30, No. 1, January 1945
139. Memoirs of Elleanor Eldridge, B.T. Albro, Providence, RI, 1843
140. A Short History of the African Meeting House and School House, Brown & Danford, 1821
141. The Negro in Colonial New England 1620-1776, Lorenzo Greene, Columbia University Press, 1942
142. Life of George Henry: A Brief History of the Colored People in America, George Henry, H.I. Gould & Company, 1894
143. "Shining in Borrowed Plumage": Affirmation of Community in the Black Coronation Festivals of New England (c. 1750-c. 1850), Melvin Wade, Western Folklore, Vol. 40, No. 3 (Jul., 1981), pp. 211-231
144. Negroes of the Island of Rhode Island, Charles A. Battle, Private Publishing, 1932
145. George T. Downing: Sketch of His Life and Times, S.A.M. Washington, Milne Printery, 1910
146. Black Yankees: The Development of an Afro-American Subculture in Eighteenth Century New England, William D. Piersen, University of Massachusetts Press, 1988
147. Black Lives, Native Lands, White Worlds, Jared Hardesty, University of Massachusetts Press, 2020
148. Where Negroes Are Masters: An African Port in the Era of the Slave Trade, Randy J. Sparks, Harvard University Press, 2014
149. Negro Churches in Rhode Island Before 1860, Robert Glenn Sherer, Jr., Rhode Island History, Vol. 25, No. 1, (January 1966) pp. 9-24
150. John Carter Minkins: Pioneering African American Newspaperman, Stanley Lemons and Diane Lambert, The New England Quarterly, Vol. 76, No. 3 (September 2003) pp. 413-438
151. Black Jacks: African American Seaman in the Age of Sail, Jeffery W. Bolster, Harvard University Press, 1997
152. The Negro in the American Revolution, Benjamin Quarles, University of North Carolina Press, 1961
153. From African to Yankee: Narratives of Slavery and Freedom in Antebellum New England, Edited by Robert J. Cottrol, Routledge Press, 1997
154. The Black Presence in the Era of the American Revolution, Sidney Kaplan & Emma Kaplan, University of Massachusetts Press, 1989
155. Re-enfranchisement of Rhode Island Negroes, J. Stanley Lemons & Michael McKenna, Rhode Island History Journal, Vol. 30, (January 1971), pp. 3-14
156. Black Sailors: Afro-American Merchant Seamen and Whalers Prior to the Civil War, Martha S. Putney, Greenwood Publishing Group, 1987

157. The Free African American Cultural Landscape: Newport, RI, 1774-1826, Akeia A. F. Benard, Dissertation – University of Connecticut, 2008

158. Black Founders: The Free Black Community in the Early Republic, Richard S. Newman, The Library Company of Philadelphia, 2008

159. Black and Native American Relations Before 1800, Rhett S. Jones, Western Journal of Black Studies, Vol.1, No. 3, (September 1977), pp. 151-63

160. Black Labor White Wealth: The Search for Power and Economic Justice, Claud Anderson, PowerNomics Corporation, 1994

161. The African American Emigration Movement in Georgia During Reconstruction, Falechiondro Sims-Alvardo, Dissertation for Department of History, Georgia State University, June 20, 2011

162. Black Labor and the American Legal System: Race, Work, and the Law, Herbert Hill, University of Wisconsin Press, 1977

163. Along the NAACP Battlefront: Kaiser Walsh Shipyard Case, The Crisis Magazine, Vol. 51, No. 7 (July 1944) pp. 226-227

164. The Colored Woman in Industry, Mary E. Jackson, The Crisis Magazine, Vol. 17, No. 1, (November 1917)

165. Votes For Women, Rev. Francis J. Grimke, The Crisis Magazine, Vol. 10, No. 4 (August 1915) pp. 178-192

166. History of Free and Accepted Masons (Prince Hall) in Rhode Island, From Whence We Came, Carl Russell Gross, Rhode Island College, Special Collections, 1971

167. In Hope of Liberty: Culture, Community and Protest Among Northern Free Blacks, 1700-1860, James Oliver Horton & Lois E. Horton, Oxford University Press, 1997

168. Constitution of the American Society of Free Persons fo Colour in the United States, J.W. Allen Printers, 1831

169. Blacks in 19th Century Rhode Island: An Overview, William H. Robinson, Rhode Island Black Heritage Society, 1978

170. All on Fire: William Lloyd Garrison and the Abolition of Slavery, Henry Mayer, St Martin's Press, 1998

171. The Tide Taken at Flood: The Black Suffrage Movement During The Dorr Rebellion in the State of Rhode Island, Caleb T. Horton, Providence City Archives

172. Forever and Hereafter a Body Politic: The African Union Meeting House and Providence's First Black Leaders, C.J. Martin, Rhode Island History, Volume 77 No. 1 (December 2019)

173. A Slave's Cause: A History of Abolition, Manisha Sinha, Yale University Press, 2016

174. A Narrative of the Life and Adventures of Venture, Related By Himself, Printed by Holt, New London, Connecticut, 1798

175. Building the Democratic Party: Black Voting in Providence in the 1930's, Norma Lasalle Daoust, Rhode Island History, Vol. 44, No. 3, (August 1985) pp.81-88

176. The Free Negro In Providence, Rhode Island, Irving H. Bartlett, Negro History Bulletin, Vol. 14, No. 3, (December 1950), pp. 51-67

177. Early Black Benevolent Societies, 1780-1830, Robert L. Harris Jr., The Massachusetts Review, Vol. 20, No. 3, (Autumn 1979), pp. 603-625

178. West Africa Before the Colonial Era: A History to 1850, Basil Davidson, Routeledge Press, 2014

179. Creative Survival: Africans as Mariners in Colonial Rhode Island, Keith W. Stokes, Small Sate Big History: The Online Review of Rhode Island History, http://smallstatebighistory.com/ (February 2020)

180. Shining in Borrowed Plumage: Affirmation of Community in the Black Coronation Festivals of New England (c. 1750-c. 1850), Melvin Wade, Western Folklore, Vol. 40, No. 3 (July 1981), pp. 211-231

181. Reading Between the Lines of Slavery: Examining New England Runaway Ads for Evidence of an Afro-Yankee Culture, Lauren Landi, Senior Thesis, Salve Reginal University, 2012

182. African Institutions in America, Hubert H. S. Aimes, The Journal of American Folklore, (March 1905), Vol. 18, No. 68, pp.15-32

183. An Imperfect Union: Slavery Federalism, and Comity, Paul Finkelman, The Lawbook Exchange, 2000

184. The Proceedings of the Free African Union Society and the African Benevolent Society, William H. Robinson, Rhode Island College, 1976

185. Dictionary of Afro-American Slavery, Edited by Randall M. Miller and John David Smith, Greenwood Press, 1997

186. Cesar Lyndon's Lists, Letters, and a Pig Roast: A Sundry Account Book, Tara Bynum, Early American Literature, Vol. 53, No. 3 (2018), pp. 839-849

187. Knights of the Razor: Black Barbers in Slavery and Freedom, Douglas Walter Bristol, Johns Hopkins University Press, 2009

188. White Americans in Black Africa: Black and White American Methodist Missionaries in Liberia, 1820-1875, Eunjin Park, Routledge Publishing, 2001

189. The Providence Society's Sierra Leone Emigration Scheme, 1794-1795: Prologue to the African Colonization Movement, George E. Brooks, Jr., The International Journal of African Historical Studies, Vol. 7, No. 2 (1974), pp. 183-202

190. Newport Gardner (1746-1826), The Black Perspective in Music, Vol. 4, No. 2, Bicentennial Number (Jul., 1976), pp. 202-207

191. Creative Survival: The Providence Black Community in 19th Century Providence, Rhode Island Black Heritage Society Exhibit and Publication, 1988

192. Strange Bedfellows: The Politics Of Race In Antebellum Rhode Island, Erik J. Chaput and Russell J. DeSimone, Common Place: The Journal of American Life, Issue 10.2 (January, 2010)

193. Jim Crow North: The Struggle for Equal Rights in Antebellum New England, Richard Archer, Oxford University Press, 2017

194. The Mustard Seed: Providence's Alfred Niger, Antebellum Black Voting Rights Activist, C.J. Martin, Small State Big History, August 1, 2020

195. History of the Providence Riots, From September 21 to September 24, 1831, Providence Committee, H.H. Brown, 1831

196. Alexander Crummell: A Study of Civilization and Discontent, Wilson J. Moses, Oxford University Press, 1989, pp.34

197. Pro Slavery and Antislavery Politics in Rhode Island's 1842 Dorr Rebellion, Erik J. Chaput, The New England Quarterly, Vol. 85, No. 4 (December 2012), pp. 658-694

198. The African Repository, Vol. 35, 1859, American Colonization Society, C. Alexander, Printer, 1859

199. Notable Black American Women, Book II, Jessie Carney Smith, Editor, Gale Research Inc., 1996
200. African American Civil Rights: Early Activism and the Niagara Movement, Angela Jones, Praeger Books, 2011
201. The Encyclopedia of African American History From 1896 to the Present, Paul Finkelman, Editor, Vol. I, A-C, Oxford University Press, 2009
202. The Formation of the NAACP Providence Branch, Edward K. Hooks, Rhode Island Black Heritage Society, 2013
203. The Crisis: A Record of the Darker Races, James W. Ivy, Editor, Vol. 65, No. 10, (December 1958)
204. African Americans Confront Lynching: Strategies of Resistance from the Civil War to the Civil Rights Era, Christopher Waldrep, Rowman & Littlefield Publishers, Inc., 2009
205. The Crisis: Record of the Darker Races, Vol. 17, No. 1, "The Colored Woman In Industry," Mary E. Jackson, (September 1918)
206. Association Monthly Magazine, Vol. XII, No. 10, "Colored Girls in the Second Line of Defense," Mary E. Jackson, (October 1918)
207. Red Summer: The Summer of 1919 and the Awakening of Black America, Cameron McWhirter, Henry Holt and Company, 2011
208. The Crisis: Record of the Darker Races, Vol. 18, No. 1, (May 1919)
209. The Birth of a Nation and the Making of the NAACP, Stephen Weinberger, Journal of American Studies, Vol. 45, No. 1, (February 2011), pp. 78
210. W.E.B. DuBois: A Biography, David Levering Lewis, Henry Holt and Company, LLC, 2009
211. The Cape Verdean in Rhode Island: A Brief History, Waltraud Berger Coli and Richard A. Lobban, Rhode Island Ethnic Heritage Pamphlet Series, Rhode Island Publications Society, 1990
212. Who's Who of the Colored Race: A General Biographical Dictionary of Men and Women of African Descent, Frank Lincoln Mather, 1915
213. An Assessment of Life in Rhode Island as an African American in the Era from 1918 to 1993, Andrew J. Bell, Vantage Press, 1997
214. Black Republicans and the Transformation of the GOP, Joshua D. Farrington, University of Pennsylvania Press, 2016
215. Encyclopedia of the Harlem Renaissance, Cary D Wintz and Paul Finkelman, Editors, Vol. 2, K-Y, Routledge Press, 2004
216. African American Led Worker Solidarity in WW2 Providence: The Story of Boilermakers Local 308, Patrick Crowley, Secretary-Treasurer, RHODE ISLAND AFL-CIO, 40th Annual North American Labor History Conference, (Oct 2018)
217. Opportunity Journal of Negro Life, Vol. XXIII, No. 1, Winter Issue, (Jan.-Mar 1945),
218. Jim Crow America: A Documentary History, Edited by Catherine M. Lewis and J. Richard Lewis, University of Arkansas Press, 2009
219. Opportunity Journal of Negro Life, Vol. XXL, No. 3, Summer Issue, (July 1943)
220. Towards Equal Opportunity: The Story of the Providence Urban League of Rhode Island in the 1940's, Richard F. Irving, Thesis at Brown University, Providence Urban League, 1974

221. From Immigrant to Ethnic: Interview with Joseph LeCount by Joseph Conforti, Rhode Island Ethnic Studies Project, Oral Interview # 15, Tape 1, Side 1, May 14, 1976
222. An Assessment of Life in Rhode Island as an African American in the Era from 1918 to 1993, Andrew J. Bell, Vantage Press, 1997
223. African American Site Survey of College Hill, Rhode Island Historical & Preservation Commission & Rhode Island Black Heritage Society, U.S. Department of Interior, National Park Service Grant, Section 8, Page 1, 2009
224. Providence External Review Authority ("PERA"), Bi-Annual Report, October 30, 2019
225. The Purpose of Power: How We Come Together When We Fall Apart, Alicia Garza, Penguin Random House, 2020
226. The State of Black Families In Rhode Island, Economic Progress Institute, May 2017, http://www.economicprogressri.org/wp-content/uploads/2017/05/SOBRI2017_Final_digital.pdf
227. 113. The Economic Impact Of Closing The Racial Wealth Gap, McKinsey & Company, August 13, 2019, https://www.mckinsey.com/industries/public-and-social-sector/our-insights/the-economic-impact-of-closing-the-racial-wealth-gap#
228. 114. A Community of Spirit: People of Color in Providence, Rhode Island, 1870-1950, Jan Armstrong, Rhode Island Black Heritage Society, 1998
229. 115. The Hosts Of Black Labor, W. E. Burghardt Du Bois, The Nation, Vol. 116 (May 9, 1923), pp. 539-41.

Indigenous People History

230. A History of the Narragansett Tribe of Rhode Island, Robert A. Geake, The History Press, 2011
231. Diary of King Philip's War 1675-76, Colonel Benjamin Church, Lockwood Publishing, 1996
232. Indian Slaves of the King Phillip's War, James G. Vose, Publications of the Rhode Island Historical Society, Volume 1, 1893
233. 1491:New Revelations of the Americas Before Columbus, Charles C. Mann, Alfred & Knopp, New York, 2006
234. Changes in the Land: Indians, Colonists, and the Ecology of New England, William Cronon, Hill & Wang, 1983
235. "We Chuse to Be Bounded": Native American Animal Husbandry in Colonial New England, David J. Silverman, The William and Mary Quarterly, Vol. 60, No. 3 (July 2003), pp. 511-548
236. The Red King's Rebellion: Racial Politics in New England, Russell Bourne, Oxford University Press, 1991
237. Guns, Germs & Steel: The Fates of Human Societies, Jared Diamond, W. W. Norton Press, 1997
238. Indian Labor in Early Rhode Island, John A. Sainsbury, New England Quarterly, Vol. 48, Np. 3, September 1975 pp. 378-393.
239. The History of the King Phillip's War, Increase Mather, J. Munsell, Editor, 1862 Edition
240. Indian New England Before the Mayflower, Howard S. Russell, University Press of New England, 1980
241. The Murder of an Indian 1638, Glenn W. LaFanasie, Rhode Island History Journal, Vol. 38, (August 1979), pp. 67-79

242. Indian Slavery in Colonial America, Alan Gallay, Editor, University of Nebraska Press, 2010
243. Native Providence Memory, Community, and Survivance in the Northeast, Patricia E. Rubertone, University of Nebraska Press, 2020
244. Narraganset Tribe of Indians: Report of the Committee of Investigation, A Historical sketch and Evidence Taken, House of Representatives, January Session 1880, E.L. Freeman & Company Printers, 1880
245. Wigwam Words, Jill Lepore, The American Scholar Vol. 70, No. 1 (WINTER 2001), pp. 97-108
246. A Relation of the Indian War, by Mr. Easton of Rhode Island 1675, Paul Royster, Editor, University of Nebraska-Lincoln Publications, 2006
247. Red Man's Land, White Man's Laws, Wilcomb E. Washburn, University of Oklahoma Press, 1971
248. Miscegenation and Acculturation in the Narragansett County of Rhode Island, 1771—1790, Rhett S. Jones, Trotter Review, Vol. 3, Issue 1, Article 4, (1989)
249. A History of the Brothertown Indians of Wisconsin, Robert H. Lambert, Author House Publishers, 2010
250. Red Yankees: Narragansett Conversion in the Great Awakening, William S. Simmons, American Ethnologist, Vol. 10, No. 2 (May 1983), pp. 253-271
251. Spirit of the New England Tribes Indian History and Folklore, 1620-1984, William S. Simmons, University Press of New England, 1986
252. The Right to a Name: Narragansett People and Rhode Island Officials in the Revolutionary Era, Ruth Wallis Herndon and Ella Wilcox Sekatau, Ethnohistory 44:3 (Summer 1997), pp. 433-62
253. Colonizing the Children: Indian Youngsters in Servitude in Early Rhode Island, Ruth Wallis Herndon and Ella Wilcox Sekatau, Colonial Society of Massachusetts, Vol. 7, (April 2003) pp. 138-173
254. Narraganset Indians History, Dr. Grace M. Sherwood, Librarian and State Record Commissioner, September 21, 1955, Rhode Island State Archives
255. "Why shall wee have peace to bee made slaves": Indian Surrenderers During and After King Philip's War, Linford D. Fisher, Ethnohistory, Volume 64, Issue 1, (January 2017) pp. 91-114
256. Narrative of the Captivity and Restoration of Mrs. Mary Rowlandson, Mary Rowlandson, 1682, Edited by Diane Janowoski, New York History Review, 2019
257. The Significance of Disease in the Extinction of the New England Indians, Sherburne F. Cook, Human Biology, Vol. 45, No. 3 (September 1973), pp. 485-508
258. "Scattered to the Winds of Heaven: Narragansett Indians, 1676-1880," Glenn LaFantaisie and Paul Campbell, Rhode Island History (August 1978) pp. 67-84
259. Daniel Gookin, the Praying Indians, and King Philip's War, Louise A. Breen, Routledge Publishers, 2019
260. God, War and Providence: The Epic Struggle of Roger Williams and the Narragansett Indians Against the Puritans of New England, James A. Warren, Scribner, 2018
261. We Are All the Sachems from East to West: A New Look at Miantonomi's Campaign of Resistance, Michael Leroy Oberg, The New England Quarterly, Vol. 77, No. 3 (September 2004), pp. 478-499
262. Flintlock and Tomahawk: New England in King Philips's War, Douglas Edward Leach, Parnassus Imprints, 1992
263. Indian Names of Places in Rhode Island, Usher Parsons, M.D., Rhode Island Historical Society, Knowles, Anthony & Company, 1861

264. <u>A Key into the Language of America</u>, Roger Williams, Edited by Howard M. Chapin, Applewood Books, 1936
265. <u>Terra Nova,</u> Cynthia Huntington, Southern Illinois University Press, 2017, pp. 61-62
266. <u>Providence and the Invention of the United States, 1607-18767,</u> Nicholas Guyatt, University of Pennsylvania Press, 2009
267. <u>Indian Legends,</u> Johanna R.M. Lyback, Lyons and Carnahan Publishers, 1925
268. <u>Atlas of Indian Nations</u>, Anton Treuer, National Geographic, 2016
269. <u>Property Rights in Transition</u>, Edited by Donn A. Derr and Leslie Small, Arno Press, 1977
270. <u>The Long Wake of the Pequot War,</u> Katherine a. Grandjean, Early American Studies, Vol. 9, No. 2, Special Issue: The Worlds of Lion Gardiner, ca. 1599—1663: Crossings and Boundaries (Spring 2011), pp. 379-411
271. <u>King Phillip's War: The History and Legacy of America's Forgotten Conflict</u>, Eric B. Schultz and Michael J. Tougias, The Countryman Press, 1999
272. <u>Native American Almanac, 50,000 Years of the Culture and Histories of Indigenous Peoples,</u> Yvonne Wakim Dennis, Arlene Hirschfelder, and Shannon Rothenberger Flynn, Visible Ink Press, 2016
273. <u>Becoming Brothertown: Native American Ethnogenesis and Endurance in the Modern World</u>, Graig N. Cipolla, University of Arizona Press, 2013
274. <u>Common Houses in America's Small Towns</u>, John A. Jakle & Robert W. Bastian, Georgia Press, 1989
275. <u>The New Deal and American Indian Tribalism</u>, Graham D. Taylor, University of Nebraska Press, 1980
276. <u>The Narragansett Dawn,</u> Princess Redwing, Editor, Vol. 2, No. 5, (September 1936)
277. <u>Act of June 18, 1934, (Indian Reorganization Act),</u>Chapter 576 of the 73rd Congress, Approved June 18, 1934
278. <u>Native Providence: Memory, Community and Survivance in the Northeast,</u> Patricia Ruberstone, University of Nebraska Press, 2020
279. <u>Federalism and the State Recognition of Native American Tribes: A Survey of State-Recognized Tribes and State Recognition Processes Across the United States,"</u> A. Koenig and J. Stein, Santa Clara Law Review, vol. 48, no. 1, pp. 77–153, 2008
280. <u>Native American Archaeology In Rhode Island</u>, Rhode Island Historical Preservation & Heritage Commission, 2002
281. <u>Memorandum,</u> Deputy Assistant Secretary – Indian Affairs, United States Department of the Interior, Buraru of Indian Affairs, July 29, 1982
282. <u>Narragansett Justice Act,</u> 105th Congress, 2nd Session, Report 105-692, September 9, 1998
283. <u>National Indian Gaming Commission</u>, Bulletin No. 04-2, 2004, https://web.archive.org/web/20120316101447/http://www.nigc.gov/Reading_Room/Bulletins/Bulletin_No._2004-2.aspx
284. <u>The American Universal Geography or a View of the Present Sate of all the Empires, Kingdoms, States and Republics, and of the United States of America</u>, Part I, Jedidiah Morse, June 1802
285. <u>Rethinking Schooling and Literacy in Eighteenth Century Algonquian Communities in Southern New England</u>, Alanna Rice, American Indian Culture and Research Journal, No. 34:3, 2010
286. <u>A Statement of the Case of the Narragansett Tribe of Indians,</u> As Shown in the Manuscript Collections of Sir William Johnson, James N. Arnold, Mercury Publishing, 1806
287. <u>Carcieri, Governor Of Rhode Island, Et Al. V. Salazar, Secretary of The Interior, Et Al.,</u> United States Supreme

Court, (2009), No. 07-526, Argued: November 3, 2008, Decided: February 24, 2009

288. *Distinguishing Carcieri v. Salazar: Why the Supreme Court Got It Wrong and How Congress and the Courts Should Respond to Preserve Tribal and Federal Interests in the IRA's Trust-Land Provisions*, Sarah Washburn, Washington Law Review, Vol. 85, No. 3, 2010

289. *The American Indian in Western Legal Thought: The Discourses of Conquest*, Robert A. Williams, Jr., Oxford University Press, 1990

290. *What The Future Holds: The Changing Landscape Of Federal Indian Policy*, Kevin K. Washburn, Harvard Law Review, Vol. 130, No. 6, (April, 2017)

291. *Memorandum on Tribal Consultation and Strengthening Nation-to-Nation Relationships*, President Joseph R. Biden, Jr., January 26, 2021, https://www.whitehouse.gov/briefing-room/presidential-actions/2021/01/26/memorandum-on-tribal-consultation-and-strengthening-nation-to-nation-relationships/

History Of Slave Trade & Enslavement

292. *Lopez of Newport, Colonial American Merchant Prince*, Stanley Chyet, Wayne State University Press, 1970

293. *The Slave Trade*, Hugh Thomas, Simon & Schuster, 1997

294. *Sons of Providence: The Brown Brothers, The Slave Trade and the American Revolution*, Charles Rappleye, Simon & Schuster, 2006

295. *Dark Work: The Business of Slavery in Rhode Island*, Christy Clark-Pujara, New York University Press, 2016

296. *The Fante and the Transatlantic Slave Trade*, Rebecca Shumway, University of Rochester Press, 2009

297. *The History of Slavery and the Slave Trade*, W.O. Blake, J & H Miller, 1858

298. *The Rhode Island Slave-Traders: Butchers, Bakers and Candlestick-Makers*, Rachel Chernos Lin, Slavery & Abolition, Vol. 33, No. 3, (December 2002) pp. 261-283

299. *Complicity: How the North Promoted, Prolonged and Profited From Slavery*, Anne Farrow & Joel Land, Ballantine Books, 2005

300. *Sins of the Fathers: The Atlantic Slave Traders*, James Pope Hennessy, Capricorn Books, 1967

301. *James DeWolf: Slaving Practices, Business Enterprises and Politics*, Cynthia Mestad Johnson, California State University Press, 2010

302. *Middle Passages: African American Journeys to Africa, 1787-2005*, James T. Campbell, Penguin Press, 2006

303. *Inhuman Bondage: The Rise and Fall of Slavery in the New World*, David Brion Davis, Oxford University Press, 2006

304. *Brethren By Nature: New England Indians, Colonists, and the Origins of American Slavery*, Margaret E. Newell, Cornell University Press, 2015

305. *The Business of Slavery and Antislavery Sentiment: The Case of Rowland Gibson Hazard – Antislavery "Negro Cloth" Cloth Dealer*, Christy Clark-Puara, Rhode Island History Journal, Vol 71, (Summer/Fall 2013), pp. 35-56.

306. *The Royal African Company*, K.G. Davies, Longmans, Green and Company, 1957

307. *The Constitution and Finance of the Royal African Company of England From its Founding Till 1720*, W.R. Scott, American Historical Review, Vol VIII, No 2, (January 1903)

308. The Fante and the Transatlantic Slave Trade, Rebecca Shumway, University of Rochester Press, 2011
309. The First Wheel of Commerce: Newport, Rhode Island, and the Slave Trade, 1760-1776, Elaine F. Crane, Slavery & Abolition 1 (March 1980) pp. 178-198
310. Slavery, Trade, and Economic Growth in Eighteenth-Century New England, in Slavery and the Rise of the Atlantic System, ed. Solow. B. L., Cambridge: Cambridge University Press, 1991
311. American Rum, African Consumers, and the Transatlantic Slave Trade, Sean M. Kelley, University of Essex, African Economic History, Volume 46, Number 2, (2018), pp. 1-29
312. Reparations for Slavery and the Slave Trade, Ana Lucia Araujo, Bloomsbury Publishing, 2017
313. American Rum, African Consumers, And The Transatlantic Slave Trade, Sean M. Kelley, African Economic History, Volume 46, (Number 2, 2018) pp. 1-29
314. Slavery and the Churches in Early America, 1619-1819, Lester B. Scherer, Eerdmans Publishing Company, 1975
315. Disowning Slavery: Gradual Emancipation and Race in New England, Joanne Pope Melish, Cornell University Press, 2015
316. New England Bound: Slavery & Colonization in Early America, Wendy Warren, W.W. Norton & Company, 2016
317. The Changing Nature of Indian Slavery in New England, 1670–1720, Margaret Ellen Newell, Colonial Society of Massachusetts, Vol. 7, (April, 2003) pp. 107-136
318. Escaping Bondage: A Documentary History of Runaway Slavs in Eighteenth Century New England, 1700-1789, Edited by Antonio T. Bly, Lexington Books, 2012
319. Slave Names and Naming in Barbados, 1630-1830, Jerome S. Handler and Joann Jacoby, The William and Mary Quarterly, Vol. 53, No. 4, (October 1996), pp. 685-728
320. Ports of Slavery, Ports of Freedom: How Slaves Used Northern Seaports Maritime Industry TO Esacape and Create Trans-Atlantic Identities, Charles Foy, Eastern Illinois University, 2008
321. Transformations in Slavery: A History of Slavery in Africa, Paul E. Lovejoy, Cambridge University Press, 2012
322. Strange New Land: Africans in Colonial America, Peter H. Wood, Oxford University Press, 1996
323. Slaves and Englishmen: Human Bondage in the Early Modern Atlantic World, Michael Guasco, University of Pennsylvania Press, 2014, pp. 186
324. Our Hidden History: Roger Williams and Slavery Origins, Margaret Newell, Providence Journal Special Section, August 29, 2020
325. Slavery, Sovereignty, and "Inheritable Blood": Reconsidering John Locke and the Origins of American Slavery, Holly Brewer, The American Historical Review, Volume 122, Issue 4, (October 2017), pp. 1038–1078
326. The Notorious Triangle: Rhode Island and the African Slave Trade, 1700-1807, Jay Coughtry, Temple University Press, 1981
327. Runaway Slaves: Rebels on the Plantation, John Hope Franklin and Loren Schwinger, Offord University Press, 1999
328. New York Burning: Liberty, Slavery, and Conspiracy in Eighteenth-Century Manhattan, Jill Lepore, Vintage Books, 2006
329. Journal of the Slave Ship Mary, Digital Georgetown University, Georgetown University Library, https://repository.library.georgetown.edu/handle/10822/1055276
330. A Newly Digitized Logbook Documents Life and Death on a Slave Trading Ship, Theresa Machemer, Smithsonian Magazine, (September, 20, 2020)

331. The Origins Debate: Slavery and Racism in Seventeenth-Century Virginia, Alden T. Vaughan, The Virginia Magazine of History and Biography, Vol. 97, No. 3, (July 1989), pp. 311-354

332. Sexual Racism: A Legacy of Slavery, Kenneth James Lay, UCLA National Black Law Journal, Vol. 13, (1993) pp. 165-183

333. Slavery and Justice: Report of the Brown University Steering Committee on Slavery and Justice, University Steering Committee on Slavery and Justice, Brown University

334. A Forgotten History: The Slave Trade and Slavery in New England, Choices Program, Watson Institute for International Studies, Brown University, June 2005

FAIR HOUSING & URBAN DEVELOPMENT

335. Rhode Island Lost A Great Citizen: Irving Jay Fain, Rhode Island Jewish Historical Notes, Volume 8, November 1981

336. Irving Fain and the Fair Housing Movement in Rhode Island, 1958-1970, Rhode Island History, Vol. 45, No. 1, February, 1986

337. A Community Apart - a History Of Public Housing In Providence and The Providence Housing Authority, Paul Campbell, The Rhode Island Publications Society, 2007

338. Making Civil Rights Law: Thurgood Marshall and the Supreme Court, 1936-1961, Mark Tushnet, Oxford University Press, 1994

339. Relocation of Families from Lippitt Hill Area, Rhode Island Commission Against Discrimination, Rhode Island State Archives, 1960

340. Remembering West Elmwood: Before & After Displacement, Lucy Asako Boltz, RICH, 2016

341. HOLC Redlining Maps: The Persistent Structure of Segregation and Economic Inequality, Bruce Mitchell, National Community Reinvestment Coalition

342. The Color of Law: A Forgotten History of How Our Government Segregated America, Robert Rothstein, Liveright Publishing Corporation, 2017

343. The Houses of Providence: A Study of Present Conditions and Tendencies, John Ihlder, Snow & Farnham, 1916

344. Machine Politics and Urban Renewal in Providence, Rhode Island: The Era of Mayor Joseph A. Doorley, Jr., 1965-74, Carl Antonucci, History & Classics Dissertatiion & Masters Theses, Providence College, 2012

345. School Desegregation in Providence, Rhode Island, Staff Report of the United States Commission of Civil Rights October, 1977

346. Labor's Home Front: The American Federation of Labor During World War II, Andrew Kerste, New York University Press, 2006

347. Citizen's Views On Urban Revitalization: The Case of Providence, Rhode Island, Marion Orr and Darrell M. West, Brown University, URBAN AFFAIRS REVIEW, Vol. 37, No. 3, (January 2002) pp. 397-419

348. Gentrification's Third Way: An Analysis of Housing Policy & Gentrification in Providence, Matthew Jerzyk, Harvard Law & Policy Review, Vol. 3, (2009) pp. 414-429

349. Urban Renewal: Title I of the Housing Act of 1949, Department of Housing and Urban Development, Maurice

Parkins Associates, P.C., Washington, D.C., 1968

350. Interstate: Highway Politics and Policy Since 1939, Mark H. Rose and Raymond A. Mohl, University of Tennessee Press, 2012

351. You Don't Have A Problem Until You Do: Revitalization and Gentrification in Providence, Fay Strongin, Housing WorksRI at Roger Williams University, 2017

352. Missing The Point, Brown Political Review, Mitchell Johnson, March 12, 2015, https://brownpoliticalreview.org/2015/03/missing-the-point/

353. A Study in Contradictions: The Origins and Legacy of the Housing Act of 1949, Alexander von Hoffman, Housing Policy Debate, Vol. 11, Issue 2, Fannie Mae Foundation, 200, pp. 299-323

354. Citizens Views on Urban Revitalization: The Case of Providence, Rhode Island, Marion Orr and Darrell M. West, Urban Affairs Review, Vol. 37, No. 3, (January 2002), pp. 397-419

355. Providence, A Citywide Survey of Historic Resources, William McKenzie Woodward and Edward F. Sanderson, Rhode Island Historical Preservation Commission, 1986

356. Homeownership Loan Corporation Redlining Maps: The Persistent Structure of Segregation and Economic Inequality, Bruce Mitchell and Juan Franco, NCRC Research, 2018

357. Housing and Displacement on Providence's East Side and Beyond, Dr. Dannie Ritchie with contributions from others, Brown University, (October 2020),

358. Elmwood, Providence, Statewide Historical Preservation Report, P-P-3, Rhode Island Historical Preservation Commission, (June 1979)

359. Mashapaug Pond Redevelopment Plan for the Huntington Expressway Industrial Park, Providence Redevelopment Agency, City of Providence, Rhode Island, 1960

360. The Culture of Race, Class, and Poverty: The Emergence of a Cultural Discourse in Early Cold War Social Work (1946-1963), Laura Curran, Rutgers University, The Journal of Sociology & Social Welfare, Vol. 30, Issue 3, (September 2003) pp. 1-25

361. College Hill: A Demonstration Study of Historic Area Renewal, Providence City Plan Commission, Providence Preservation Society, City Plan Commission, Providence, Rhode Island, 1967

362. Demonstration Cities And Metropolitan Development Act of 1966, Public Law 89-754, 89th Congress, 2nd Session, November, 4, 1966

363. Profile of Youth-1966: A Report Prepared at the Request of Senator Claiborne Pell of Rhode Island for the Subcommittee on Employment, Manpower, and Poverty, of the Committee on Labor and Public Welfare, United States Senate, U.S. Government Printing Office, (August 1966)

364. Images of America: South Providence, Patrick T. Conley and Paul Campbell, Arcadia Publishing, 2020

365. Revealing the Empowerment Revolution: A Literature Review of the Model Cities Program, Brett Webber, Journal of Urban History, No. 38, (2012), pp. 173-192

366. For a Revolutionary Position on the Negro Question, Harry Haywood, Liberator Press, 1975

367. School Desegregation in Providence, Rhode Island, U.S. Department of Health, Education & Welfare, National Institute of Education, and Staff Report of the U.S. Commission of Civil Rights, October 1977

368. Congressional Record: Proceedings and Debates of the 90th Congress, First Edition, Tuesday, August 22, 1967, pp. 24801- 24807

369. The Bus Stops Here: A Study of School Desegregation in Three Cities, Anna Holden, Agathon Press, 1974

GENERAL SOURCES

370. Reminiscences of Newport, George Champlin Mason, Published by Charles W. Hammett, 1894
371. An Album of Rhode Island History, 1636-1986, Patrick T. Conley, The Donning Company Publishers, 1986
372. A Dependent People, Newport, RI In the Revolutionary Era, Elaine Forman Crane, Fordham University Press, 1985
373. History of Providence County, Rhode Island, Richard, M. Bayles, W.W. Preston, 1891
374. Providence In Colonial Times, Gertrude Kimball, Houghton Mifflin Company, 1912
375. Rules and Orders of the Fellowship Club, The Newport Historical Magazine, No. 1, Vol 4, (July 1883) pp. 166-178
376. The Latino in Rhode Island, Marta V. Martinez, The History Press, 2014
377. The Browns of Providence Plantations: The Colonial Years, James Blaine Hedges, Harvard University Press, 1952
378. Owners and Occupants of the Houses and Shops in the Town of Providence, Rhode Island in 1798, Compiled by Henry R. Chace, 1914
379. Beyond The Bridge: 375th Anniversary of Bridgetown, Barbados, Edited by Woodville Marshall & Pedro Welch, Barbados Museum & Historical Society, 2005
380. The Making of America By England's Merchant Adventurers, John Butman and Simon Target, Little & Brown Publishers, 2018
381. First Founders, American Puritans and Puritanism in an Atlantic World, Francis J. Bremer, University of New Hampshire Press, 2012
382. Memoir of Roger Williams, James D. Knowles, Lewis & Penniman Press, 1833
383. Race & Redemption in Puritan New England, Richard A. Bailey, Oxford University Press, 2011
384. Neither Justice nor Mercy": Public and Private Executions in Rhode Island, 1832–1833, Stephen Chambers, The New England Quarterly, Vol. 82, No. 3 (September 2009), pp. 430-451
385. The Molasses Act: A Brief History, Ken Shumate, Journal of the American Revolution, January 24, 2019
386. An Historical Discourse on the Civil and Religious Affairs of the Colony of Rhode Island, John Callender, Second Edition, by Romeo Elton, Knowles, Vose & Company, 1838
387. Colonial Acts, The Newport Historical Magazine, Vol. 4, No. 1, Newport Historical Society, (July 1883)
388. History of Newport County, Rhode Island, Edited by Richard M. Bayles, L.E. Preston, 1888
389. Unwelcome Americans: Living on the Margin in Early New England, Ruth Wallis Herndon, University of Pennsylvania Press, 2001
390. An Equity Profile of Rhode Island, Policy Link, US Program for Environmental and Regional Equity, February, 2013
391. Report on the Poor and Insane in Rhode Island, Thomas R. Hazard, Made to the General Assembly, Joseph Knowles Printers, 1851
392. Moses Brown: Reluctant Reformer, Mack Thompson, Omohundro Institute of Early American History and

Culture, Williamsburg, Virginia, university of North Carolina Press, 1962

393. The Pilgrims of Plymouth, Oliver Wendall Holmes, (New England Society of New York, 1855), Documents of American Prejudice, S.T. Joshi, Perseus Books Group, 1999

394. William Larned: Overseer of the Poor: Power and Precariousness in the Early Republic, Gabriel Loiacono, The New England Quarterly, Vol. 88, No. 2 (June 2015), pp. 223-251

395. Poor Laws and the Construction of Race in Early Republican Providence, Rhode Island, Gabriel Loiacono, Journal of Policy History, Cambridge University Press, Volume 25, (November 2, 2013), pp. 264-287

396. The Providence Washington Insurance Company: Two Hundred Years, Robert L. Sherman, Rhode Island History, Volume 57, Number 1, (February 1999), pp 2-30

397. Reluctant Charity: Poor Laws in the Original Thirteen States, William P. Quigley, University of Richmond Law Review, Volume 31, Issue 1, Article 4, (1997), pp. 111-178

398. Disorderly House Keepers: Poor Women in Providence, Rhode Island 1781-1832, Andrew T. Polta, A Thesis Submitted In Partial Fulfillment Of The Requirements For The Degree Of Master Of Arts In History, University of Rhode Island, 2018

399. Faithful Bodies: Performing Religion and Race in the Puritan Atlantic, Heather M. Kopelson, New York University Press, 2014

400. A Dreadful Deceit: The Myth of Race From Colonial Era to Obama's America, Jacqueline Jones, Basic Books, 2013

401. The History of the State of Rhode Island and Providence Plantations, Volumes I-V, Thomas Williams Bicknell, American Historical Society, 1920

402. A Lively Experiment: Reflections on the Charter of 1663, Rhode Island Council for the Humanities, 2013

403. Bodies Politic: Negotiating Race in the American North, 1730-1830, John Wood Sweet, University of Pennsylvania Press, 2003.

404. Rhode Island In Rhetoric And Reflection, Public Addresses and Essays, Patrick T. Conley, Rhode Island Publications Society, 2002

405. Middle Class Providence, 1820-1940, John S. Gilkeson, Princeton University Press, 1986

406. New Israel New England: Jews and Puritans in Early America, Michael Hoffman, University of Massachusetts Press, 2011

407. Roger Williams and the Creation of the American Soul, John M. Barry, Penguin Books, 2011 pp. 206

408. The Economic and Social History of New England: 1620-1789, William B. Weeden, Houghton, Mifflin and Company, 1891

409. The Boisterous Sea of Liberty: A Documentary of America from Discovery Through the Civil War, Brion Davis and Steven Mintz, Oxford University Press, 1998

410. The Works of John Adams, Vol. 10 (Letters 1811-1825), Charles Francis Adams, Little Brown and Company, 1856

411. Records of the Colony of Rhode Island and Providence Plantations in New England, Edited by John Russell Bartlett, Volumes I-X, 1865

412. Early History of Rhode Island: A Social History of the People, William B. Weeden, Grafton Press, 1910

413. Celebrating Ethnicity and Nation: American Festive Culture from the Revolution to the Early 20th Century,

Genevieve Fabre, Berghahn Books, 2001

414. The Works of Samuel Hopkins, D.D., A Memoir of His Life and Character, Sewall Harding, Doctrinal Tract and Book Society, Vol I, 1854

415. The System of Doctrines, Contained in Divine Revelation, Samuel Hopkins, D.D. Isaiah Thomas & Ebenezer T. Andrews Printers, 1793

416. Piety in Providence: Class Dimensions of Religious Experience in Antebellum Rhode Island, Mark S. Schantz, Cornell University Press, 2000

417. Warning Out in New England, Josiah Henry Brenton, W.B. Clarke Company, 1911

418. Encouraging Faithful Domestic Servants: Race, Deviance, and Social Control in Providence, Jane Lancaster, Rhode Island History, Vol. 51, No. 3, pp. 71-87

419. Christian Slavery: Conversion and Race in the Protestant Atlantic World, Katherine Gerbner, University of Pennsylvania Press, 2018

420. The Definitive Journals of Lewis & Clark, Joseph Whitehouse, Volume 11, University of Nebraska Press, 2001

421. American Work: Four Centuries of Black and White Labor, Jacqueline Jones, W.W. Norton & Company, 1998

422. Cities in American Political History, Richardson Dillworth, Editor, CQ Press, 2011

423. Gender and Law Policy, Katherine T. Bartlett, Et Al., Wolters Kluwer Publishing, 2021

424. The Irish Bridget: Irish Immigrant Women in Domestic Service in America, 1840-1930, Margaret Lynch-Brennan, Syracuse University Press, 2009

425. Unwelcome Americans: Living on the Margin in Early New England, Ruth Wallis Herndon, University of Pennsylvania Press, 2001

426. Down and Out in Early America, Billy G. Smith, Pennsylvania State University Press, 2004

427. Women and Freedom in Early America, Larry L. Eldridge, Editor, New York University Press, 1997

428. Social Turmoil and Governmental Reform in Providence, 1820-1832, Howard P. Chudacoff and Theodore C. Hirt, Rhode Island History, Vol. 31, No. 1, (February 1972)

429. History of Providence County, Vol I & II, Ed. by Richard M. Bayles; W.W. Preston & Co., NY. 1891

430. King's Pocket-book of Providence, R.I., Moses King, Cambridge, Mass., Tibbitts, Shaw & Co., Providence, RI, 1882

431. Landscape of Industry: An Industrial History of the Blackstone Valley, Worcester Historical Museum, University Press of New England, 2009

432. Robert Stafford of Cumberland: Growth of a Planter, Mary R. Bullard, University of Georgia Press, 1995

433. Legal History of the Color Line: The Rise and Triumph of the One-Drop Rule, Frank W. Sweet, Backintyme Books, 2005

434. The Story of a Sub-Pioneer, Sara M. Algeo, Snow & Farnham Company, 1925

435. They Call Themselves The K.K.K.: The Birth of an American Terrorist Group, Susan Campbell BArtoletti, Houghton Mifflin Harcourt, 2010

436. The Klu Klux Klan in Rhode Island, Norman W. Smith, Rhode Island History, Vol. 37, No. 2, (May 1978),

437. A State By State History of Race and Racism in the United States, Patricia Reid-Merritt, Editor, ABC-CLIO, Incorporated, 2018, pp.772

438. The Forgotten Diaspora: Jewish Communities in West Africa and the Making of the Atlantic World, Peter Mark and Jose Da Silva Horta, Cambridge University Press, 2011

439. Between Race and Ethnicity: Cape Verdean America Immigrants, 1860-1965, Marilyn Halter, University of Illinois Press, 1993

440. Housing Act of 1959, Hearings Before the Committee on Banking and Currency, United States Senate, Eighty-Sixth Congress, First Session, January 22-28, 1959, pp. 818

441. The Providence Survey: A Study in Community Planning, Community Chests & Councils of America, Inc. (May 1936)

442. The Ships from Field's Point Providence, RI 1942-1945, C. Roger Wallin, Dorrance Publishing, 2017

443. Providence Industrial Sites, Statewide Historical Preservation Report, P-P-6, Rhode Island Historical Preservation Commission, (July 1981)

444. Congressional Record: Proceedings and Debates of the 90th Congress, First Edition, Tuesday, August 22, 1967, pp. 24801- 24807

445. Demographic Turning Points for the United States: Population Projections for 2020 to 2060, United States Department of Commerce, U.S. Census Bureau, Jonathan Vespa, Lauren Medina, and David M. Armstrong, Issued March 2018, Revised (February 2020)

446. Health Equity Considerations and Racial and Ethnic Minority Groups, Centers For Disease Control and Prevention, National Center for Immunization and Respiratory Diseases (NCIRD), Division of Viral Diseases, July 24, 2020

447. Hispanic Women, Immigrants, Young Adults, Those With Less Education Hit Hardest By COVID-19 Job Losses, Pew Research Center, FactTank/News in the Numbers, Rakesh Kochhar, June 9, 2020

448. R.I. Department Of Health Data Shows People Of Color Are Overrepresented In Positive Test Cases For COVID-19, Brown Daily Herald, Corey Gelb-Bicknell, May 1, 2020

449. An Equity Profile of Rhode Island, Policy Link and University of Southern California Program for Environmental & Regional Equity, February 19, 2013

450. Selected Articles on Child Labor, Edna D. Bullock, H.W. Wilson Company, 1911

451. Urban Institute, Urban Policy Center, https://www.urban.org/policy-centers/justice-policy-center

452. ACLU Criminal Law Reform Project, American Civil Liberties Union, 2020, https://www.aclu.org/other/aclu- criminal-law-reform-project

453. An Unjust Burden: The Disparate Treatment of Black Americans in the Criminal Justice System, Elizabeth Hinton, Assistant Professor, Department of History and Department of African and African American Studies, Harvard University, LeShae Henderson, Special Assistant, Research, Vera Institute of Justice, and Cindy Reed, Senior Editor, Vera Institute of Justice, Vera Institute of Justice, For The Record (May 2018)

454. U.S. Department of Justice, Office of Justice Programs, Bureau of Justice Statistics, Prisoners 2019 Summary, E. Ann Carson. Emily Buehler, Stephanie Mueller, Danielle Kaeble, NCJ 255115 (October 2020)

455. Remarks of Senator Jim Webb, Subcommittee on Crime and Drugs U.S. Senate Committee on the Judiciary Hearing on the National Criminal Justice Commission Act of 2009, June 11, 2009

456. Jews in Cape Verde: The Rhode Island Connection, Richard A. Lobban, Jr., Ph.D., Rhode Island Jewish Historical Notes, Volume 12, No. 3, (November 1997)

457. Latino History in Rhode Island: Nuestras Raices, Marta V. Martinez, History Press, 2014

458. Immigrants in Rhode Island, American Immigration Council, 2020

459. What New Immigrants Could Mean For American Wages, The Hamilton Project, Brookings Institute, August 2013

460. The Racial Achievement Gap, Segregated Schools, and Segregated Neighborhoods – A Constitutional Insult, Richard Rothstein, Economic Policy Institute, Race and Social Problems Vol. 6, No. 4, December 2014

461. Evenness Vs. Isolation In Schools: The City Of Providence Illustrates How Segregation Gauges Can Move In Opposite Directions, Jill Barshay, U.S. News & World Report (June 2018)

462. U.S. Supreme Court Brown v. Board of Education of Topeka, 347 U.S. 483 (1954), Decided May 17, 1954

463. Brown v. Board at 60: Why Have We Been So Disappointed? What Have We Learned?, Richard Rothstein, Economic Policy Institute, April 17, 2014, https://files.epi.org/2014/EPI-Brown-v-Board-04-17-2014.pdf

464. Are Clinicians Contributing to Excess African American COVID-19 Deaths? Unbeknownst to Them, They May Be, Adam J. Milam et al. 2020, Mary Ann Liebert, Inc., Health Equity, Volume 4.1, 2020, pp. 139-141

465. Health Equity Considerations and Racial and Ethnic Minority Groups, Centers For Disease Control and Prevention, Feb. 12, 2021, https://www.cdc.gov/coronavirus/2019-ncov/community/health-equity/race-ethnicity.html

466. R.I. Department Of Health Data Shows People Of Color Are Overrepresented In Positive Test Cases For COVID-19, Corey Gelb-Bicknell, Brown Daily Herald, May 1, 2020, https://www.browndailyherald.com/2020/05/01/r-department-health-data-shows-people-color-overrepresented-positive-test-cases-covid-19/

467. The COVID Tracking Data Project, The Atlantic, February 12, 2021, https://covidtracking.com/data/state/rhode-island

468. Closing The Racial Wealth Gap Requires Heavy, Progressive Taxation Of Wealth, Vanessa Williamson, Brookings Blueprints for American Renewal & Prosperity Project, Wednesday, December 9, 2020, https://www.brookings.edu/research/closing-the-racial-wealth-gap-requires-heavy-progressive-taxation-of-wealth/

469. Sovereignty and the Sacred: Secularism and the Political Economy of Religion, Robert A. Yale, University of Chicago Press, 1992

470. Fair Employment Practice Legislation in the United States, Federal, State, Municipal, W. Brooke Graves, Library of Congress Legislative Reference Service (April 1951)

NEWSPAPER ARTICLES

471. Sachem Thomas Ninigret Death, Boston Evening Post, April 12, 1769

472. Prince G. Wright Fashionable Hairdresser Advertisement, Providence Journal and Country Advertiser, December 18, 1799

473. Creditors of Narragansett Indians, Rhode Island American, September 24, 1811

474. Notice: Union African Society, Rhode Island American, December 29, 1820

475. African School, Rhode Island American, June 9, 1820

476. Annual Meeting of African Union Society, Rhode Island American, December 26, 1821

477. African School, Rhode Island American, June 10, 1831

478. Committee's Report on Onley Lane Riot, Rhode Island American, September 30, 1831
479. Execution of Walmsley, New England Artisan, and Laboring Man's Repository, Thursday, Jun 07, 1832
480. Capital Punishments in Rhode Island, Rhode Island American, November 16, 1832
481. Increase of Blacks, Providence Gazette, July 28, 1824
482. Hardscrabble Defense, Independent Inquirer, December 30, 1824
483. Riot And Murder, Rhode Island American, September 23, 1831
484. Another Riot, Rhode Island American, September 24, 1831
485. The Late Riot, Providence Patriot, October 1, 1831
486. Snowtown Outrage, Rhode Island American, November 10, 1832
487. Petition of Alfred Niger, et. al To Be Exempt From Taxation, Pawtucket Chronicle and Manufacturers, January 14, 1831
488. A Voice From Providence, The Liberator, William Llyod Garrison, Publisher, November 5, 1831
489. Anti-Abolition Meeting, Providence Journal, November 4, 1835
490. Meeting of Narraganset Tribe of Indians, Newport Mercury, August 14, 1843
491. The Narragansett Indians of R.I., Niles National Register, August 26, 1843
492. Colored Freeman Right of Suffrage, Daily Transcript and Chronicle, March 31, 1846
493. George C. Willis Obituary, Manufactures and Farmers Journal, January 21, 1858
494. An Act Relating to the Narragansett Indians, Manufactures and Farmers Journal, February 2, 1859
495. George Thomas Downing, Esq. The Anglo American, April 11, 1863
496. The Colored School Question, Providence Evening Press, July 12, 1865
497. Westerly And Its Witnesses, Providence Evening Bulletin, April 6, 1867
498. The History of the Indian Church, Providence Evening Bulletin, May 16, 1867
499. National Labor Convention, Baltimore American, October 2, 1869
500. The Narragansett Tribe, Democrat and Weekly Sentinel, August 23, 1879
501. Van Horne Nominated, Fall River Daily Evening News, March 31, 1885
502. Mass Meeting of Colored Citizens, Newport Mercury, April 14, 1882
503. Emancipation Day Observance at Rocky Point, Newport Mercury, August 4, 1888
504. Home For Aged Colored Women, New York Age, April 26, 1890
505. Vest On Secession, Parson's Daily Eclipse, August 21, 1891
506. Want A Big Strip of Land: Narragansett Indians Hold A Powwow and Discuss Their Claims, The Boston Globe, September 26, 1893
507. Last of Indian Chiefs: Gideon Ammons, A Famous Narragansett Indian is Dead, Fall River Daily Herald, December 5, 1899
508. Yankees Honor a Negress, Mitchell Newspaper, July 18, 1902
509. Negroes Do Not Care For Their Own Race, Evening Bulletin, March 25, 1904

510. George T. Downing Obituary, New York Age, July 20, 1905
511. In Memory of George T. Downing, New York Age, January 4, 1906
512. Rhode Island Colored Women's Club Meeting, New York Age, March 5, 1908
513. Negro As Publicity Promoter, New York Age, October 28, 1909
514. Miss M.E. Jackson Head of State Clubs of Colored Women, Providence Evening Bulletin, February 2, 1910
515. Nigger Dead: Men At Theatre Mourn, Providence Evening Bulletin, December 16, 1911
516. Dr. Willman H. Higgins Elected to Republican City Committee, New York Age, October 12, 1911
517. Negroes Decide Bull Moose Is Friend To Race, Providence Evening Bulletin, October 4, 1912
518. Emancipation of Slaves Observed, 50th Anniversary, Providence Evening Bulletin, January 2, 1913
519. Mary H. Dickerson Obituary, New York Age, July 9, 1914
520. Dr. William H. Higgins Re-elected as City Official, New York Age, October 16, 1914
521. Alexander Gorham Obituary, New York Age, December 23, 1914
522. Record Price Paid For Birth Of A Nation, Evening Bulletin, August 28, 1915
523. Providence Preachers Make Denial, New York Age, November 4, 1915
524. South Seeks to Keep Its Labor Out of Army For Planting Work, Providence Journal, May 24, 1917
525. Rhode Island Union of Colored Women's Clubs, New York Age, June 1917
526. Negro Silent Protest Parade, New York Age, August 1917
527. Advice of Rev Lucas to Colored People Avoid Trouble in Public Places, Newport Mercury, July 27, 1917
528. Silent Protest Parade Is Held By 1400 Negroes, Evening Bulletin, October 15, 1917
529. YMCA Sending Workers Among Race Women, New York Age Newspaper, January 3, 1918
530. Openings for Colored Women in Providence, New York Age, July 20, 1918
531. Rhode Island Negro Community Welcomes Home Servicemen, New York Age, June 1919
532. YWCA Worker to Attend Conference, New York Age, March 1, 1919
533. Civil Rights Bill's Passage Demanded, Pawtucket Times, April 16, 1920
534. Lawton Attacked In Negro Meeting For His Attitude, Evening Bulletin, April 16, 1920
535. Colored Women's Caucus Meeting, New York Age, October 2, 1920
536. Drawing Religious Line in the Matter of Lynchings, New York Age, November 20, 1920
537. Seventh War Colored Voters Desert Caucus, Evening Bulletin, January 28, 1921
538. Observe Emancipation Day At Rocky Point, Providence Evening Bulletin, August 2, 1922
539. Thanks Bulletin For Stand on Dyer Anti-Lynching Bill, Providence Evening Bulletin, November 11, 1922
540. Colored Independent Political Association of Rhode Island Formed, New York Age, February 25, 1922
541. Dr. Higgins Elected To School Committee, New York Age, November 18, 1922
542. Mary E. Jackson Obituary, New York Age, May 19, 1923
543. Stockett Thanks Women of Rhode Island After Appointment, New York Age, February 6, 1926
544. Sensational Charges Made Against Ku Klux Klan in Rhode Island, New York Age, October 1928

545. Atrocities in America Characterized as True and Honest Citizen, Newport Herald, March 11, 1928
546. Urges Enactment of Anti-Lynching Law, Newport Mercury, October 17, 1930
547. Seeks Quick Passage or Anti-Lynching Bill, Newport Mercury, March 26, 1937
548. John F. Lopez Addresses Newport NAACP, Newport Mercury, February 12, 1943
549. Walsh-Kaiser Shipyard Hires 250 Negroes in Providence, New York Age, April 17, 1943
550. Jim Crow Boilermakers Union Under Fire in Rhode Island, New York Age, June 3, 1944
551. RI Council for Fair Employment Holds First Meeting Here, Newport Mercury, February 21, 1947
552. Any Housing Bans Decried By Mayor, Providence Journal, January 7, 1950
553. Segregation Stand Hit, Providence Journal, January 14, 1950
554. R.I. Rent Control Bill Vigorously Attacked, Providence Journal, 1950
555. Attitude Towards Negroes Gradually Chaining Here, Providence Journal, December 13, 1950
556. Andrew Bell Jr. Named Chairman of R.I. Council For Human Rights, Providence Journal, February 6, 1951
557. Emancipation Day Marked By 15,000, Providence Journal, August 2, 1951
558. Mrs. Hunt Cited For Race Work, Providence Journal, February 2, 1954
559. Urban League Eyes Progress In Race Relations in 15 Years, Providence Journal, January 9, 1955
560. Roberta J. Dunbar Obituary, Providence Journal, November 3, 1956
561. Anti-Segregation Action Weighed, Providence Journal, June 6, 1956
562. A Shameful Suppression of a State Ruling, Providence Journal, July 23, 1956
563. Let's Have No Color Line in Public Housing, Providence Journal, June 22, 1956
564. No Place for Discrimination, Providence Journal, June 9, 1956
565. Governor Lists Total Integration Housing Policy, Providence Journal, September 21, 1956
566. Segregation Core Dead, Says Rev La Farge, Newport Daily News, February 20, 1956
567. Urban League Set to Aid Court Suits on Housing, Providence Evening Bulletin, May 16, 1956
568. Law Should Include Private Housing, Irving Jay Fain Editorial, Providence Journal, August 1, 1957
569. NAACP Official Censures Solons from RI For Civil Rights Votes, Newport Daily News, October 24, 1957
570. Fair Housing Law Proposed, Providence Journal, October 29, 1957
571. Urban League to Assist West Broadway Residents, Newport Daily News, April 26, 1957
572. Redevelopment Moves Forward in Providence, Newport Daily News, April 4, 1958
573. Spokesman See End of 30 Firms On Lippitt Hill, Providence Journal, October 24, 1958
574. Housing Discrimination Bill Provisions Are Outlined, Newport Daily News, December 4, 1958
575. Urban League Speakers Urge Newport Act on Poor Housing, Providence Journal, July 1, 1958
576. A Message Concerning Fair Housing, Providence Journal, April 4, 1959
577. Lippitt Hill Plan Gets Opposition, Providence Journal, May 15, 1959
578. Discrimination Keeps Negroes In Lippitt Hill, Providence Journal, October 10, 1959
579. Negro Housing Cruz of Lippitt Hill Job, Providence Journal, October 25, 1959

580. 500 Jam House Chamber to Hear Opponents of Fair Housing Law, Providence Journal, April 8, 1959
581. Fair Housing Law Would Benefit R. I., Providence Sunday Journal, January 18, 1959
582. Discrimination in Housing Found in Newport County, Newport Daily News, April 6, 1960
583. Why Should You Oppose A Fair Housing Bill, Providence Journal, March 6, 1960
584. What Is… The Case For Fair Housing? Providence Journal, March 29, 1960
585. Industrial Park OK'D For Mashapaug Pond, Providence Journal, May 6, 1960
586. So-Called Fair Housing Bill, Providence Journal, May 20, 1960
587. The Case Against The So-Called Fair Housing Bill: Statement of William D. Slattery, Providence Journal, April 14, 1960
588. City Relocates Firms, Providence Journal, January 31, 1960
589. NAACP Hears of Fair Housing, Newport Daily News, May 15, 1961
590. Attack at Providence, Rhode Island, Monroe News-Star, November 7, 1961
591. Urban League Insists Job Bias Continues, Newport Daily News, February 14, 1961
592. South Providence Negroes Aroused By Police Treatment, Springfield Sun, August 9, 1962
593. Negro Leaders Still Differ With Police, Providence Journal, August 24, 1962
594. Chafee, Democrats to Meet On New Fair Housing Session, Newport Daily News, July 3, 1963
595. March for Fair Housing, Providence Journal, June 3, 1963
596. Fair Housing Measure Killed By House, Newport Daily News, April 10, 1964
597. Student Plan March for Civil Rights Law, Newport Daily News, March 16, 1964
598. Sit In Planned at State House, Providence Journal, March 13, 1964
599. Fair Housing Bill Offered by Gov. Chafee, Providence Journal, January 24, 1964
600. Providence "Segregated," Newport Daily News, 1965
601. Doorley Pledged To Promore State Fair Housing Bill, Providence Journal, February 16, 1965
602. Housing Made Law by Chaffee, Newport Daily News, April 12, 1965
603. Providence Negro Rally to Promote Racial Unity, Newport Daily News, August 1, 1966
604. Providence Seen Ideal For Core City Project, Providence Journal, June 25, 1966
605. Two Providence Grants Increases, Providence Journal, June 25, 1966
606. Proof Asked By Doorley, Newport Daily News, October 1, 1966
607. City Battle Snipers, Newport Daily News, August 2, 1967
608. Only Negro Delegate Talks Republican National Convention, Newport Daily News, August 14, 1968
609. Doorley Defends His Thinking On Arena, S. Prov, Evening Bulletin, March 7, 1968
610. State's Urban Coalition to Hold First Officials Gathering, Providence Journal, May 15, 1969
611. State's Urban Coalition to Hold First Officials Gathering Today, Providence Journal, May 15, 1969
612. Providence Closes Riot Struck School, Newport Daily News, May 14, 1969
613. NAACP Sues US & RI Firms, Unions, Providence Journal, December 27, 1972

614. Providence Asked to Act on Arsonists, Newport Daily News, February 25, 1974
615. Discrimination Seminar Raises Hackles, Newport Daily News October 15, 1974
616. NETC Commander Posts EEO Policy on Discrimination, Newport Daily News, May 30, 1975
617. Bias Suit Filed Against N. E. Telephone by Providence NAACP, Nashua Telegraph, December 24, 1976
618. Judge Sets Election Dates for 10th Ward, The North Star, June 14, 1977
619. To Many In R.I. Narragansett Indians Are Invisible, Nashua Telegraph, May 10, 1976
620. Dunes Club Manager Tells Shelby Jordan Premises Are Private, Providence Journal, July 17, 1980
621. Historian Is Rooting For Former Slave, Providence Journal Bulletin, August 1 1981
622. Rosa Parks Takes A Bus Ride Aimed At Helping S. Providence Overcome, Providence Journal, July 1, 1984
623. State Land Returned To Rhode Island Indians, New Mexican Newspaper, October 12, 1985
624. To Indians, No One Could Buy, Sell Earth, News Record, December 3, 1993
625. Call for Calm After Shooting Of Policeman By Colleagues, New York Times, January 30, 2000
626. Carcieri Apologizes To Narragansetts, The Day, December 22. 2009
627. Carcieri 'Fix' Still In Limbo More Than A Decade Later, Indian Gaming, February 24, 2020
628. Providence Activists: Summer of Protests Leaves Unfinished Work For Social Justice, Providence Journal, December 5, 2020

SELECTED HISTORIC RUNAWAY ADVERTISEMENTS

629. York – A Very Black Looking Fellow, Providence Gazette, March 30, 1763
630. Moses Perry – Molatto Man Providence Gazette, May 23, 1772
631. Dick – Mulatto Man, Providence Gazette, May 30, 1772
632. Mingo- Tall Man, Providence Gazette, October 9, 1773
633. John Jones – Apprentice Lad, Providence Gazette, April 4, 1776
634. Negro Woman, Providence Gazette, March 4, 1777
635. Silvia – Negro Servant Girl, Providence Gazette, March 18, 1785
636. Stephen – Indian Boy, Providence Gazette, August 7, 1787
637. Maria Wanton – Indentured Servant Girl, Providence Gazette, November 17, 1798
638. Barshaba – Apprentice Negro Girl, Providence Gazette, August 25, 1788
639. Lemuel Ware & Davis Partridge, Providence Gazette, December 21, 1795
640. William Briggs – Indentured Apprentice Boy, United States Chronicle, August 15, 1799
641. Ephraim Curtis – Potter Trade, United States Chronicle, April 4, 1791
642. Catherine Gardner – Indentured Black Girl, Providence Gazette, May 27, 1803
643. Phillip – Mulatto To Indian Looking Man, Providence Gazette, January 13, 1806
644. Isaac How, Indentured Apprentice, Providence Gazette, May 24, 1806

www.ingramcontent.com/pod-product-compliance
Lightning Source LLC
Chambersburg PA
CBHW050736110526
44591CB00003B/38